WomanEucharist

Sheila Durkin Dierks

ry

Cover design by Traci Schalow

For additional information contact: WovenWord Press, 811 Mapleton Avenue, Boulder, Colorado, 80304.

ISBN 0-9658137-9-7

———————————————————

Library of Congress Catalog Card Number
97-60762

WomenEucharist
Dierks, Sheila Durkin

Includes bibliography and index
1. Catholic women and sacraments 2. Feminism — religious aspects
3. Women and theology

For dear Lael,
who in many ways
made this book happen
just by being born

This book is not mine alone.

The stories you hear are those of women from across the nation, many nameless, who have been kind enough to share their lives.

To each of you, a thank you which is deeper and more profound than you might imagine. Your voices have been the muses of this work. I have heard you sing to me of joy and unhappiness and discouragement and hope through three years of writing. You have been known to me collectively as The Chorus of Yes!

Throughout the writing of this book many friends, who are also experts in various germane areas, have supported and prayed the continuation of this work. I am grateful to my sisters: Ellen/Sr. Mary Cabrini Durkin OSU who blue-penciled well and challenged me to think clearly, while believing that this work should be published; and Frances Durkin Colletti who read and encouraged and was amazed and delighted by the voices of all the respondents, thereby giving me hope.

I am deeply thankful to Paul Turner, whose goodness and sense of pastoral vocation gives me tremendous hope for the priesthood. His incisive comments, close reading and sense of humor got me through numerous bad patches.

Members of my New Jersey WomenEucharist group, especially Jackie Hickey, Valli Re, Alyce Parrino, and Jane Nirella, read and commented and critiqued. Their honesty shaped the text. Members of my Colorado WE group kept praying with me and kept my creative juices flowing with thoughtful, prayerful liturgies.

I could not have written this book without the wonderful computer know-how of my son, John.

Kitty Steed, my friend and cousin, believed in me and in the work. She read every word and kept me moving forward.

Meinrad Craighead was kind enough to listen to me and to reassure me on numerous occasions that this work has a life of its own and is destined for the light of day.

Vicki McVey, dear friend and thoroughly exact proofreader and comma minder, was singularly crucial in bringing this book to its final form.

Especially, thanks to my husband who, more than anyone, has lived this book in all its agonies, with me. He has walked with me the anger-into-hope road.

Now let it go forth and have life!

TABLE OF CONTENTS

Dear Women Friends:

I am a writer doing research on the quiet revolution of women gathering to celebrate Eucharist. This growing reality is being joyfully experienced all over the United States and there is a need to document and share it.

I am grateful for your willingness to help us all by lending your voice and experience.

The questionnaire is long. Feel free to answer those questions which you can. There may be some to which you do not know the answers or which do not apply to you. If you are concerned about confidentiality do not sign your name or return address your envelope. If you wish to identify yourself but do not wish your name to be used, please indicate. I am deeply aware of the need for confidentiality for many of you, I have heard from women who might lose their jobs, or whose religious communities would be deeply affected if their participation was known; but I am hoping that you will see as a counterbalance the call to share our experiences together, so that we will not be, like so many women, unheard.

Please don't feel limited by the questions since I would love to hear, and share, your stories and observations on things which are important to you but which I may not have directly addressed in the questions. Please answer as fully as possible.

I am a custom weaver by profession, a wife and mother of four, aged 12 to 25. My last book was on the Catholic Worker Movement, (*Catholic Worker Houses:Ordinary Miracles* 1987) I am part of a circle of women who celebrate Eucharist monthly, and a family group who celebrates twice a month. I am also an active member of a parish community.

I anxiously await your Good News.

Blessings,

Sheila Dierks

QUESTIONNAIRE

1. How did your group come into existence?

2. Is the group Catholic? Interdenominational?

3. How often do you meet?

4. How is planning done? Are there planning guidelines?

5. Do you use a traditional liturgical format? If not, what do you include, exclude? Where does this model come from?

6. What resources do you use and find helpful?

7. What Scripture translation(s) do you use? Do you use readings from other than Scripture in your liturgies?

8. How do you adapt language?

9. Who is the celebrant (specific individual, changing individual, pair of women, the whole group, etc.)? How was this decided?

10. How does the group homilize?

11. What images does the group employ in relationship to God (Father, Son, Spirit) ?

12. How is transubstantiation viewed by the group? Is there a particular Eucharistic prayer you use? Do you write your own? (If so, could you include examples?)

13. How is the historical/sacramental Jesus a part of your celebration?

14. What is the group's relationship to the institutional Catholic Church?

15. Does the group feel it is a part of a rebelling or alienated or emerging Church?

16. Does the group have any qualms about your celebrations? Any fear of discovery?

17. Have there been women who have taken part and then ceased coming? Do you know their reasons for leaving the group? Please share what you can of their reasons.

18. What is your spiritual response to your celebrations?

19. Do you continue to be active in a parish community? If yes, in what ways?

20. If you are no longer active in a parish, what led to the separation?

21. Does this group better meet your spiritual needs?

22. If you are active in a parish, do you feel the need to conceal the existence of your group? The nature of its activities?

23. Are you married or have a significant other? How does that person view the group?

24. Are there other relationships in which knowledge or your group and its activities would cause tension? Please explain.

25. Do you have uncertainties, misgivings about your participation? If so, could you share them with me.

26. Are you afraid? Rejoicing? Other emotions?

27. Do you feel that what you are doing is radical/revolutionary? How?

28. What experiences in your life have led you to be a part of the group?

29. What books have you read that led you here?

30. What is the impact of this experience on your life?

31. How do you view the future of your group?

32. Do you think the existence of your group and others like it will have an impact of a positive or negative nature on the institutional Church?

33. What have I forgotten to ask? What would you like to say that has not been included elsewhere?

PREFACE

✳Before we can pray,
before we can dream,
before we can witness
to justice and peace,
we must be a single circle,
a single, unbroken circle,
a wide open, welcoming circle.
Let us build this circle of love.[1]

In researching various aspects of women's lives and Eucharistic tradition, I have become intensely aware that I and the respondents whose ideas and experiences make up the fertile ground of this work, stand in a mighty large circle. Among those with us are Thomas Aquinas and Julian of Norwich and Martin Luther, Matthew Fox and Catherine of Siena and Hans Küng and Miriam Therese Winter, the participants in the Council of Trent and Edward Schillebeeckx, Flannery O'Connor and Augustine and Frank Sheed and Rosemary Radford Ruether, Paul of Tarsus and members of Dignity and tens of thousands of women and men all of whom have brought various levels of belief, curiosity and learning to the search for how JesusGod is present in life and ritual.

I find the image of a circle quite satisfying. It is easy to enlarge without breaking. All sorts of people can wander in and join hands. In this circle I visualize the only requirement for entry is that you too are searching for how Jesus is near you. Circles are noncompetitive. There's no being first or being last. Everyone has a place no higher or lower and everyone has a part in the seeking action. Many of those to whose work we will refer can be faced across the circle, rather than seen distantly down a long line of centuries. We all bring, inescapably, the texture of our own time and experience to our search. This is a gift for it allows us to see within our own generation, within our own circumstance, the presence of God, and gives us contemporary language and image with which to articulate it. (Imagine the language of the Mayflower crew describing the flight of Apollo space missions. Both are about transportation, after all.)

This rootedness in time can also be a stumbling block if we insist that our role is articulating for everyone the shape of relations between God and the human family. While God is eternal it is impossible for us to climb out of our own skins, our own place in salvation history, and speak the language of understanding which would define for all time how God is present in community, in word, in bread and wine. To do that would be to deprive others now alive and the generations which follow the wonderful seeking conversation with the Almighty which is a key to intimacy. We cannot and should not try to deprive those sisters and brothers the pleasures of discovery in which faith struggles and grows.

One marvelous outgrowth of this study for me is the wonder that we take our place in a great tradition, the tradition of examining, praying our circumstances of life. We no longer face the curse of the Black Plague, and the destruction of the monastic libraries by barbarian hoards, the estrangement of an iron curtain. We do find the struggle of materialism and the threat of ecological destruction. We suffer with friends who are HIV positive and cry out, how can God be present in this mess? The Catholic Church is not a mere museum of beliefs, with gatekeepers who cry *anathema sit.* Every age must be able to enter the museum, handle the treasures and while recognizing their value to those who came before, also be able to add to the treasure from what is available now. There are poets, artists, humans of every age who help us to name and experience the glory that is now. If we continue to support an institution which sees its perfection as spoken with finality by St. Thomas Aquinas we will continue to cause suffering and experience irrelevance in this moment.

In not claiming that this work is cast in stone, we are relieved of the burden of inflated expectations. I neither wish to put these voices forward as the only ones which hold truth, nor wish to claim that this is the last word on the subject of women and the Eucharist. We are part of a conversation, part of a large and wonderful group of people all circled around our God and describing the view from here. I respect those others in the circle who honestly share their views, while calling to awareness those whose stated views no longer reflect what they actually see. The institutional Church has mouthpieced ideas whose time has passed, has defended views which are no longer defensible.

(Remember the length of time it takes the institutional Church to accept Gallileo or condemn slavery or embrace the Jews.) It is possible that we all have, at times, continued to support a position we no longer genuinely believed for fear of appearing foolish or for fear of losing face. I call upon us to put aside such fears of embarrassment. While we will continue to have a conversation with the past, we have no need to defend the dead whose views very much sprang from the concerns of their own life circumstance, and can be accepted as such. Our views are very much the same, and quite possibly will be seen by even our children as slightly out of date.

There is a photo of me taken as a pudgy pre-adolescent in front of the family Christmas tree in 1955. I wear a dress which at that time I thought of as really great. Looking at it now I am bemused by what ever led me to that fashion statement. The photo, and similar life experience, is instructive. It reminds me that fashion changes but we still wear clothes (some changes being surface only.) What I looked like then does not in any way make me less lovable or more dispensable now. So too the body of Christ which we call church. Recognizing that which came before, we can accept it for what it is, an expression of a time, and a group of people seeking God in temporal circumstances and trying to express that relationship in word and ritual. The question now is not to focus our eyes backward and concentrate our energies on defense (or offense) of what now seems out of date, but instead to recognize the conversation with the past and keep on asking how we seek and speak our truths in this year of the Lord.

I invite you, as you read to imagine us all, the Body of Christ, in that enormous circle all facing in toward the body of Christ, each sharing a God-given vision of what is seen. Let us remember that everyone deserves a respectful Spirit-prompted hearing, respectful because God's voice can be echoed in each one of ours.[2] In reverent listening we may be blessed to discover some ideas which are new, some which we have heard before but which may deserve greater attention, some which call for prayer of understanding, and some with which we cannot agree. Let us expect the Spirit to be conspiring with us in our search for God in our day.

✪✪✪✪✪

INTRODUCTION

Bind me-I still can sing-
Banish-my mandolin
Strikes true within-
Slay-and my soul shall rise
Chanting to Paradise-
Still thine.[3]

Theology is not carved lapidary
from the quarry of eternal truth
(he said),
but flashes fresh in each new age,
dancing just beyond the horizon of longing.[4]

For every woman we have named, there are a hundred who speak; for every hundred
who speak, there are a thousand who know; for every thousand who know, there ten
thousand who do not yet know.[5]

    This book began almost a decade ago, around the lunch table in a local restaurant. I had invited half a dozen interesting women to meet on a monthly basis to talk about how it is that God enters into our lives. The group was enormously popular and women marked calendars at the beginning of each year so there would be no conflicts with our monthly date.

    We had no set agenda, nor readings-in-preparation. We knew we were coming together to explore the Creative Presence in our existence. It was prophetic that we should gather in a circle and share food as we talked of God's love. There was no short-age of topics. The participants dealt out tales of cancers, children's engagements both happy and sad, domestic free-for-alls, births of wonder, the spectrum of life. No event was shrugged away as trivial. We challenged ourselves to see God in these experiences. There were tears and a lot of joking. As intimacy bloomed so did willingness to bare our souls. In response, respect flourished, evidenced by the fact that no one demeaned the experience of another, nor marched out canned judgments.

We were there in support of each other, and in the recognized reverence for the journey. In the years that we met the number of regular participants grew to almost twenty who came to talk of the actualities of God present in our lives.

As the group matured we sensed that our meetings were not complete, lacking the ritualization which we as mostly Catholic believe is central to our lives. We needed to pray these moments, distress and happiness together. We wanted to pray them with the prayer of Eucharist. So, in awe we began. We knew of no other groups of women who were involved in such an endeavor, [6] but we took our cue from the Christians of the early Church. Gathering in our homes, we praised and thanked God, shared Scripture, blessed and shared bread and wine. We did, and do this in memory of Jesus. "Everyday they devoted themselves. . . to breaking bread in their homes. They ate their meals with exultation and sincerity of heart, praising God. . . "[7]

For many Catholic women the daily struggle to remain faithful to their Church requires that they deny their own experience and sense of call, and if not their own, that of their sisters. Many women recognize that not only the "who" of celebration, but also the "what" and "how" has been determined by men for almost two millennia. The canon of who is acceptable, what shape the skin must be in order to preside, and the rubrics of the celebration presided over have had input from only one group of the baptized. Women chafe under the inequity, often finding that we must attend liturgy with intellectual, emotional and spiritual blinders on in order to remain practicing members of a faith community. To pray with people whom we love and know as faith-family, we must ignore excluding language, insensitive homilies, poor liturgy. The pervasive nature of sexism in the church, indeed sexism deified and presented as religious necessity is a burden of stone strapped to the backs of women. Many of us find ourselves chronically angry as we depart from Sunday Eucharists. Rosemary Radford Ruether comments, "It is precisely when feminists discover the congruence between the Gospel and liberation from sexism that they also experience their greatest alienation from existing churches." [8]

Thousands of women have ceased formal practice of faith as they experience heightened consciousness of their own capabilities and what seems to them the virtual certainty that their voices will not be heard, their talents never fully employed in the church of their baptism. As women begin to identify and claim their own spiritual authority, they often come to admit that the institution is blindly out of balance with the values preached and lived by Jesus, and that the valuing of power-over and the maintenance of the status quo have become paramount for that institution. It is sadly noted that many feel that they are not missed; they count for so little that their passing out of the parish doors for the last time is not noted or regretted.

And where do they go? Those who wish ordination may turn to the Lutheran church which first ordained US women in 1970 or to the Episcopalians where women were irregularly ordained in 1974 and officially in 1976. Those two denominations joined Methodists and Presbyterians who have allowed women as clergy since 1956. Other Christian denominations have also opened their doors kindly to Catholic women.

Women who feel a lack of hospitality in Catholic parishes go to a variety of churches where they are welcomed, or finding that nowhere drift away from formal religious practice. Some have experienced such unfortunate treatment at the hands of the official Church and in the name of Jesus that they have left Christianity behind and, in search of a spiritual community which affirms them, have joined the New Age or Goddess movements.

In this age of spiritual seeking there is a swelling alternative to remain in pain or find a new home. Women in small but growing numbers are gathering in informal groups, often in private homes, to celebrate Eucharist without inviting or including a priest to act as presider or celebrant.

I have identified over 100 such gatherings in the United States. They reach out their arms from Seattle to Miami, from southern California to Vermont. They are six women, they are 30 joined in the name of Jesus. They meet regularly (my definition: at least once a month). Many are on a journey of discovery, some feel that they are finally home.
In my curiosity about these spiritual communities I queried 30 groups by questionnaire and accepted the invitation of five to visit, celebrate Eucharist and explore in depth their motives and experiences.

What follows in this book is not meant to be a sociological study. I am not trained for that, nor am I primarily interested in statistics. My goal is to share the voices of many women; to experience each story as individual and important to an understanding and appreciation of how significant numbers of women are experiencing the spirit of Jesus present in their lives and to seek the connection points (and sometimes the points of diversion) with the formations of our childhoods and earlier adulthood.

Community without hierarchy, we sit in a circle. Community without sexism, we experience each other as image of God, and God as Mother, Breath, Ruah, Shekinah. Community without rigidity, we may all participate in shaping the celebration to reflect our own journeys and how God is a part of them. Community without slavery to fixed space, we can rediscover our bodies in gesture and dance, free-flowing movement. Community without judgment, we may, as women, finally offer our best gifts without fear that they will be refused because of our gender.

This is WomenEucharist (WE) and in many ways, we claim the middle ground. WE chooses to affirm our deep connection with Jesus through the celebration of Eucharist together. It is the native tongue of our spirituality.

Women often say, "I don't do theology." We have understood from years of training that theology is the purview of the specially educated, most frequently of the priest. Theology has for so long been hands-off territory, confined to the seminaries, where women could not tread. Of course, we, many of us, are theologues, doing God-thinking every day as we seek to imagine what God must want when we are sad or injured, content or rejected, joyous or angry, how our loving God accompanies, guides and instructs us when we are confronted with crises, what God wishes when we are faced with challenge, how God must love us to send a Godchild to teach us how to live and die.

In my conversations with women in all parts of the United States I discovered that what is at issue is not solely inclusive language or the ordination of women, though both are part of the problem. Rather, women are identifying that we have different styles of celebration and prayer which are not acknowledged or respected by the institutional Church; styles which perhaps we do not even know, having seldom or never been in a position to pray in our own ways. We have an inkling that if we continue to practice our subjugation in canonized liturgies we cannot possibly live what we celebrate.

Since the hatching of The Women's Ordination Conference in the early 1970's, the thrust has been away from women's ordination as the only issue, and toward a reordered priesthood for women and men in which talent is more important than gender, in which feminine experience is cherished and in which access to ministry and decision making is open to all.

A most striking fact about participants in WomenEucharist groups is that most are beyond the age we might think of as the rebellious years. In the groups with whom I visited (and most of those who indicated age on the questionnaires) grey hair is a constant. Many participants are over the age of forty, with some well into retirement years. I met several women who had passed eighty.

The majority are cradle Catholics, who can only be called in Dorothy Day's words, "Faithful daughters of the Church." They are distinguished by their years of membership, often their years of employment. A good number are, or have been, vowed members of canonical orders. A significant number indicated that they hold advanced degrees in divinity, theology, scripture or liturgy.

It is a sign of spiritual maturity that these women continue to attempt to separate that which is liberating from that which is unhealthy in the church. More than half of the respondents volunteer a fair bit of time to parish needs. It is interesting that many who are involved are so in spite of their perception that injustice dwells there. Religious education teachers, bible study group leaders, liturgical planners, parish council members, musicians, justice and peace activists. As one respondent put it, "My group of women gathering to pray is what makes it possible to remain in my parish."

It is valuable that, in this age of options, so many who find little joy in the institution do not just walk away, but instead remain, seeking new ways to celebrate and explore the spirit of Jesus present in themselves and their communities through the expression of Eucharist.

WHAT THIS BOOK IS AND IS NOT ABOUT ✪

This book is not about hating or rejecting men.

This book is about creating a space for women to encounter their spiritual lives in loving community while being free from male judgment and safe to speak, pray, invent, and ritualize the most sacred and the most daily elements of their lives.

This book is not about rebellion, though it is about revolution, in the sense of a movement expressing vigorous dissent. The revolution has its genesis in the lives of women, one by aching one. It is about revolving away from the individual experience of rejection, denial of gifts, patronization, condescension, played out against the words of the Scriptures, the promise of God-life betrayed again and again by the Church of our baptism.

The vigorous dissent confronts the centuries old concept that the male sex holds the keys to the kingdom, defines the New Covenant, has the corner on all official under-standing of morality, spiritual life and growth. This dissent rejects the idea that only through maleness can the most important and unifying act of our sacramental Church be experienced. This dissent confronts the idea that women's prayer must be mediated by a male priest, that it is only through a male-dominated community that a woman can find her salvation.

This book is not about pathology in religion, rather it is about a revolving toward spiri-tual wholeness. Certainly, the curtains have been parted to disclose what many of us have experienced individually: there has been much abuse of power over others and this abuse is the root of heart-rending damage done in the name of Jesus by the Catholic Church. Many have found the institution to be an impediment to spiritual maturity, as it often seems to encourage infantilism in adults, especially female ones.

We gaze at a long history of institutional abuse of many groups, but *always* against women, and marvel at how the faith has survived, especially among women. In this moment, however, there are many who recognize that we, as Christians, are responsible for the now. We are not indifferent to our moment in Creation history. We cannot contin-ue to blame the institution if we have, for at least part of our lives, made the mistake of having faith in it, and substituting it for faith in the love of God.

This book is not about final answers. Few who participated in the research for this book believe that women gathering to celebrate Eucharist is the ultimate solution to the problems which confront us. Many of us wish for ways to include men, families, in coequal worship. As Rosemary Radford Ruether dreams it, "I assume the name for this liberated humanity would then no longer be 'Women-Church,' but simply 'Church'; that is, the authentic community of exodus from oppression that has been heralded by the traditions of religious and social liberation but, until now, corrupted by reversion to new forms of the *ecclesia* of patriarchy."[9]

Most express that this is part of an ongoing discovery, a process, an evolution in which we, because the ways of our childhood are not sufficient to our adult spiritual experience, attempt to encounter how God interacts with us. For many this is extremely painful, often lonely. It is in the gathering, the sharing, that the pain is eased, the loneli-ness lessened. It is also relief, delight, God's presence with an intensity never before experienced, and yet most see it as an oasis, a long sought place of safety in the desert, not home yet, but wonderful for now.

SOME PROCEDURAL NOTES ✪

Of course, our little group which went from lunch to Eucharist discovered we are not alone, and it is in curiosity about this that the book took life. My main source of leads to other groups was through word of mouth. One friend tells another that she has a friend in Minneapolis who gathers with other women to celebrate, another knows someone in Miami or San Francisco. I also discovered the network of WomenChurch to which I am greatly indebted.

When I learned the name of a woman in another city, I would phone and explain my interest, ask her to describe her group and request that she share a set of questions with each participant. No one refused. There was a wonderful sense of community by telephone. People were eager to share news of their gatherings and hear about others.

There is great curiosity about what other groups are doing, who is imagining their own worship materials, and what rituals and styles of celebration call forth joy.

Groups were mailed the appropriate number of questionnaires (one per member), each accompanied by a stamped envelope addressed to me and a cover letter. I guaranteed anonymity by telling those who had concerns about disclosure to not sign or back address their responses.[10]

The questions cover two main areas: one devoted to the specifics of organization and planning, the other to the personal and spiritual experience of celebrating. (See questionnaire.)

The return mail brought 126 responses to 377 sent out. I organized them by postmark of place of origin. The answers of four groups, while wonderful, are not used as material here because the majority of their rituals are not or are no longer Eucharistic. The 104 usable responses from 26 groups averages exactly four respondents per group, however I received as few as two per group and as many as 8 from others.

I received responses from three men who are included in two groups. Their answers are here and may sometimes be identifiable by certain comments they make. The men are participants in groups which include families.

That we struggle with language will be apparent in many of the voices. Our vocabularies for this undertaking are still shaky. We are thoroughly suspicious (with cause) of language which we have used for the decades of our lives without much thought. It is language which has imperiled us, defeated and corralled us while masquerading as normal. We have a hard time differentiating *Church*, as in the institution identified with the Vatican and Bishops, (sometimes called Papalist) [11] from church, as recognized in the gathering of the people of God. Because of my unwillingness to assume what exactly we mean when we choose to capitalize or lower case a word, I have recorded the word *church* as it is written by each respondent. You may notice that in the responses of the survey participants, (identified always by a double star ** at the beginning of each response), there are other language and capitalization differences which I have made no attempt to standardize. To do so would be to somehow imply that I know better than they what they intended to say.

Each chapter will be preceded by a FORETHOUGHT, placed there in order to give a preview of what ideas will be addressed and how they work together about a particular aspect of this journey of ours.

I have made every effort to proportionately represent ideas which came in the returned questionnaires.

I received numerous invitations to visit, talk, and pray. I chose the groups I would visit based on their ability to share specific insights. It is no wiser to assume that the numerically dominant group, (white, middle-aged women) has a corner on answers than to assume that men do. I talked with a several Latin American women and African American women whose experience of church in a white culture has had its own special difficulties. Lesbian women also spent time sharing the particular struggles they face.

So this is our story, our voices braided together, individuals in God-focused community, singing songs of liberation, walking together on a new (yet aged) path, feeling mutual strength in prayer and ritual, uncertain at times about the future but hopeful, trusting that we move in the Spirit.

✪✪✪✪✪

SOME NOTES ON VISIONS, VALUES AND ANGER

FORETHOUGHT ✪

What elements bring women to the point of WomenEucharist (WE)? For those who are Catholic and female, much of the material is already familiar and has been lightly or deeply felt in the walk of faith and ritual.

I speak briefly about the history of discrimination against women and about how alternate visions (how life ought to be) and the values which support this vision come into being. We then discuss the development of anger when opposing values clash. Last, I work with the responses of WomenEucharist members to show how this all happens within our church.

The material here is not upbeat or fun to read. It will make some of you mad (again). For others, the material may help in comprehending what women's struggles in the church are all about.

While I believe that this material is important I encourage those who find it heavy going or unrewarding to jump to the next chapter and read this as a post script to the book.

✪✪✪✪✪

⁎. . . the woman is as it were an impotent male, for it is through a certain incapacity that the female is female. [12]

⁎There is another kind of subjection, which is called economic or civil, whereby the superior makes use of his subjects for their own benefit and good; and this kind of subjection existed even before sin. For good order would have been wanting in the human family if some were not governed by others wiser than themselves. So by such a kind of subjection woman is naturally subject to man, because in man the discretion of reason predominates. [13]

⁎A woman who has a head full of Greek, like Mme Dacier, or carries on fundamental controversies about mechanics, like the Marquise de Chatelet, might as well even have a beard. [14]

⁎The real man wishes for two things: danger and recreation. Hence man wants woman as the most dangerous plaything. Man should be brought up for the purpose of war and woman for the relaxation of the soldier: everything else is foolish. [15]

⁎What is woman, what is proper for her? [16]

⁎Devil Woman, Devil Woman, don't follow me,
Devil Woman, let me be, just leave me alone,
I want to go home. [17]

⁎Men define intelligence, men define usefulness, men tell us what is beautiful, men even tell us what is womanly. [18]

It has been happening for thousands of years. Men decide what women are and then tell us.

What do we discover when women finally gain access to their own voices, and share with the world their vision of themselves? But that was a long time coming.

What has occurred is a slow and mighty separation in the visions which men and women hold about the capabilities, roles and responsibilities of females. As long as the majority of men and women accepted women's position as subservient, as God's intent, as the natural order, the shared vision held power for both groups. The creeping and anguished change in vision is first apparent in the desire of women for formal education, systematically denied them. When women began to see themselves as capable of learning beyond gender-based preparation for tasks, one by one they sought it. A long struggle had begun. "With a few notable exceptions, such as the education of girls in Sparta of Classical Antiquity and the monastic system of education in Europe, . . . girls were disadvantaged in every known society of the Western world in regard to the length of their training, the content they were taught and the skills of their teachers." [19] (While this refers to girls in the Middle Ages, Gerda Lerner comments about the 20th Century," . . . no matter what the variation for a particular group to be considered {ethnicity, age, region, religion}, what remains unvaryingly true is that women's access to education remains below that of males of their group.")[20]

Even women who were taught to read were frequently not provided with equal training in writing, thus making it difficult or impossible to express themselves except to those who were near. Even when permitted to learn penmanship, access to the printing press was often difficult and those women who did publish often did so using a man's name or under a man's protection. Because men visioned women as intellectually incapable authorship was often challenged. "The Renaissance humanist Laura Cereta (1469-99) was accused by male writers of presenting her father's works as her own, because no woman could have written such learned letters. . . . Many British women authors, from the 17th to the 19th century, sought to forestall such accusations by having male authorities endorse their works." [21]

At the opening of the 15th century Christine de Pizan, a self-taught writer and thinker who, astounding for her time, wrote for a living, raised the fundamental question of the basic humanity of women. In the debate which flowed for more than three hundred years in Europe, the issues of women's core capabilities were argued. "Were women capable of absorbing education, exercising reason and controlling their feelings?"[22]

The argument was part of the work which opened (faintly) a vision of women: able, intelligent and fully participant in the labors of the world, and ministers toward the kingdom to come.

However, the misogynist concept of the lesser humanity of women is so thoroughly a part of church and state belief and policy that every generation of women has had to do battle with it.

Sarah Grimke called out with passion for men to join in this vision in the 19th century. She asked that no particular favors be granted to women, only that men take their feet off the necks of women and allow them to stand tall as God intended. [23]

Joan Chittister OSB in 1991 pleads the situation eloquently for our generation, "So what is the question before the human race, the response to which may well decide the future of life on earth? And what is the answer? The question is surely, 'Is thinking women's work?' And the answer is certainly, 'Are women human?' The question is 'Should women be in decision-making positions?' And the answer must be, 'Are women human?' The question is, 'Do women have anything to contribute to international relations and ecology and peace and human development?' and the answer must be, 'Are women human?' The question certainly is, 'Can the Church possibly be whole without women?' And the answer without doubt is, 'Are women human?' It is time to answer the real question, the basic question, the fundamental question. 'Are women really human beings or not?'"[24]

The vision of full humanity has been slowly subscribed to by women, and by some men, down through the centuries, but generationally it has had to be repeated as a new group of men come forward and take control.

Slowly, and repeatedly, women have come to envision themselves as more than, other than subservient, ill-educated sex objects, born solely (soully?) for the purpose of meeting men's need and bearing babies.

The vision of full equality has borne fruit in a set of values which support that dream.

Visions precede the values which come to underpin and enforce them. Women are coming to envision themselves as coequal in the process of seeking the center of meaning in life, not mediated or dictated by males. The institutional Church persists, in spite of what it says in many teaching documents, in a vision of women as unequal, ineffectual in entering into divine relationship, unimportant as a sex in understanding and participating in and contributing to the work of salvation.

What are values and how do we know them?

A value has been defined as a recognition of the worth, or truth or beauty of an idea or object or action. It tends to involve critical thinking and behavior. How people decide to use their lives is a good sign of what they value.

Webster's lists *value* not only as a noun, but more importantly, as a verb "to hold in high esteem, to rate in usefulness, excellence." Values are something you do.

With the separation in visions of women's place and worth has come a separation in the values which we experience. Behavior is the disclosing dye of our values system. One of the best signs of what we value can be determined through looking at how we behave to ourselves and others on a daily basis. As adults, people who value good health, for the most part, live healthy lives. People who value personal security lock their doors and keep their hands on their wallets. Those of us who value thriftiness shake out plastic bags and reuse them, and smooth out the aluminum foil and put it away for the next leftover.

Values are reflected emotionally in our lives. We feel stress or anger when our values are contravened by others. An example that every teacher and every parent knows is the statement from a child, usually delivered with some anguish, "It's not fair!" Children often hold fairness as an important value and respond emotionally when their encounters with the world feel unfair. That is a pain filled experience which continues throughout life.

Along with emotional and behavioral components, values also have an active part in our thinking processes. However, this part may not consciously emerge unless challenged, thus triggering the negative emotions which tell us we are in conflict. In other words, if your values system is parallel to the dominant values of your culture, you will feel synchronicity and few values struggles, and therefore, few reasons to explore your values intellectually. If you are discovering your values to be in frequent disharmony with your society, the disharmony causes psychic pain and a search for solution, either a reordering of values or a strengthening of the ones you already affirm.

Research shows that girls and boys learn very different values in our society, but that from the ages of 11 to 15 girls begin to tamp down their own values and assume the dominant male values, which are seen to be normative. Girls learn early that their values, practiced openly will bring conflict with the male experience and therefore they go underground with them, using them primarily in the female sphere. [25]

Values such as cooperation struggle with competition, relationship ideals war with individualism. Primacy of rights is set against primacy of responsibility.

Girls often "see" or value themselves in a circle, while boys "see" or value themselves on a ladder. The circle is infinitely expandable so that many people can be included, while there is only so much room on the step of a ladder and in order to move toward the top you may have to knock someone else off. Since linear, hierarchical values are perceived as normative, girls either give lip-service to those values, or if they persist in acting out their own they are seen and judged as less by people in authority. Academic life, seen as a competitive effort, allows one or two to shine and win the prizes; seen as a cooperative effort, allows many to share their gift so that everyone can take part in success. Though the cooperative model is winning greater acceptance in schools, the hierarchy of class rank still compels many to not share information, but rather to withhold in order to "beat" the competition. This process makes other students the enemy, rather than helpers in learning.

The evidence shows that girls do not desert their values system in early adolescence, they merely do not actively display it in a masculine world. The values of relationality and cooperation are often still visible when girls and women work on a project. The growing affirmation of consensus decision making in female groups, rather than majority rule, is an example of this. The willingness of women to share information with their group in order to accomplish a goal, in whose success they all take part, is another. Even when the dominant culture is very strong there are whispers, faint stirrings, signs that women's values have not died. Even so there are women, who for their own preservation and sanity have completely accepted the White Male System evaluation of themselves and their roles. Kate Millett observes in *Sexual Politics,* "Many women do not recognize themselves as discriminated against; no better proof could be found of the totality of their conditioning."[26] Many women's values do not begin to reemerge out of the interpersonal sphere until their middle years, "Women in their fifties have come to care more about how *they feel* than about what *others think.*"[27] This is middle age reaffirmation for some, a silver-haired psychic metamorphosis for others. This emergence may explain the predominance of women over the age of forty in the groups I visited. Another way of putting it is that we are all involved in the long term, ongoing process of conversion that is the implicit call of our Baptisms. "For most people a genuine conversion experience probably takes place . . . in the period of older adulthood, when conventional *personas* shaped by socialization break down and people begin the process of more authentic individuation."[28]

In the middle years many people reassess their life structures. What has worked and what has not? The decade of the forties used to be seen as the one in which you had, finally, the answers. More and more of us have come to experience it as the decade in which you have fewer certainties and more questions than ever. It is the time for moving away from the power that society, both secular and Church, have held, and toward the personal power of lived experience.

In all five groups which I visited I ask them to spell out the values which they experienced as lived by the patriarchal Church, and the values which were lived out by small groups of women gathering for Eucharist. Here are the results, which represent answers duplicated often.

PATRIARCHY	WOMENEUCHARIST
Authority	Collegiality
Group Submission	Personal autonomy
Transcendence	Immanence
Power of no	Power of yes
Rights of authority	Responsibilities of authority
Rigidity	Flexibility
Orthodoxy	Heterodoxy
Obedience	Exploration
Telling	Listening
Unilaterality	Multilaterality

These are the values which women experience as lived in their individual encounters with the hierarchy and they are values well testified to in a variety of literature. This does not mean that individuals within the institution assign no importance to the values put forth by women. However, they seem to fall to a lower place on their values scale, because they are less frequently *behaved*. It does not mean that women, even the ones who responded to the question, do not also occasionally behave in a manner which connotes rigidity, or authority-over, but that in the greater part women *behave* in ways which show their values to support a horizontal as opposed to a vertical authority model.

What happens when those in authority regularly contravene the values of a group over whom they are deemed to have power? The result is anger.

An important study, released in 1993, investigates for the first time ever the patterns of anger in women. I will reference it heavily here because it is the only document so far that deals specifically with cause and response. Much of the material will not be a surprise to Catholic women. Though we were not specifically studied, some conclusions can be drawn from the material which are appropriate to the situation in which many women in the Church find themselves. (A large-scale study of Catholic and Protestant women and their feminine spirituality groups tells us that Catholic women are the angriest of all. "More women feel alienated in the Catholic Church than in any other denomination in this study . . . *four out of five Roman Catholic women who participated in this study say they often feel alienated from the institutional church.* Those feelings of alienation are intense. . . . There is a remarkable agreement among Catholic Sisters and Catholic laywomen on this issue: 82 percent of the Sisters and 81 percent of the laywomen surveyed often feel alienated from their church.") [29]

I did not ask specific questions concerning anger in the questionnaire. I should have. So many women referred in their responses to their own anger and related feelings of distress that I think it is appropriate here to make some comments on this emotion and how it relates to the values with which many women identify.

**I feel so powerless in my parish, in the Church. I know the priest wants me to sit down and be quiet. I know I have a lot to give, and I want to, but I see that he listens and responds to any man more than he does to any woman.

**I expect the church to be responsive to the values that it preaches. It just doesn't make sense to sing, "The Lord hears the cry of the poor" and then to stop clothing distribution because you don't like the looks of the people who come.

**Our pastor says things like, "I'm deeply sensitive to the needs of women." But a bunch of us got together and investigated inclusive language lectionaries and we bought one and he didn't like it, so we found another one and he said it was fine, but he never uses it. We asked him why and he said he is waiting for the bishops to tell him what to use. I get so angry that he has so much control and it never seems to occur to him that the community counts.

**I do not know if I shall resolve enough conflict to become part of a parish again. Longstanding anger and the inertia of priest, hierarchy, breaks my heart.

** I consistently got angry with the meaninglessness of ill-prepared homilies, with the lies and lack of respect for parishioners' intelligence and with the absence of integrity.

**My departure is very painful to me. When I go to a parish and the grand "pooba" priest dominates the liturgy it makes me angry. What a shame.

**I am a religious and have worked in the chancery for eight years, I head the social ministry office. I work with the bishop regularly and have sat on numerous commissions for the diocese, but in all those years the bishop has never once asked my opinion on any church issue. This makes me so angry. It is as if I don't exist.

**The last few years I went to a parish but I grew angry and weary of the lack of response to my efforts to get changes toward inclusive language, involvement of women and justice issues. The domineering patriarchal system is too much for me to bear any longer.

What in the world has happened? The behaved values of the Catholic Church haven't changed much, but Catholic women's have.

As we find, tentatively, an equal footing in the work place, as we sit through affirmative action meetings mandated by employers, as we see the courts rule in favor of women in sexual harassment cases, as we read newspapers which no longer consign us to the Homemakers' section, as we look on at women of other denominations having their ministries confirmed, we are seeing our own Church as the last bastion of outright sexism in the country.

I believe that the cause of our anger is based in an enormous conflict of values. Though we all profess the same creed, though we all read the same scriptures, we have heard significantly different messages.

A tremendous obstacle for women is the opprobrium directed at the expression of anger. We all learned to be ladies.

Women's psychological preparation for adult life does not usually educate for the healthy uses of anger. Many of us come from families in which the modeling was women as peacemakers, women as passive, women as the forces of stability within the home, as the ones who smooth over all those difficulties.

Part of the education of well-brought up girls is the control of direct expression of anger. We know from our environment that women who display anger are bitches or shrews. Anger displays are more often accepted from boys than girls, and more often on television, from men than women.[30]

In fact, angry women are often seen as out of control, someone you didn't want to grow up to be. Perhaps we admire and try to emulate the woman serene in the grocery store coping beatifically (Mary-like?) with the high decibel tantrum of her three-year-old in front of the candy rack. How we would cringe if she began to shout, acting out her own anger, our sympathy instantly with the child who has been transformed now from noisy aggressor to tiny victim. How we turn away in the street, or in a meeting or in the grocery store or in the Church from the messy uncontrolled loudness of an angry woman.

What would we have learned if there was some story from the Bible telling us of

Mary's anger when Jesus didn't come home with everyone else from Jerusalem, in fact, didn't even bother to mention that he was going to hang around the temple for awhile? The Lucan story depicts her as "sorrowful" after having searched a crowded and threatening city for days. Common sense reminds us that even a special woman like Mary might have been somewhat taken aback, perhaps even angered, by what seems to be her 13-year-old son's lack of basic good manners. Or, if she could accept and hold in her heart her son's behavior, why do we not see anger, righteous anger, rush forth from Mary as she watched her beloved child humiliated on the cross by an occupying and oppressive Roman army?

Mary, as the paradigm of feminine behavior, gives women few clues about appropriate uses of anger.

Scriptures which Mary may well have known warn us against this prickly emotion.

Proverbs 15:18 says, "An ill-tempered man stirs up strife, but a patient man allays discord." Proverbs 27:4 reminds us that "anger is relentless, and wrath is overwhelming. . . ." Sirach 8:16 cautions, "Provoke no quarrel with a quick-tempered man/ nor ride with him through the desert;/ For bloodshed is nothing to him;/ when there is no one to help you, he will destroy you." (sic)

What a vivid and compelling image, the one so angry that murder follows quickly. A caution to those of us that grow irate, we will have no control over our actions. James 1:19-20 calls us to "Know this, my dear brothers: everyone should be quick to hear, slow to speak, slow to wrath, for the wrath of a man does not accomplish the righteousness of God." (sic)

Catholic women bonded to the Church by decades of training in the proper behavior of holy women, in which anger was a sin and unquestioning acceptance was the ideal, learned to sublimate the emotion. The voices of women now report that many of us lived years of quiet anger, often participating in behavior which we believed to be against our own best interests and the best interests of our families, because Church teaching so dictated. The symptom, ignored, led frequently to depression and feelings of lack of control in our own lives.

"Thus the woman who begins to feel this appropriate anger may choose not to appropriately express it. As with any repressed anger, the result is depression and sadness: loss of energy, of zest, of a taste for life, inability to pray or to relate in a trusting and loving way with anyone. This feeling of isolation can lead to severe self-doubt and self hatred, as if she herself were to blame for the predicament. . . .The price of repression is personal diminishment."[31]

One of the difficulties of being angry is that mostly it is done privately, as a shameful emotion. Even when the anger bubbles to the surface it is the slightly revealed sign of the turbulence beneath. In large part, people do not get angry as a group activity, though they may join together in a common cause to vent or confront the anger which they have felt individually.

"Well into adult life, I regarded human emotions like envy, anger, sexual desire, and jealousy as diseased parts of myself that had to be suppressed or preferably cut out of my life altogether."[32]

Thus when just anger comes with the horrible dawning of the truth of oppression there is a transforming moment. Many of us practice denial because to admit the anger is going to be too much to handle, but the transforming moment is also the beginning of conversion, of being able to see the world around through a new lens, one that recognizes oppression of women in everything from tabloid newspaper photographs, to the percentage of women murdered and abused, to the lack of equal medical care, to the dearth of women in the sanctuary during a liturgy.

For many, the recognition is almost more distressing than discrimination itself. To be able to say, "This is women's role" is to be able to accept, though painfully, a set of experiences because they are our lot, as they have been for the millions of women in all the generations who came before. Though unfortunate (and for many women, fatal) some sense of perverse logic pervades this reasoning, as if discrimination, rape, denial of talent, sometimes denial of food, early death from curable illness, come as the "birthright" of the female. Imagine the overwhelming distress when it is discovered that none of this needed to be. It is worse than an ugly practical joke. In fact, as women view the world through the new prism of understanding we realize the almost-hopelessness of our position. Everywhere, in government, in the workplace, in the rural communities of India and Haiti, in the high schools of middle America, in the welfare lines, on the stage in Atlantic City, even in the enforcement of living wills (where only 3 in 10 women will have their wishes followed) women will suffer discrimination, some of which will lead only to dis-ease, some will have fatal consequences.

The continued bombshells of realization might first be met with rage, "We must do something, don't you see what is going on?" Then the enormity of the situation begins to make itself felt. There is nowhere, nowhere that is free, is safe. Hopelessness. Depression, not only about the world around but also at the world internal. The new viewing of the world upsets all the systems of life. Our eyes become suspicious eyes.

The worst blow of all may be the discovery that our faith life is built in an institution that not only is a cultural party to misogynist belief, but that the institution is one of the main perpetrators, having taught it as a matter of faith to seminarians who by word and action maintain and nurture the concept of women as unequal.

Feminist consciousness, once raised, can only deepen. Consciousness-raising makes it impossible to ever go home again. Once sensitized to the reality and the effects of patriarchy, one can only become ever more aware of its pervasiveness, more convinced of its destructiveness, more resistant to its influence on oneself and one's world. The feminist Catholic may begin with a mildly disturbing realization that the religious language of her tradition is heavily sexist, that she is being victimized in her ministry by the irrational fear and hatred of women that has been bred into an all-male, celibate clergy, that the God-imaging in the tradition is overwhelmingly masculine, that she is being restricted in totally unnecessary ways in the exercise of her sacramental life because of her sex. But once she has begun to see, begun the critical process of analysis, she will necessarily gradually be overwhelmed by the extent, the depth, and the violence of the institutional Church's rejection and oppression of women. This precipitates the inward crisis which the feminist Catholic inevitably faces: a deep, abiding, emotionally draining anger that, depending on her personality, might run the gamut from towering rage to chronic depression.

"This experience, which must be distinguished from the episodic anger we all experience in the face of frustrations or everyday mistreatment, should probably be called existential anger. It is not a temporary emotion but a state of being. . . . Waking up angry in the morning and going to bed at night angry, especially for a person who has been socialized to women's responsibility for keeping peace in family and community and who has learned from childhood that a good Christian does not even feel, much less express anger, is a personally shattering experience. . . .

"In her heart the feminist Catholic knows her anger is not only justified but mandatory, just as was Jesus' anger at the oppressive hypocrisy of the clergy of his day. . . . She wishes she could focus her anger on institutional arrangements and doctrinal positions, but the source of her suffering and the cause of her anger are most often real people, usually males in power positions who really cannot be honestly excused on the grounds of stupidity or ignorance because they *do* know what they are doing. These people are simultaneously her personal oppressors and those for whose salvation Jesus died."[33]

And that is a major foundering point, these others are brothers in Christ, co-equals to inherit the kingdom, they have inherited the same scripture, the Gospels of liberation, and yet, in the midst of hearing it, preaching it, they also use it as a means of unjust control.

When our values or moral code are assaulted anger is appropriate. The level of our anger is proportionate to our understanding of the offense. If we deem it to be intentional or malicious our response is heightened.[34]

What do we do with this anger? Susan Thomas delineates three ways we cope. The classic way, the good girl way, she calls "anger-in" or sublimation.

**I have never felt I could talk about my anger with the Church. For a long time I felt like there was something wrong with me, other women seemed happy enough. It took me twenty years, until the late seventies, to find out that a lot of those other women sitting in the pews with me were angry, too.

**There is a Sunday-only associate at our parish and my stomach knots every time he is the celebrant. He actually used the word "bitch" from the altar once.

The second, acting out our anger, involves venting and blaming, but we experience almost no positive rewards[35] from this type of response; the anger, vented, just won't go away, especially if the behaviors which caused the rage occur over and over. Many women fear that venting may cause a rent in relationships, with the recipient of our anger retaliating or turning away.[36] And while we might be able to dream of yelling at the bishop, not many of us will, so those around us stand as surrogates. A dangerous business it is since we hold relationships to be highly important. That valuing may well lead to a sense of grief if we damage even difficult relationships.[37]

**Several years ago I had a shouting match on the steps of the church with my pastor after Mass. I wasn't that mad at him but I was so fed up with the way liturgies are conducted in our parish. He and I still speak to each other, but it's never been comfortable since and I think he has never forgiven me.

"Anger-discuss" is the third way of confronting the beast. Dicussion is the only way of expressing anger which actually aids good health, while not talking about anger is a significant predictor of heart disease in women of middle age"[38]

**There are five of us who met with our pastor and tried to explain how we feel when we aren't included. He really gave us a sympathetic hearing, and said he would do what he could, but that there was a lot that just wasn't up to him. We've seen some positive changes and we know he is doing what he can. I just feel a lot better walking into church when I know at least he heard us. Things aren't great, I need my woman's group for that, but they are better.

Catholic women wrestle with the Leviathan: "once you but lay a hand upon him, no need to recall any other conflict!" [39] Even discussing the mess with an unyielding institution has proved to be dangerous. What do you do with anyone who thinks all truth is deposited in his own pocket? How did Sr. Theresa Kane feel after she talked to the Pope?

Given the ways in which we respond to anger, what is likely to set us off? Power, justice and responsibility issues in which what we confront is not congruent with our ideology is a significant factor in making us really mad.[40]

Refer back to the statements of women from the questionnaire. Their anger acknowledgments refer to experiences in which power, justice and responsibility values were denigrated or ignored.

Catholic women are coming in large numbers to believe the power of their baptism is not so great as the power of men's in that there are stringent limitations on how one can minister and to whom, and under what circumstances, and it is the baptized male who makes the determinations.

Issues of justice values have a high level of anger surrounding them for women (and, by implication, power and responsibility issues, for, who has the power to change things, and having that power, who has the responsibility?). As an example, here is a tiny taste of the topics which The National Coalition of Catholic Nuns, "sensitive to the way in which institutions and structures can work against the good of persons"[41] sees as in violation of justice over the past twenty years.

Domination of Communities of Religious Women by Priests

"We recognize the interdependence of men and women and we fully agree that neither men nor women can arrive at wholeness without the other. At the same time, we uphold as inviolable the right of self-determination for religious women." [42]

Statement against Segregation

"NCAN calls upon the teaching Sisters of Mississippi Catholic schools to resist, to protest, and to strike if necessary rather than accept white children escaping desegregation."[43]

Support for New York City Gay Rights Bill.

"As Roman Catholic nuns who passed a resolution in 1974 that 'it is immoral and should be illegal to discriminate against any person because of his or her sexual preference,' we lament that 12 years later the City of New York has not yet provided legal protection in employment, housing, land, commercial space and public accommodations for a substantial minority of its residents."[44]

Perhaps it is that those who have faced injustice in their own lives are deeply touched and angered by it in the existence of others.

So what do we do when holding it in doesn't work, shouting gives us heart attacks and discussing our right to equality is met with never-statements?

Carolyn Osiek describes several ways of coping. One is the *rejectionist stance*, in which ". . . the only way to cope with the pain is to remove its cause as a significant factor in one's life."[45] A second is the *marginalist position* on the fringes of the Church, "Lacking the clear call or the courage to leave, neither can they fully belong."[46] A third way is *revisionist*, which sees that "the patriarchal pattern of dominance and submission are serious but not fatal wounds that can be healed." They remain in the Church, but with a critical stance. [47] Finally, there is the *liberationist viewpoint*, which calls for conversion beginning with oneself, and continuing to trumpet the needs and rights of the oppressed, believed to be Jesus' call, and opposing every position which does not lead to freedom.[48]

Using my question "Are you still active in a parish?" as a guide I found many had chosen the rejectionist path. Sometimes they also identify with some aspects of the liberation position.

**No. Years of sexism piled up. When the pope came I just stopped altogether.

**It no longer fills my needs.

** "Occasion of sin" was a phrase I used when I left the parish.

**No, The parish was too Father-oriented, and never tried to offer anything for me as a lesbian woman, or for my sisters and brothers who are gay.

**Twenty years ago I majored in theology in college and took seriously my work and the work of Vatican II and realized that the hierarchical church was not my church.

**No. The Church is pretty sterile, sexist. The official attitude toward women and the practices re women, the papal/Vatican move toward increasing control and emphasizing dogma rather than the Good News.

**No. The liturgies ceased being meaningful prayer for me; too large and impersonal, with poor homilies and all male presiders.

**No. I have had to struggle with sexism and repression by the institution of men and women trying to express spirituality.

**Absolutely not! I was a canonical religious for nine years. I finally came to believe that my presence in the Church during liturgies gave silent assent to the continued injustice done to women.

The rest are divided about equally into marginalists and revisionists. Hints of the liberationist position are heard in both groups.

This is the way in which marginalists view their institutional participation:

**I attend a parish mass but there are lots of painful memories.

**Yes, but just for Eucharist.

**Sometimes I go for the special celebrations, Christmas, etc., because my women's Eucharist group hasn't created them.

**I stopped being a lector because the messages were often not what I could proclaim.

The homilies are sexist, or guilt-driven and I could not actively participate in a liturgy based around those things in good conscience. I still go to Sunday Mass.

** I have been active in a parish and work as a campus minister but it becomes increasingly painful for me. Because of work and long felt associations I have not completely severed the connection, but this year I have thought more seriously about it than ever before. I feel excluded or not fully welcomed as a woman and a lesbian. The recent letter on gays and lesbians has upset me greatly.

**I am a teacher in a parish school and attend mandatory school liturgies but that is all.

** I still identify with the parish because it was in this place that my spirituality started. I go with my friends when it is significant for them, even though it is painful for me. I await the day when Church is a more just setting. Pain for pain's sake is not a healthy thing.

**I go to Sunday Mass once or twice a month to connect with friends outside my women's liturgy group.

**I sing in the choir but at times I don't participate because of the lifeless leadership of a priest who fears change.

**I'm semi-active. I still attend council meetings and sometimes think I can still make a difference by voicing opinions but grow disheartened. I play the organ and piano for occasional liturgies.

**I still have children of school age, so we attend Sunday liturgy, trying to make sure we get the better of the two priests. My real spiritual needs are met in my women's group and in the soup kitchen where my whole family works.

There is such a longing to belong, such memories, so much awareness of where formation comes from, but so much pain in embracing the daily/weekliness of parish life. One of the saddest messages for the institution is the loss of all that talent, all that willingness to share in building up. Some are gone completely, some just barely holding on.

There is a surprisingly large number of revisionists, those still extremely active in their parishes, giving their gifts, supporting the life of the church while searching for ways not only to change that institution and also meet their own spiritual needs. "Women who are defecting in a parish place are helping to raise feminist consciousness, an essential step before the tradition can consider systemic change. Such women are potential change-agents within local congregations." [49] Many of them have parish-shopped so that they worship where weekly personal experiences are somewhat mediated by thoughtful and sensitive staff. There is a delightfully subversive nature about many of them. Osiek's liberationist position is somewhat more visible in the responses of this group.

** I've chosen to join a parish that has liturgy which attempts to use inclusive language. It has developed a mission statement which is read in place of the Creed. I do centering prayer with a group there.

** I teach CCD. I spend a lot of time talking with the kids in my class about the call of Jesus to justice, and about how it is God we worship and not the Church, and that the Church has made lots of mistakes and continues to do so, This isn't just ancient history, this is right now. I keep asking them, challenging them, to look at the Gospels from a justice perspective.

**I am a lector and the coordinator of a group I organized, the Women's Concerns Ministry, a small group of feminist Catholics who advocate for change in the parish.

**I do still participate in a parish, probably because I haven't suffered so badly. Our parish towers above the others in our city for forward thinking and sincere pastoral ministry. I am sixty two years old and this is the first parish in which I have participated.

**I am a eucharistic minister and the coordinator of the Homeless Ministry.

**I am a Eucharistic minister and feel I have a ministry in the prayer of the faithful. I pray for people with AIDS, especially children, their families and our Church.

**I participate in daily and Sunday liturgies. I also have an active part in many ongoing programs at the Newman Center. It is an unusually liberal place.

**I worship, do adult education, lector, am a eucharistic minister. I plan occasional liturgies and have given homilies. I also help others with funeral and wedding liturgies.

**I am a member of the parish social ministries committee and go to mass two or three times a week.

**I attend daily Mass and am a eucharistic minister and lector.

**I facilitate a women's issues group in our parish. There are about twenty of us who meet once a month. When I see them gathered I am just amazed, it is absolutely the backbone of this parish. With the exception of the ushers, not one single activity, from CCD to parish dances would happen, no way, if this group walked out. This is the most enlightened, best educated group in the parish in terms of theology and social justice. A number of them are degreed in those areas. There are a couple of ex-nuns with liturgy and pastoral ministry degrees. Everyone has done and is doing her reading. We have begun to talk about what would happen if we "struck" for greater justice. The idea is so tempting.

What would happen if the women of the Church struck, struck for the vision of complete equality, struck to demand that the values of collegiality and responsibility and flexibility and exploration and acceptance be normative? The women quoted above have already done so in a quiet way. They have carried their anger out of those buildings, either permanently, or temporarily and joined to praise God, transforming anger into prayer and action to build the church of the people and to work for their own spirituality in a safe house, the house that our Church should be but isn't.

How badly bruised the Church of the Institution is, how rattled and wounded the church of the people is. Wounded and wandering. Trying to "be" church while seeing Church as the enemy, our separated brethren.

We're so angry and still we come; we're so angry and so we go. We cry for justice, plain as the sun in the East, plain as the words of the Son, and have rules of their making, rules of their convenient imaginations quoted back, and so we go aside, praying together and invite that friend of women, Jesus, to join us. We are, we have been sexually abused, abused because of our sex, and we suffer, We ALL suffer.

✪✪✪✪✪✪

HOW GROUPS COME
INTO EXISTENCE

FORETHOUGHT ✪

In this chapter I will try to share some of the issues and concerns which respondents mention as goads to the genesis of their own WomenEucharist groups. Issues which surfaced frequently are poorly developed liturgies, male dominance of ritual, scandal in the institution and a lack of awareness of justice issues within parishes, as well as a felt push from the Spirit.

I attempt to work out some ideas on how Eucharist becomes more "real" as it addresses the issues of order, community and transformation. Of course, there are many threads which come together to bring us toward a new consciousness and new action, and some of those I have tried to name late in the chapter.

✪✪✪✪✪

Who ever walked behind anyone to freedom? If I can't walk hand in hand, I don't want to go. [50]

Most of us do not have the courage to set out on this path wholeheartedly, so God arranges it for us. [51]

For some there is an event in which the institutional Church by some action, crosses an invisible boundary line. For others it is slow steady piling up of experience and study, or it is the slow and steady pull of the Spirit.

REDISCOVERING LITURGY ✪

**The experience of the growing pain of stoic liturgies. We desired the reality of Eucharist. We met to discern what we might do for enriching our lives as individuals and in community.

**We started by sharing with the Medical Mission Sisters in the 1960s. We were invited to their Sunday liturgies. They taught us how to plan liturgies and work together as a community. When the cardinal closed the liturgies at MMS in 1973 we continued to celebrate elsewhere.

**We had a mutual desire to celebrate the changes in the liturgy.

**My wife and I, unhappy with all-male purist liturgies, decided to begin a feminist inclusive worship group at home and invite others to join us.

**We're mostly Catholic women who were frustrated with Church liturgy and yet wanted to celebrate together.

**Our parish liturgy committee could plan a beautiful liturgy, carefully following the guidelines of the diocese, and focusing on the felt needs of the community, and our pastor, as often as not, would chose not to follow it. Not only that, but he would substitute inappropriately, not sensitive to the congregation. As for inclusive language, forget it. After years of requests by the liturgy committee, he is still saying, during the Creed, "for us men and for our salvation."

**I'm not even sure that what my parish does would be called liturgy. That's a word that implies, for me, prayerful planning, thought, intention. We have routine. Bloodless, uninspired, no joy. I finally couldn't stand it anymore and went looking for a place where people could deliberately intentionally join together in celebration,

**There were two women hungering for an inclusive meaningful Eucharist who invited others with the same hunger.

The Constitution on Sacred Liturgy called us again to an earthly liturgy which is a foreshadowing, a sweet taste of the heavenly liturgy, a sacred action surpassing all others.[52] For many women these are ideals yet to be attempted in the locus of parish and how we hunger for them! Liturgical revisions often embraced the letter but not the spirit of Vatican II. In many parishes where creative effort brought forth the heart of the document the liturgies have fallen on hard times as that creative effort slumped, thirty years later, into disuse. We moved from one sort of lock step, the rigid ritual of pre-conciliar days, to the new lock step of liturgical reform, which once accomplished sometime in the 1970s is now complete and we as a congregation can turn to new areas of interest.

The experimentation and enculturation which should continue to be a part of Eucharistic planning in order to fully integrate the life of the congregation into the celebration is frequently lacking in contemporary American parishes. We continue to look for a place where our lives as Christians are embraced in Eucharist, coming from it and flowing back into it.[53] What many cannot understand is why the sacrament which should be so dynamic, so affirming, so revealing of God's love continues to limp along pro forma. Perhaps a major reason is that we mostly in parish life do things "by the book." That is to imply that the movement of the Spirit had best be in the book or we are not permitted to feel it. To call for prayerful liturgy planning is to comprehend that we not only speak to God but that we listen hard for the reply. One response calls liturgy "uninspired," meaning that God has not breathed Godspirit into it. We need to conspire, breath with God, as we enter into ritual so Eucharist can pulse with love and concern, both God's and ours.

It is important to listen to the voices of these women. You may recall that many of them have been long in the church and, thirty years after the Vatican Council, are still trying to get it right. They continue to feel a discontinuity between belief and ritual practice. It is not that they do not live what they celebrate, they are unable to celebrate what they live.

**Why can't we ever be glad, be really happy in Church? I mean, all of us together, and let each other know it?

What can the phrase "reality of Eucharist" (cited in the quotes at the top of the chapter) mean? I suggest that the respondent did not deny the reality of Jesus present in her own parish Mass, but rather, that it is not evident that the celebrant and the congregation believe that it is true. Perhaps they are unable to make that truth evident through the ritual which they are in the midst of performing. We recognize gradually when rites, even sacramental ones, no longer deeply enter into our lives. Perhaps the symbols no longer cry out to us. Perhaps these rites have become so thickly encrusted that we cannot see through to the bare bones of meaning. Perhaps they praise and thank God with phrases which are no longer a deeply felt part of our personal language. Perhaps we can no longer see clearly how we as the Body of Christ are meshed with he who inhabits the body of Christ.

Eucharist, Jesus present, is only an idea, a concept without some medium through which it becomes real, that reality of Eucharist of which we spoke before. The medium, for our public celebration, is ritual. Ritual is an endlessly human attempt to provide a space in which we who are human encounter God who is human and also divine. It is the very humanness of ritual, the very weakness of its human attempt to embrace the divine which requires that we must keep on finding ways to make it better, make it more fitting to our developing understanding.

"Ritual is no universal remedy for the difficulties that face the proclamation of the good news today, but then nothing else is either. . . it will be enough to recall that ritual goes very deep into the human condition; that it can speak to the whole person as nothing else can; . . . that it looks forward to the salvation promised; that it acknowledges the natural world and faces the darkness in that world; that it proclaims the Lord's death and resurrection; that it falls silent in the face of the mystery of God's loving redemption." [54]

Though we chafe at petrified rubrics, we still know the need to celebrate in ways that are certain, fixed though flexible. The wonderful sense of order which we experience when we are able to repeat meaningful ritual gives shape and order to our world. Good ritual is a pathway along which we can move into sacred space, bringing our lives and, through God, have them make sense.

"In its ordering function, ritual performs the world, bringing it from chaos . . . into actualized (actionful) form. It is not as if there were first a world and then someone thought of representing it ritually. It is rather that the perceived and imagined world is an extension, a projection, of the ritual forms a people practice. This is the sense in which it can be said that through rituals ` the rivers flow, and all things flourish.'" [55]

"Real Eucharist" shapes our perceptions, gives order to our lives. It puts the events of our existence into sacred perspective, assisting us in seeing the world through the prism of God love. It reinforces us against the battering of hopelessness, pumps up our joy. It provides a psychic arena in which we can encounter our God. The ritual is not the act of worship, rather it is the setting where that act can take place. If the setting, the arena, is foreign or uncomfortable or repressive or stressful or forbidding, we are deeply hindered in the act itself.

We ask, where is the first virtue of community liturgy, hospitality? Good liturgy does not happen until the congregation feels welcomed, wanted, in communion. Without greeting, without enfolding we remain individuals locked in our private worlds, inhabiting the same space, but not bound by ties of knowing, and affirming. There is growing certainty that large, uninvolved groups have a real tough time being the deeply personally committed people of God. How can we, as women who often find personal richness in relationship, praise God well, thoroughly and constantly in a body of strangers?

We wonder, where is the joy promised as the sign of God's presence in contemporary liturgy? When the face of the priest, his words, his body contain no hint of rejoicing, when the posture and demeanor of the assembled reflect boredom, how is it that the liturgy has failed to speak of the joy of Jesus among us?

As people who have come to believe that God is deeply and passionately indwelling, we want that reflected in our liturgical encounter. We want to recognize in our ritual that the life and experience of each of us is a part of the community's journey toward holiness. We ask, can this happen when we do not know the names, much less the stories of those around us? How is it that we can grow toward wholeness if we do not see and respect the paths which others walk? It is these stories, individually and together, that we carry into liturgy so that they may be transformed.

Some of those stories are boring, or repetitive or angry or unbalanced. Some of them we would prefer to avoid. Doing community is messy and loose-ended. We have to be open wide to the unexpected, called to be patient and careful and simple, we have to have our journey boots on. We have to dispose of stocked-up, one-size-fits-all answers. We need to remember remember remember that this woman, this man is Jesus.

So we come together to hold each other gently, to treasure each other. No need to fight or fear, we are free to grow.

FACING PATRIARCHY ✪

**We came into existence because of the pain and anger and frustration of the all-male symbolism at the altar. I believe very many groups were influenced into existence by the regular scandals surfacing today concerning the sexual addictions of Catholic priests and bishops.

**People just do not buy the all male symbolism anymore in the wake of clergy scandals. They begin to question. This is the case with me. Since at least a third of the women have been sexually assaulted at one time or another these revelations are a huge factor.

**Four years ago women were very "hiddenly" being put down by a priest who came to take the place of our regular priest. One lady said she would not tolerate that and asked a small group to her home for Eucharist.

**We're mostly Catholic women who were frustrated and felt the pain of non-inclusion.

**Our group began because we decided we could wait no longer to be fully included. It will be wonderful for our sons and daughters if they finally have a church where they can worship equally but most of us feel that we'll be long dead before half the human race is counted as equal by the Church.

** So many of us talked about how discouraging it is, week after week, to hear our sons and husbands preached to. The Church has no idea what damage it does.

**We're a group of women who finally just decided to get on with it since no one was going to do it for us.

The wound of sexual scandal has gashed open parishes across the country, and we have been bloodied again and again by the terrible events in our own dioceses, and others. We live now in fear of, in suspicion of our own priests. Whereas, formerly they might have been dull or disenchanted or delightful and enthusiastic, we now see them as possible physical and psychosexual threats to our families and parishes. Uneasy basis for praying together in trust and hope.

The breach between clergy and communicants widens as each new charge is made, each new court case and chancery settlement becomes part of the week's news. When the assistant who was assigned to the parish years ago is indicted questions are raised about what secret damage he may have left as his legacy. Accusations and convictions flowing from events two decades old are not uncommon. Whose family will next bear the scars? The family of Church bears them all.

For some women, especially those who have personally suffered sexual abuse, attempting worship in a church riddled with such distrust may be impossible.

The frequent examples of sexual misconduct in the American Church serve as excellent, horrible symbols of many of our struggles. Such behavior, especially pedophilia, relies on misusing power for personal pleasure or gain. Many women and children have experienced powerlessness at the hands of men and with it the feelings of worthlessness and guilt which so frequently accompany their inability to protect themselves from ones with greater physical or psychological or theological authority. Women congregating together for worship seek a place where there is no need to have authority over each other, respecting instead the right each has to personal autonomy and integrity. "Integrating and nurturing power are a sign of the holy."[56] This is power that frees, that encourages, that calls forth, not power that competes, controls and inhibits. It is power-with, not power-over, and we need to practice it.

Pedophilia requires that the victim be perceived as an object, someone not in relationship with, something not equal to the abuser. Consideration of the possible effect of one's actions on another, a necessity in God-shaped relationships, is absent from the decision to abuse. Women often feel objectified and abused in parishes where the ordained male finds women useful for the non-power-sharing jobs of secretary, cook, teacher of young children, while having no interest or vision of equality in the work of the Christian community.

"At the same time that the church excluded women from full participation in the sacramental system and from any participation in church leadership, legitimating their oppression in the family, and collaborated in their societal marginalization, the church used women for virtually all ecclesial tasks that men did not care to perform while underpaying them, denying them all access to power, and leaving them totally dependent on the good will and tolerance of male power figures."[57]

**My mother cooked and cleaned for Father and took out his garbage, and he never looked at her or asked her what she thought, or saw her as more than her job.

Women have certainly been objectified, as less intelligent, as emotional, as temptress, as unclean, as the major workhorses for all those messy jobs. Women gathering for Eucharist seek the honoring of individual gift, and the vitality of each person's contribution, the escape from objectification.

Sexual misconduct relies on secrecy in order to continue. The pedophiliac performs his deeds in secret, often threatening the victim if the abuse is revealed.

How often the institution has operated in secret, separating itself from the community of believers by the cover-up and denial in matters sexual and financial. Bishops who do not demonstrate accountability for money and for abusive priests, and threaten those who would wish to disclose stand guilty. Rosemary Radford Ruether calls this the female inferiorization of the reduction of women to silence, [58] a state in which women learn that it is dangerous to attempt to name their own oppression in a situation which still holds some power in their lives. They often know from experience that their expressions will be devalued or looked upon as disruptive and hysterical. Keeping silent means that women suffer discrimination alone, often thinking they are crazy. It is one thing to identify patriarchal sexist abuse in impersonal society, but to name it in one's own parish community means taking a chance on becoming a pariah. "The woman who experiences dissenting thoughts alone, without a network of communication to support her, can hardly bring her own dissent to articulation. Without a social matrix, she will simply be terrorized into submission by the authorities that surround her. . . ." [59]

Women gather separately to find their own voices in order to speak out their experiences of discrimination. Naming them, they can uncover ways through ritual and prayer, to address and heal them.

It is so very difficult to be present week after week at liturgies which reflect only half the population, which deny the value of the women present by failing to include them prayerfully, by idolizing the male in God, so firmly implanted in ritual. Many women leave Sunday Eucharist disheartened and angry, for themselves at being non-valued, for their daughters who do not hear the Word call out to them, for their sons and husbands who hear from the altar the deification of the masculine gender. As one respondent said, "Going to Sunday Mass has become an occasion of sin for me."

Along with order and community we seek transformation. There is no point in ritual if nothing can change, if life will remain the same after we have received the last blessing and gone home. We must believe that change can happen, that our God will hear us, not hard-heartedly, but intimately engaged. To fully celebrate we must affirm our own and our community struggle toward the liberation promised by the Gospels.

Real Eucharist is "an action of God together with the people of God, ritually performed to celebrate freedom and to hasten the liberation of the whole world." [60]

We seek a community where people will take a chance on openly believing, profoundly hoping, that God is here and in love liberation happens. As women, we seek the dissolution of oppression for ourselves, our sisters and all who are held down. "Ritual is, at least, the preparation of groups of people for the spiritual work they must do; and the struggle for liberation is a spiritual work—that is, a work of moral courage . . ."[61]

Those most deeply in need of liberation are the ones called to free Eucharist from the bonds of status quo, a strait jacket if there ever was one, and beg the Spirit to join in the search for the justice and peace we are promised.

RECOGNIZING SEXUAL ORIENTATION ✪

**We come out of an active Dignity group. We formed a committee to speak specifically about women's concerns and our Eucharist group flowed out of this.

**Several of us who met through a lesbian consciousness group are Catholic and we were able to share our sense of estrangement from the Roman Church. We felt totally unincluded in parish life, which is mostly heterosexual and family centered. There is no recognition in any mainline Catholic Church I have ever worshipped in that there is any such thing as faithful lesbians who really want to worship and be included in the life of the parish. Besides that, the Church's teachings say that I am immoral, in a state of sin because I love my partner and want to live a full life with her.

**I needed to find a place where my whole person, my spirit, my body, my lesbianism, could be accepted without shame. I firmly believe that God made me the way I am, and for a purpose and I suffered so long, feeling shamed by my church.

**My partner and I had to find a place to pray where we didn't have to hide what we are.

Lesbians have a double burden, gender and sexual orientation. Most parishes have little specific to offer them, and it is easy to feel excluded on both levels.

We live in a time when there is tremendous dissension and unrest about the position of homosexuals in society. May they teach in schools, may they participate in same-sex marriages? May they participate in the health coverage of their partners? Does "don't ask, don't tell" make it possible for them to serve in the armed forces? The heterosexual population frequently exhibits phobic behavior in response to gay/lesbian issues.

In the midst of the furor, theologians struggle with how homosexuality can be viewed as "disordered" (Vatican letter on pastoral care of homosexuals, 1986) on one hand and as "God's gift" (Bishop Mugavero, Brooklyn, 1976).

Meanwhile, gays and lesbians attempt to find their own paths to God on a road littered with the stones of prejudice. In moving from positions of denial of their sexual orientation, and searching for God's meaning for their lives, some have begun to speak of and act on their own personal visions.

Carter Heywood comments, "Deprived of civil and religious trappings of romantic love, we may well be those who are most compelled to plumb the depths of what it really means to love. Our deprivation becomes an opportunity and a vocation to become conscious of the things we have not seen, and to make others conscious of these same things." [62]

Lesbian women seek in WomenEucharist groups a space which is not a battle ground. They can pray toward becoming aware of their own gifts for seeing God's image and acceptance in their own experiences and those of other oppressed people, and gradually find ways to share their graced insights with others.

This is how Carter Heywood views the pain:

"The 'Fathers' are not with us. Our families do not know how to be with us. Our church believes it must be against us. The Bible admonishes us. Jesus was silent about us. The authorities that be despise the threat we pose —and despise it all the more if we happen, or appear to be, wise and happy people. It is much easier to tolerate a sad and pitiful homosexual than a proud and creative gay man or lesbian. If we affirm ourselves, we are seen as sick; if we renounce ourselves, we are called healthy. And we think *we* are crazy!" [63]

And so it is non-judgmental community ritual that lesbians can join in their work of transformation and liberation.

ADDRESSING SOCIAL JUSTICE ✪

**We began as a group of families meeting at the Catholic Worker House for Saturday night mass. We all sought an alternative liturgy with a social justice slant.

**We began as a parish group to promote justice for women both within the Church and society. We did a lot of self-education with study groups and discussions. At one point, four of us just decided we were ready to celebrate.

**It began as a group of women activists who took actions of public protest to various government actions. Worship became necessary.

**A group of us need a good liturgical service coming from a perspective of social justice.

**I work in a battered women's shelter, and have for almost ten years. The burnout factor is a constant problem for many of us. I keep looking for ways to counteract it in me and I find praying together with others who understand the misery I see and feel there helps me enormously to keep going. My parish liturgies don't really speak to this, they seem more to support the status quo, even though they read words about freeing the oppressed, they don't seem to really feel them or act on them, so sometimes I need to pray and have Eucharist with others who are truly working with the people who suffer. My faith is in large part based on belief that the words of liberation are true, will be true some day, for the women and children I work with.

Women have been reading Scripture for a long time, looking for the good news of their own liberation. Those who have done long duty as social workers, civil rights workers, soup kitchen servers, volunteers in shelters search for the tidings that there is freedom, justice for all in God's family. Some women are beckoned by social justice struggles because they see the relationship between their own oppression and the pain of others who are unable to grasp enough power to be self-determining. [64]

The planet is webbed with torment, some involuntary, such as flood and earthquake, and much more voluntary, such as unemployment, famine, racial struggle, war. Always, it is the powerless who suffer most. Children starve, women are beaten, men and women of color are the first to lose jobs in times of cutback.

Those who would read Matthew 25, and attempt to feed and clothe and visit in the name of Jesus, those who believe that "Yahweh is close to the brokenhearted and rescues those whose spirit is crushed"[65] also seek liturgy which specifically encounters the needs of those who are damaged by injustice, and so they gather for Eucharist. Catholics involved in working with the impoverished and the diminished struggle with what seems to be the Dr. Jekyll and Mr. Hyde faces of the Church. On the one hand the institution is visibly compassionate, with hospital beds for AIDS patients, parish-sponsored food drives, international relief. On the other hand, the institution is often allied with the secular power structures in promoting the very subjugation responsible for misery. Stories concerning the dealings of the Vatican Bank, Opus Dei and the Banco Ambrosiano[66] encourage cynicism and a sense that at the highest levels the Church of Rome continues to care little for the struggles of the poor.

Having been invited by the Gospels to see the pain of the world and respond to it in the promise of Jesus, many gather for Eucharist with others who share the daily labor.

SO WE GATHER ✪

**I came home from the 1985 WOC conference in St Louis determined to get a SF Bay Area WOC group going. Within a few years we evolved into a women's liturgy group instead of a discussion/action group.

**A few of us came together to organize a day on women in the Church. Later we wanted to keep doing things. We began using the Church facility (for liturgies) but later began meeting in a private home to free ourselves.

**We had formed a Women's Concerns Ministry in our parish and a major aspect of it grew into this liturgy group (nearly all the same people). We meet for this in a participant's home.

**We began as a parish group to promote justice for women both within the Church and society. We did a lot of self-education with study groups and discussions. At one point four of us just decided we were ready to celebrate liturgy.

**I received materials and a questionnaire from WomenChurch about their 1983 conference so another woman and I invited a group of women to gather and discuss the issues. The group evolved to a one time a month gathering for potluck and worship. We continue to invite people to join us when they express interest.

**A small group of two or three women shared their beliefs about eucharist and began to share together once a month ritually.

**Two women invited their friends to discuss the role of women in the Church and that is where we began. That was 1980.

**Eight years ago members of the . . . religious congregation and others started a prayer group which developed into our primary liturgical experience.

**It evolved out of a group of women who got together for discussion, loosely known as the Women of God (WOGs). We all wanted something richer in our worship; we felt that it was time for us to begin celebrating Eucharist together. One of our group visited other WomenChurch groups and expressed her desire to begin having liturgies.

**We evolved from a post-Vatican II group of educated Catholics.

Some responders see these beginnings as not unlike the beginnings of the family of church.

This is a Pentecost experience. We gathered, perhaps frightened, uncertain, wondering. Then the Spirit came, and we were filled up and began to express ourselves in foreign tongues (for it is certain that to say that women can celebrate is two thousand years foreign) and we began to make bold proclamations (for to say that all we need do is ask and Jesus is with us is audacious indeed).

**Three of us working on doing it on a monthly basis. The first one was Pentecost 1989.

The Gospels testify that for the followers of Jesus the day of Pentecost evolved from those first meetings on the beach, flowed through the feeding and the healing and the stories and the Supper and finally through the death and resurrection. Conversion, the Jesus-spark within, the sacred power to testify in faith happened over years as Jesus' friends saw, and learned and got side-tracked and bickered and listened and learned again.

So it is with us. We have spent our lives in our own evolutionary following of the Gospels. And we have, like Magdelene and Peter and James and John, heard and wondered and been afraid, but faith, the Jesus power, is amazing. For finally two, three of us gathered together in uncertainty and came to actively believe that when He said "Do this in memory of Me" He was talking to us.

What comprised this evolution? Ask yourself, what made yours? What is the spiral of experience, prayer, encounter, meeting, sorrow, doubt, event, joy, which guided you?

The civil rights movement, Rosemary Radford Ruether, spiritual direction, feminist studies, being employed in the chancery, doing Bible study with a parish group, Thea Bowman, getting a divorce and trying to get an annulment, working as a member of the Jesuit Volunteers in Central America, being part of an RCIA team, volunteering with the aged, growing up, reading Boff, Vatican II and Xavier Rynne, The Grail, having a daughter, Women's Ordination Conference, meeting Jesus through Cursillo, John Courtney Murray and his growing edge of tradition, WomenChurch, *America* magazine, being in a religious order which tried hard to do community, Andrew Greeley, the bishops' 1979 Ad Hoc Committee on Women in Society and the Church, studies in Marxism, Sr. Theresa Kane, hearing "confession" as a hospital chaplain because there was no one else, getting raped, Leadership Conference of Women Religious, Anita Hill, organizing a women's issues reading group, Dignity, *The National Catholic Reporter*, Diann Neu and Mary Hunt and WATER, the ecumenical movement, other women with Good News, meditation, Meinrad Craighead and God as mother, assertiveness training, Thomas Gumbleton, The Vatican Bank, the diocesan spiritual center programs, Miriam Therese Winter, The Gnostic Gospels, doing social work in a women's prison, Elisabeth Schüssler Fiorenza, trusting the Spirit, *Humanae Vitae*, Sojourner Truth, maturing prayer life, Call to Action, *Daughters of Sarah*, a woman retreat director, Gloria Steinem, Bernard Haring, having a seminar with Matthew Fox and believing in creation spirituality, The Catholic Worker, Mary Daly, belonging to a "good" parish, being sick and afraid and having other women care, Galatians 3:28.

Women are, in great numbers, beginning to cautiously trust their own lives, and the lives of those around them to help burnish and shape their paths toward God. "What we need are stories from spiritually mature women in our time and culture who are demonstrating the sacred in today's world. We need to hear from women we can relate to, women like ourselves who fall in love, raise children, run businesses, speak from pulpits, commute on freeways, work for peace, and go through divorces. We need to hear directly from these women about the unfolding of the sacred in their lives in their own words, in the language of their own hearts."[67]

This is a slow process, this constant conversation with our past, the unlearning of some and affirming of others, and two steps forward, one step back approach to recognizing our own wisdom, as we see God present in our sisters and their lives.

**I looked around at the people who are the wisest people I know. They have been more faithful to God in their lives, they have prayed more, they have looked hard for what God wants for them and from them. One has suffered the crib death of a child, another has had to deal with the drug abuse and imprisonment of a son, another has had a very difficult marriage to a man who suffers from chronic depression, another has had her own struggle with alcohol. They have been brave enough to tell the truth, and to let me see that they look for, sometimes desperately, how God calls them through all this. And here we were, all gathered in a circle, about to begin to celebrate Eucharist.

✪✪✪✪✪

CELEBRATION AND SELF: HOW DO I GET THERE?

FORETHOUGHT ✪

All groups are composed of individuals, and in the case of WE, individuals who have come to hear their call to this celebration as they move toward self-authorization. In this chapter I attempt to show through the words of the respondents how they have grown singly toward celebrating communally. Most frequently mentioned influences in self-authorization are role models, reading, education, work and prayer.

✪✪✪✪✪✪

*God made me and I am good,
 because I am a woman.
I share in God's own Motherhood,
 because I am a woman.
The image of God is image of me,
 because I am a woman.
God will give the victory,
 because I am a woman.
God said, Daughter, don't be sad
 because you are a woman.
And I said, I am very glad,
 because I am a woman!* [68]

What is coming already makes a claim on the present. [69]

*The blessed virgin Mary was the first human person who could say of Jesus, 'This is my body, this is my blood. ' She was the first altar of the incarnation's mystery.
"Was she not, then, the first priest, the first minister of the sacrament of the real presence? How might those who hold that women are symbolically inadequate for the priesthood think about this?* [70]

. . . nothing is impossible with God. [71]

**There is one organizer per gathering but we are all presiders.

**The team which prepares the liturgy will act as guide but we all celebrate and consecrate together.

**We have revolving leadership. What matters is to involve the group in liturgy.

**Most often the whole group shares the celebrant role. Often the Eucharistic prayers are read by all in attendance.

**We all agreed to take turns presiding. We all want our turns, me especially!

**We rotate responsibility at the end of each gathering. We simply ask who would like to plan the next time. New members are encouraged to try it but are not pressured.

** I don't think we think in terms of a celebrant, as a single individual. We seem to have a planner, introducer of the theme, but we are all full participants in the ritual. We believe that it is not necessary *to have one single mediator but that God is present in and through every individual who joins in the celebration.*

**Though the woman who hosts gives direction, everyone participates.

**We are all celebrants. We never decided.

**In the beginning the group asked that I be the celebrant because of my M. Div. degree but then in time, they wanted it rotated or offered to others who would also accept this role. When I am the celebrant I like the participation on the part of the members. I like it that they want to do something they think significant.

**The celebrants switch from month to month. There is either a couple or a single person who prepares the liturgy. The text for the eucharistic prayer is usually passed from member to member with each reading a paragraph. It is a random situation as to who will have the book at the point of the words of institution. I do not recall how we settled upon this procedure but it began early in our group's history.

**We have a woman whom we as a community ordained in 1980 following the completion of an advanced theology degree, and our year long process of discernment about her charisms and about the meaning of ordination.

**We take turns. The person who put together the liturgy is the leader and brings the readings for others to read. We all have copies and we love to take them home and ponder them. We seem to agree that by our creation we are priests ourselves.

**We simply share bread together. God is with us.

**We all take turns celebrating. All members have been ordained by the group.

**The celebrant changes monthly but we all say the words of consecration together.

**There is one organizer per gathering, but we all are presiders.

**The celebrant is the one who prepares the liturgy, but it is not done so the leader is set off from the rest of us.

**The team who prepares the liturgy will act as guide but we all celebrate and consecrate together.

**A major difference in our group is that no one believes that one person has a lock on wisdom relating to the scriptures. We are not children. We have lived complex lives, struggled, had disappointments and victories. Everyone can listen to the spirit speak and share that wisdom.

Organizer, team, revolving leadership, whole group as celebrant, director/host, preparer, guide, planner, introducer.

It is late on a winter Sunday afternoon. The sun is deep in the west. In a family room of a colonial house on a suburban street in the midwest eleven women are assembled. Three are going over the readings, from poet May Sarton and the Gospel of Luke. Two are setting a low table with candles, a bowl of water, a plate with a small loaf of fresh bread and a wine glass filled up with burgundy. Several of us are in the kitchen making coffee and putting out plates of fruit and cookies. There is a ramble of voices and laughter as friends catch up on the last month in each other's lives. The doorbell rings, signaling the last expected participant and we are ready to begin.

Quiet settles. We find seats on the couches, on the floor. Joan, in a red sweater, the mother of the family who lives here, welcomes us, her friends, and tells of the theme which has been planned for today: the waters of Baptism which keep on flowing in each life. Her face glows. Someone pushes the play button and "The Fountains of Rome" fills up the room, washing over us.

A white-haired woman in her fifties calls us to worship: "O God, from whom all goodness flows, come to us." Our voices respond, "God, make haste." Her voice rises: "Let justice flow like water" and we answer, "And integrity like an unfailing stream."[72]

The first reading is shared by Beth, pregnant, sitting tailor-style on the floor.

"Here is a glass of water from my well.

It tastes of rock and root and earth and rain. . . ."[73]

A contemporary psalm of praise is prayed antiphonally by the whole group. The Lucan Gospel of Jesus' baptism is told as a story by a rotund woman in blue. She sets the scene, the river bank, the hot sun, the gathered men and women, excited that this strange man, John, might be the Promised One and Jesus, in the flowing water. The story teller pauses: "And then the heavens opened, and a mighty voice came, 'You, you are my Beloved. My favor, my love rests in you.'" We sit in silence, captive to the story.

The sharing begins as the women speak about their own experiences of baptism. One talks about being a sponsor in an RCIA program and how that has enhanced her understanding of Jesus in her life and in the life of the community. Beth, the pregnant woman, tells of the planning for the baptism of her soon-to-be-born child. Another points out that the story of Jesus' baptism calls him "Beloved," and that this is the beginning of his public ministry. How does it feel to know that your own baptism makes you, identifies you as, God's beloved also? How does that affect the ministry of each baptized person? A woman over sixty responds that she has a very hard time thinking about herself as beloved; so do several younger women. Someone points out the frequency of water in our lives: dishes, laundry, children's baths, our own tears, and how often we have the chance to see the good work that water does. There is some laughter, much earnestness as we break open the idea of belovedness and how it affects the work of daily life. The discussion weaves among us for almost a half hour, then Joan gathers up the threads of the sharing into an introduction to the prayers of petition. There are prayers for family, friends, sick acquaintances, and for the shared ministry at a soup kitchen.

Several women begin the Eucharistic prayer, and voices rise and fall as each takes her turn. At the words, ". . . and so, Jesus said to his friends," the hands of all the women in the room are extended over the loaf and cup.

Lavonne and Susan come forward and break the bread and pass the wine. "This is the Body of Christ," "This is the Blood of Christ," as plate and goblet are passed from hand to hand.

The women stand, and holding hands, their voices rise, "We are called, we are chosen, we are Christ to one another, we are promise of tomorrow . . ." and the group dissolves into a sea of hugs, the sign of peace.

Who is the celebrant here? We all are. Who is the community? We all are. Who is the planner/ organizer? Probably Joan, the woman in the red sweater. Helen, the woman who led the song, will host next month. She will plan with Lavonne who baked the bread for today's celebration. Teresita will be back from Puerto Rico by then and will bring her guitar, so there will be live music for the singing. We all expect to join the celebration of the baptism of Beth's new baby before that.

**It was only leading up to the first liturgy that it felt strange to dare to celebrate. In the midst of doing it seemed like the most natural thing in the world, being there in a circle of friends, asking Jesus to be with us, telling him we love him, sharing with him and each other our lives and trying to open his words and stories to understand what they have meant for us and what they will mean in the future. No heavens split open, striking us down for daring to violate the Holy. Rather, I, at the conclusion of our first gathering, looked at the faces of these women and thought, "This is holy, this is what we have been called to do all along."

This is what we were called to do, and the reason that Jesus offered us, and everyone the simplest of mediums, the family meal, with the simplest of elements, the daily bread of every, any culture, and wine, so that everyone, everyone might be able to celebrate and remember him and what he did for us and how he wants to lead us to our Creator. It is congruent. It is that simple.

He did it this way so that anyone, regardless of circumstance, could find a bit of bread and a friend or two, and sit together around the kitchen table or under a tree and talk of the goodness of the God, and read Jesus' words and bless the bread and see him present, in the stories, and in the bread and in each other.

When women gather, often out of desperation, sometimes in fear, always in hope, and begin this experience for ourselves, we discover what we were born and baptized to do. In the voices of the respondents there are no reverberations of false excitement or even of rebellion. This is the natural Christian prayer experience. This is simply what we are encouraged to do in memory of him, and we do it. The wonder is why we waited and struggled so long.

In gathering we discover that most likely we are replicating, 2000 years later, the way in which the earliest of his friends joined in his memory. [74]

This action seems to be organic in nature, a step on the continuum of developing understanding of what it means to be a Christian. A response, not only to the long and often fruitful journey of our Christian foreparents, it is also a natural outgrowth of contemporary theology and social reality. Many women find in these celebrations the building up of heaven in the here and now.

What seems, from outside, to have been impetuous has in fact been developing for centuries.

"The history of theology makes it abundantly clear that each age has its own contributions to make to the understanding of the life of faith. These are conditioned by a variety of cultural and historical circumstances. In one age, with its peculiar questions provoked by a special religious experience and understanding of reality, some aspects of the theology of sacraments may be highlighted while others, which received attention previously, are neglected. A new age, stimulated by its own religious needs, may rediscover those forgotten aspects and contribute to the overall intelligibility by building on earlier knowledge." [75]

It is significant that the groups I surveyed have met an average of five years. It is also important to note that they often began with no knowledge of other groups. In other words, the varied influences which I will name came to maturity in the hearts of women of faith in various parts of the United States at approximately the same time, *but most often these women believed they were alone in what they chose to do.*

**We thought we were crazy, even though deeply we knew that celebrating together was what we must do. I clung to the phrase, "Lord, to whom shall we go, for you have the words of everlasting life." That kept me going, and soon it was all right.

They saw dimly, or not at all, that they were part of a maturing process of Christian Catholics in their developing understanding of Eucharist and community.

The quantum leap of concelebration is cataclysmically counter to almost everything we ever learned in the classroom or in the pew, so what would be so compelling that groups of women doing just that could emerge spontaneously across the country?

While there is an abundance of causes for any significant change in the belief and behavior of groups, I would like to spotlight modifications the responders single out as *most significant in self-understanding* which seem to have had the greatest role in recentering us in celebration.

AFFIRMING OURSELVES ✪

**We need sensitivity to women feeling ignored, left out.

**I feel anger at Church making me feel second class.

**In second grade, I was sent to the principal's office for drawing my "vocation" as a woman priest!

The first and most exquisite pain is the pain of self-censure. The cost is borne by women as individuals. When women fail to develop their own talents because they believe their elders and "wisers" that certain jobs are unavailable to women, that certain charisms cannot be theirs, that they could not be called to certain ministries because they are female, there is the primary loss of possibility within their own lives. The process of reclaiming what was falsely denied is long and mostly painful. Glimpses of joy make the process worthwhile.

Self-affirmation is the first step toward celebrating Eucharist. We must find ourselves worthy, first personally, then in relationship to God and finally in the earthly community.

This struggle for individual woman is millennial. Gerda Lerner comments on women in the centuries before ours: "The concept that women are born inferior, have a weaker mind and intellect, are more subject to emotions and sexual temptations than men and that they need to be ruled by men, had a devastating effect on women's minds. Even extraordinary women, talents which occur once or twice a century, had to struggle against this notion which deprived them of authenticity and authority. Each thinking woman had to spend inordinate amounts of time and energy apologizing for the very fact of her thinking."[76]

The feelings of inferiority are still deeply internalized by many of us but we are beginning to see massive changes in women's ability to self-affirm.

So how do we, in the last tenth of the twentieth century cope with, struggle to overcome our own individual, deep-in-our-hearts feeling of unworthiness? How do we affirm ourselves?

POWER OF ROLE MODELS ✪

**I grew up with a number of Irish women relatives who were very devout Catholics but also strong women—their strength and courage as part of an immigrant culture has always inspired me.

**I still can remember the shock wave that went through my whole body when I went to the wedding of my niece. Her fiancé was a Lutheran and his pastor was on the altar with the priest. His pastor was a woman. All through that wedding I kept saying to myself, "That could be me. I could do that." It was earthshaking, mind bending.

**My experience with the Medical Missionary sisters was wonderful. They taught me to live my beliefs and accept responsibility for my own religious and spiritual development.

**The other women of Dignity have challenged me to be more inclusive, authentic and trusting of the Spirit.

**I learned my faith from women primarily, although my Presbyterian father taught me to love and revere scriptures. But women, the Sisters of Mercy, were my teachers along with my mother and my aunt. From them I learned a loving, nurturing God.

It is difficult to over estimate the importance of women seeing other women exercising capability. As the number of women in the labor pool rises we are able to see about us women performing competently in all manner of jobs. This visible competency encourages us and affirms us. What we see in evidence we can model in ourselves. The skills in others implies the possibility of such skills in ourselves. This is true in the Senate, in the classroom, on the factory floor, at the altar. Women need to see women handling the bread and wine which has been sanctified, not just as eucharistic ministers but as consecrators, with the deed recognized and affirmed as sacred. [77]

Whom we should most praise and remember are those first lonely women who dared to stand alone, and by their thinking, speaking, writing and sometimes in their dying, dared to challenge traditional gender roles. "In the workshops I offer, . . .I have found that women are comforted to hear the stories of other women and grateful to see how these women have changed their lives. Living examples remain the best source of inspiration." [78]

I've come a distance since my role models, Nancy Drew and Sue Barton, were replaced by Sr. Theresa Kane and Rosemary Ruether. . . .

Whom do you see as a role model for your own personal competency?

POWER OF READING ⊙

**I became a feminist when I read Mary Daly's *Second Sex* where I read for the first time (and I have an MSW from Catholic University) what the Fathers of the Church had to say about women.

**I have, for some years, been averse to many of the decrees coming down from on high that just don't wash with the message of Jesus. The frustration has churned in me with no kindred spirits to support my thinking. Finally, I found Matthew Fox OP and his *Coming of the Cosmic Christ.* That was my turning point, my metanoia.

**Constant reading and meditating since the age of fifteen changed me.

For thousands of us, reading the works of feminist writers has been our own private gateway to affirming our goodness beyond traditional gender assumptions. The authors of the second wave of the feminist movement do a great deal to present women with a different view of themselves than the ones traditionally taught. Entering silently into a community of words, we confront concepts about self which are often hugely different than those on which we were weaned. Reading opens us to the intimacy of the struggles of other women, but allows us to do it in reflective quiet. That special circle of word and reflection is a personal world builder. In that space we find that we are not alone, we are not crazy. A family of understanding exists, even though its members may be thousands of miles apart. *Lectio divina*, or divine reading, encourages us to read at a deeper level, to listen to the words with not only our minds, but also our hearts and enter into this kind of absorption, which engages our imaginations as well as our intellects.

People like Andrea Dworkin, Gloria Steinam, Maya Angelou, Sandra Cisneros, Mary McCarthy, Carol Gilligan, inform us about our own power, not derivative, but personal. Women who began to crack open the nut of religion and our place in it: Mary Daly, Rosemary Radford Ruether, Sandra Schneiders, Starhawk, Toinette Eugene, Mary Hunt, Judith Plaskow, Ada Maria Isasi-Diaz, Carol Christ, Mary Jo Weaver, help to give us a dif-ferent possibility of ourselves in relationship to Church and to the people of God. They begin the healing from the treachery of false teachings about women's role, nature and relationship to God.

It is impossible to overstate the importance of access to the printing press for the liberation of us all. The ideas that pop up in print can be examined and embraced in private, tried on. Do they fit me? Do they need alterations for my life? When I look in my interior mirror, do these ideas look like me? Do they have *meaning* for me?

To see reflected back our own perhaps haltingly held beliefs from the pages of a well known feminist writer is to see ourselves affirmed in print.

What books and articles have you read which encouraged you?

POWER OF EDUCATION ✪

**I went through Catholic Education through college. Part of college was a year in Rome where I saw the Catholic Church as a part of superstition and legalism. I learned to abhor rules and laws that are mere form, not nurturing of persons.

**I began to find myself as a person, and especially as a spiritual person when I studied feminine spirituality in college.

**My family wasn't much for education. I went to work right after high school and got married when I was 19. When my youngest started kindergarten I went back to school, too. First to the community college to brush up on my skills and learn to run a computer so I could go back to work. Now I am in my third year of college. I am amazed at how much wonderful stuff there is to learn.

.**Bernard Häring was at Brown the second semester of my graduate work in 1966. I was a very different Catholic after a semester of his daily homilies. I was empowered.

**Critical theological and scriptural studies changed me.

**I took a Master's degree in creation spirituality with Matt Fox in 1979-80 in Chicago and that certainly transformed my thinking.

**My time at Holy Cross College where I studied liberation theology changed me—my time in seminary and my studies in mixed groups for ritual and worship, my coming to understand what needs I have and my dissatisfaction with the institution.

**I have made workshops and retreats on feminism, as well as having three adult blood sisters who are supportive and actively involved in this issue as well as I.

**The primary motivator (to join a women's celebration group) was the educational experience I had at Mundelein College, Chicago. It was my introduction to feminine spirituality.

**My introduction to academic liberation theology and Women's Ordination Conference in college as part of a theology degree gave me vocabulary to name my experience, and I began to work for change.

** I believe my college experience made me open to a (women's Eucharist) group. It was a Catholic Jesuit college, where I came to know my religion as an adult.

There are still occasionally families which educate sons and not daughters, but they are increasingly dinosaurs. Access to the classroom is a powerful tool for individual affirmation and women hold as many seats in the student chairs as men do. There is such a wonderful availability for students today: scheduling that fits with employment hours, weekend seminars, televised classes, week-long intensive learning, summer Masters programs. Every offering enlarges our understanding, introducing us to ideas both secular and sacred, permitting us to expand ourselves in a systematic way, polishing our notions by interactions with others. It is no wonder that learning has often been restricted to the few, especially to men. If you learn what I learn you will know as much as I know. It is also instructive that lobbying for women's education has been a constant theme in the women's rights movement in America. Every generation learns again how important learning is.

What educational experiences have increased your sense of autonomy?

POWER IN THE WORK FORCE ✪

**I started to grow as a feminist when I finally got out of the house and began a job. All those years before I believed that men were somehow smarter, better. Deep down I never thought I could "make it." I laugh now when I think back. In my first job I realized that I could do the work as well as and sometimes a lot better then the men in my department. It didn't make me think less of them but it sure made me feel a lot better about myself and about other women.

**My order pushed me to get a Master's degree. Then I left teaching and went to work in the Chancery. I soon was representing the diocese at conferences. The thing that amazed me was that there people listened to me.

A regular paycheck is not a guarantee of human goodness or self-worth, but employment can reflect capability. Women who find their talents and education rewarded can make great strides in the journey of self-esteem. Anyone out of a job for even a matter of months may catch herself slipping into a morass of uncertainty as the world goes on without her. Anyone who has had to live, dependent on the paycheck of another, or worse yet, the welfare check, can easily come to believe herself less good, less worthy, not pulling her own weight.

The job which calls forth our talents, challenges the goodness in us, increases our sense of autonomy and provides a reasonable level of support is a field in which our self esteem can grow.

One women speaks of this experience:

"Because of a very tumultuous childhood (divorced parents, drinking and abusive father), gaining an education and entry into a respected profession like teaching gave me a permanent sense of self-esteem. As it provided me with a lifetime earning power and kept my standard of living through a divorce . . . teaching gave me a sense of independence that stands me in good stead. . . ." [79]

The emancipation into the workplace has had a great liberating and leveling effect. Women begin to see themselves as the mistresses of their own destiny, destroying the mythic concept of the board room, the stock room, the operating room, the union hall, the cockpit. No more standing behind the throne, no more fear of becoming "masculinized" by the tumult of the world; women often can find instead that they bring their own feminist, communitarian concerns with them and begin to reshape the workplace into a more human environment.

Which employment experiences have encouraged your sense of capability?

POWER OF PRAYER ✪

**I first began to believe in myself in my prayer. As I was growing up I bought all the business of God as a man (I come from a very religious Hispanic family) and I saw it in my daily life. The priest was "God," my father was "God." I finally began to say to myself, how can I pray to the man God, how can I ever be like him or have him understand me? Then it came, like a voice, but more of an understanding, this God made me a woman, and if I am an image then God must be like women,too.

**I had to pray through much injustice, not only in my life, but in lives around me. I had to look deep into my prayer to find a God who would not choose such injustices, such pain. I pray now to God our Mother, seeing there a loving and compassionate God. This has given me a great sense of myself, that I, too, as a woman can be a bearer of justice and caring in the world. This has led me to hold my head up, to be strong, to try and push for God's justice around me. When we were little we used to giggle about being a temple of the Holy Ghost. Now I know what that means.

**I always felt disconnected from God, like I needed someone else to explain me to him. Other people seemed to have a direct line, especially men, especially priests, who wrote and spoke with such authority about praying. Then several years ago, I came across a book of Meinrad Craighead's paintings, called *Mother Song*. They somehow reminded me of the holy cards I grew up with, but they were also completely different. They were compelling to me. I looked at them over and over again. Finally I realized that the cards were supposed to make us think of what was sacred, but these pictures had that effect on me, much more strongly than any of the ones from my childhood. They were so much about God visible in female form. That was the beginning of depth and reality in my prayer. I began to value my feminine in relationship with God.

**My prayer and my life flourished when I began to believe that my own life, my own experience, was good ground to stand on.

**My life has always been outward, trying to prove I am good through all the things I could do. It was through prayer that I found I no longer had to prove anything. In God, who loves me I am good because I am.

**My prayer life has moved me to be more authentic to my basis: the theological, ethical and spiritual movements of my heart.

**I've known a personal God from the age of seven when we met in my first Eucharist.

**My experiences with meditation have influenced my beliefs. I've had very positive "travels" with meditation, which I've been doing for sixteen years.

**The Cursillo movement and the introduction of charismatic renewal, and a spiritual center encouraged me in experiencing God, not just worshipping. I joined a 12 Step program which opened me up to a new kind of spirituality.

Prayer, especially the deep personal one of our own heart, slashes through walls which block us off from God. Feminist prayer removes that which make us non-image of a male God. If we can believe that our words, our experiences have meaning for our Creator, that God knows and treasures the groanings which are at our depth, then we can carry all that is into the heart of the Sacred. That certainty of acceptance blossoms in personal joy, a gift of the Divine, and in gratefulness, for everything made is holy. As we see God's love reflected back on us we grow in stature in our own eyes, accepting ourselves as holy images.

Sandra Schneiders gives us a profile of what can be named as the heart of feminist spirituality It is rooted in personal experience, and reintegrates all that has been considered less worthy in patriarchal religion, especially our bodies and all of non-human nature. Feminist spirituality also rejects abstract and cerebral approaches, basing itself in interconnections, e.g., of personal growth to social justice. "Feminist spirituality starts with a commitment which faces simultaneously inward and outward. The changes and growth which must happen in women if they are to be and to experience themselves as fully human, daughters of divinity and its bearers in this world, are the same changes that must occur in a society, namely, the reintegration of what has been dichotomized . . . the liberation of that which has been enslaved."[80]

Clare Wagner, a spiritual director, says, "While the reality of women praying is not new, the same cannot be said for the ways they pray. . . . The changes . . . come from the fact that they are beginning to understand themselves and God in new ways. As a result, they have new expectations of their relationships with God. . . . I see women becoming aware of the fact that a relationship with God is their baptismal right. What's more, they see that their own experience is a valid and valuable arena for developing this relationship."[81]

It has been a wake-up call. What can it mean that we contribute to an understanding of God through our prayer? Many of us are hesitant at first to see our private interchange with God as having any bearing on a larger world, but Bernard Lee points out that that is exactly what happens when we pray out of our own experience. "Good theology has always been a faithful reflection of faith experience. Fidelity to experience is a touchstone of valid theological reflection." [82]

Women are drifting away or working away from memorized prayer (which is after all, always someone's else's composition), as they self-authorize in their spiritual lives. We cautiously experiment with new ways of speaking to God, and of God, a bit of work which Wagner sees as wonderful. "More and more frequently, God is entering the prayer of today's women as other than the father image. This is good for women because it allows them to reflect freely and creatively. . . . it is also 'good for God' because it increases the ways God's presence among us can be expressed." [83]

Enablement and empowerment are gifts of one's own genuine personal encounter with God. "Enabling concerns a woman's own life and her own healing. Being empowered . . refers to a woman reaching out and helping others. . . . My experience in working with women shows they need a great deal of enabling and healing. I see them come to prayer sessions wounded by all kinds of things—oppression, eating disorders, low self-esteem. . . . If they are attentive to God and allow themselves to be touched, they experience healing and are able to begin the journey to wholeness. . . ." [84]

If God's greatest glory is a human deeply and fully alive, then we are most God-like when we most fulfill our Divine spark, and that is when we are most completely ourselves, we see ourselves as *changed,* in using our gifts, in honoring our own reflected worth, in the joyfulness of our grateful and healing worship.

How has your prayer encouraged self-understanding?

Role models, reading, education, work and prayer, all these experiences (and doubtless, many others) help us to emerge into our own place of personal giftedness, a most treasured and wonderful spot.

"Women and men who have entered seriously into the feminist movement, for example, have not merely understood themselves differently. Their selves are made into different selves by a change in the meaning structures to which they give power. How such people go about being human changes significantly." [85] When we discover ourselves as different from the way we previously defined ourselves, or that we allowed society to define us, we can challenge all the imposed limitations to which we have previously given credence. [86] We take tremendous power when our eyes are open to the understanding that we need no longer accept another's demarcation of our boundaries.

"Disbelief . . . is the dawn of liberation. Not until I am able to disbelieve the way that those in power have defined me will I be free to imagine alternatives to the status quo. And imagining alternatives is the first step toward their becoming possible. To disbelieve, we need not yet have an alternative to offer. We need not yet sense that others share our disbelief. These will become important if disbelief is to move us toward effective action, but disbelief alone is enough at the start." [87]

Disbelief in the judgments of others, growth in self respect, can lead women to say and say again as one respondent did,

**I am finally glad that I was born a woman.

Steps toward self-respect and self-acceptance happen before and simultaneously with the participation in a community of equals. Women seem to value mutuality or con-nection highly in relationship to individuation and autonomy.[88] In the next chapter we will explore how women exercise an ethic of care within a group context.

✪✪✪✪✪✪

CELEBRATION AND COMMUNITY: HOW DO WE GET THERE?

FORETHOUGHT ✪

No experience occurs outside of its own place in history. WE is very much a product of this generation, a part of the events of the last three decades. In this chapter I enumerate some of the secular, religious and spiritual community experiences which lead to the development of WE groups. These experiences, as named by respondents, help us to trace the path of growth in group consciousness which leads us now to celebrate the Eucharist.

✪✪✪✪✪

✳ *it's not that
everybody's trying
 to get into the act,
as Jimmy Durante
says—it's that
EVERYBODY IS
 IN THE ACT.*[89]

✳*The theological process is an intrinsic part of the liberation task because it is one of the ways in which the community becomes the agent of its own history.*[90]

✳*May God. . .grant that the human family by carefully observing the principle of religious liberty in society may be brought by the grace of Christ and the power of the Holy Spirit to that "glorious freedom of the children of God"(Rom. 8:21) which is sublime and everlasting.* [91]

AFFIRMING COMMUNITY ⊙

**Since 1948 every experience, amazing, remarkable, led step by step with others to feel the importance of any group seeking to build the earth and follow steps for change to bring us closer to the people of God.

**Solidarity with women has become increasingly important to me.

**I believe that when we are joined together, when we dream together, when we suffer and pray and plan together, we are more than the sum of our parts.

We innovating women live in a world continually inflected by the nuances of societal flow. As we re-vision ourselves we look at our environment with new eyes and a fresh understanding of the meaning of community and how we fit in it.

There are several aspects of the American experience which give our community and our church its particular character.

THE MYTH OF POSSIBILITY ⊙

This country continues to be infected with possibility in mythic proportions. (I use *myth* here in the sense of a belief that embodies a visionary ideal.) It is not only those who come to our shores who believe that all things are possible. Our history and our now are full of stories of individuals who rose from struggle to accomplish goals. We revel in these stories. They affirm a basic belief, that pain can be conquered, that visions can become reality, that impediments are not insurmountable. Where was it commanded that the now must be the future?

The New York Times story of three winners in the 1994 Westinghouse Science Talent Search reaffirms our belief. One Chinese girl, one Ukrainian girl who came as a child, one young black man raised in homeless shelters and foster homes, took scholarships. [92]

This only-in-America success story, and thousands like it, stoke the certainty that persistence, faith and hope will carry us to our goal.

And if one can succeed, how much more powerful, how much more effective are two or more, united for support, in search of transformation?

We believe, believe that when we gather, when we work, when we study, picket, poll, march, pray, beleaguer, implore, insist *as a group*, we are significant, our voices will be heard, transformation will happen. It transpires because we understand ourselves and our beliefs better when we discern together and because our desire for alteration is no longer private. I'm not crazy, others see the same problems that I do!

Even in defeat (such as the failure of the Equal Rights Amendment), we mostly are certain that if we had tried harder we could have overcome. In other words, it is not the concept of group power that is challenged, but the methods we used, or the time we spent, or our inability to stay focused. Every group effort informs us for the next one.

GRASSROOTS MOVEMENTS ✪

**Studying theology liberated me to be a part of the grassroots movement.

**I learned early, in college, that many of us together got things done. We might not have power but we had numbers and conviction.

The myth of possibility of freedom exploded into our lives as individuals joined in common life in the Civil Rights Movement in the 1960s.

Here many of us not only got our first blooding in the power of community commitment, but were also unexpectedly gifted with the concept that scripture could be a most powerful tool for confronting oppression.

Those of us who took part actively, or who watched it on TV saw scripture put to use on a daily basis to justify, legitimate, a movement toward removal of unlawful authority. Collapsing historical and Biblical time, Martin Luther King Jr. rallied us to the new people of God who had to flee the pharaohs of bigotry and cross over the Red Sea of oppression. "The Bible tells the thrilling story of how Moses stood in Pharaoh's court centuries ago and cried, 'Let my people go.' This was an opening chapter in a continuing story. The present struggle in the United States is a later chapter in the same story." [93]

For many Catholics who had grown up in a church which was only guardedly biblical, the explosion of scripture as the base for a nonviolent revolution was a revelation.

**It was during the Civil Rights movement in the '60s that I first discovered that scripture applied to us, here and now, that the stories didn't just tell us about something that happened long ago, but could be read now and have meaning right now. That understanding has powered me through demonstrations and marches for thirty years. It has powered my own personal search for liberation. I love the immediacy of Scriptures.

The Civil Rights Movement was a church-based movement of the anawim, the forgotten, the powerless. The demand for justice flowed out of the worship space and into the streets, strengthened by the dream of an exodus people fleeing oppression and demanding autonomy, a demand based on the radical freedom offered by Jesus. We saw (or were) young and old, black and white, male and female, kneeling *nonviolently* (like Jesus) under the blows of angry whites, bonding in a conviction of scripture-based community in exodus from oppression.

The Civil Rights movement would be important to the Women-Church movement because it passionately activated a Biblical liberation model in our time, facing oppression nonviolently, and lobbied for community concerns in grassroots solidarity.

Sara Evans points out the influence of the civil rights movement on women, "The initiation of a new feminist sensibility came from two groups of middle-class women, both inspired by the civil rights movement. The first group consisted primarily of professional women. The second . . . drew on younger radical activists and posed a broader cultural challenge to accepted definitions of femininity and sexuality." [94]

**The Women's movement has been a big influence in my life.
**The women's revolution has had a tremendous impact on my life. My mother was a charter member of NOW, and I saw in her life and mine (and then in our world) that unless we act together our status will not change. Now I have daughters to look out for. They might not understand what it is we are doing but in the future I will know that our protests, our campaigns for equality will pay off in their lives.

Every mass of people gathered into one voice which garners media attention reinforces our belief. No better example than the Women's Rights Movement. We, who felt insignificant, uncertain, as one, found that we could fill the Mall in Washington DC as many joined in common understanding. As the stories of women gathered force, we began to identify the inappropriate uses of power by men over women, and we stepped forward together in print, at meetings, in offices and factories and in litigation to apply pressure for alteration of attitudes, conventions and laws. Every large gathering informed us and vested us with the courage to build the smaller community. Then when we turn on our televisions, open our morning papers, and see groups gathered for community action, we know how they feel because we have been there ourselves.

**Peace and justice are the emphasis of my life.

**Growing up in the San Francisco bay area in the 1960s I was conscientized to justice issues and have always felt justice to be at the core of my being.

**I have a risk-taking personality. I've been involved in anti-institutional activity in many arenas.

**All my early justice work was based in parishes and we always prayed our commitment. Everyone's opinions were important, mainly because there were so few of us!

**Even though I never marched with Caesar Chavez, our family could take part in the lettuce and grape boycotts, could pray for those people, and could tell our grocery stores that we wouldn't buy those products.

**Our Catholic Worker community always has had a prayerful peace agenda. We protest on the day of the week that we don't serve meals. We have done much prayer and discernment about this.

The United Farm Workers' non-violent boycotts and the peace movement followed, as did the struggle for gay and lesbian rights. All these were grassroots gatherings seeking transformation, all finding solace and encouragement in the scriptures. They share the common traits of non-violence, community recognition of individual gifts or charisms, discernment and action, they are also dignified and enforced by prayer.

The myth of possibility also lives in an endless round of self-help groups, like Alcoholics Anonymous and Tough Love, Gray Panthers, Native American Rights, neighborhood organizations to stop the placement of incinerators, parish councils, environmental defense clusters.

Women laboring in grass roots movements could not help but glimpse the connection between them and the struggles of women. The possibilities for others were possibilities for them, too.

VATICAN II AND THE PEOPLE OF GOD ✪

Vigorous community-based movements in the United States coincided with the new wind of Vatican II (1962-1965) and its introduction into this country.

**The Civil Rights movement and then Vatican II merged in my mind to an absolute conviction of lay power in the Church, including me as a woman. The peace movement and the women's movement followed and strengthened me.

The bishops gathered in Rome and over many months produced a set of documents which would rock the people of God. As we broke open the conciliar writings we found that we were like a sacrament [95] and that the Spirit lives in our hearts. [96] We found that our growth as sacramental and spirit-filled was not complete, implying that change was not only possible but necessary in our seemingly immutable institution. "While she slowly grows to maturity, the Church longs for the completed kingdom . . ."[97] We knew that was not just the heavenly kingdom but the one happening now.

Many of us heard and pondered the concept of our common priesthood,[98] in which we are all included. How did it differ from and how did it resemble the sacramental priesthood? How did we as the faithful participate in Eucharist?[99] Like so many refugees out in the cold, when the warmth of the Eucharist was offered we rushed in.

We found that the *sensum fidei*, or "instinctive sensitivity and discrimination which the *members* of the Church possess in matters of faith"[100] (my italics) might imply that we as lay men and women had a valid role in expressing our vision of the life of the parish community.

We were reminded that in many areas of the world where there are few or no priests, lay women and men are vital to making Jesus present.[101] We found assurance in the idea that when we follow those who came before in sharing the Gospels we supply the needs of our brothers and sisters and are vital to pastors and faithful alike.[102]

And how were we to know and understand our mission? Among other ways, ". . . the Sacred Synod forcefully and specifically exhorts all the Christian faithful . . . to learn 'the surpassing knowledge of Jesus Christ' by frequent reading of the divine Scriptures. 'Ignorance of the Scriptures is ignorance of Christ.'"[103]

Calling Eucharist "the summit of the whole of the Church's worship and of Christian life,"[104] it was made available in the vernacular,[105] with the note that "the use of the mother tongue can frequently be of great advantage to the people,"[106] while permitting that the scriptures could be proclaimed by women.[107]

Reintroducing and reemphasizing the Eucharist as a community meal (recommended at the Council of Trent) led the bishops to call for receiving both the elements of bread and that of wine,[108] the council opened the way for reception in the hands,[109] again returning us to the concept of a holy meal.

Recognizing the imperative to return the Eucharist to the people who had spent mute centuries as uninvolved viewers, the Council reasserted the need to reshape the celebration so that people could be more active and aware participants. We were informed that this indeed was what we had a right to because of our baptisms.[110] In order to make this possible, signs and symbols of sacrament must be intelligible to the participants, for a sign which is unknowable cannot be effective, and in being intelligible those symbols must represent the "sacred reality" of Jesus.[111]

COMMUNITIES OF GROWTH ✪

As we studied, discussed, and implemented the documents it became apparent that the bishops had provided the game plan for the people of God to take back the Church. Certainly some of the plan was unclear. Many specifics had to be discovered, but the broad outline spilled out in the pages of the documents. The experimentation filled many of us with tremendous enthusiasm, a sign of the Spirit present, not only in the documents, but also in us.

One aspect that slowly became visible was that the people of God had a right to the benefits of a rebalance of power. With the restatement of our own gifts and responsibilities, with our rediscovery of our role in a royal priesthood, we also saw that mature conscience, polished in community, informed through Scripture, conspiring with the Spirit, could stand, speak and act with authority. "Communities of faith are coming alive today in a renewed sense of their vocation and conscience. They are listening, carefully, to discern their own special instincts of faith — about justice, or sexuality, or celebration. As they listen, and learn to trust these instincts, they become more authoritative in the faith.

And they remember that this authority comes from the Spirit and is an authority shared with other, different communities."[112]

The impositions of hierarchy began to yield to the common wisdom of the assembled. Women and men grew to understand that it is not only our right but also our duty in good conscience, to return authority to its intended place, centered in community. We began to act, when called, as the loyal opposition, a function without which intelligent community dies.

"As the reforms of Vatican II excited American Catholics to a deeper participation in our faith, these events also quickened our consciences. It became clear that to be called to contribute our giftedness to a community is to be called to be "conscientious"— to develop the trustworthy resources of personal conscience. Without such reliable inner authority, we can participate in community only as children or as victims." [113]

This self-identification of the community of authority led many to begin to question the nearly unchallenged assumption that power came from the top. By 1993, 74% of surveyed Catholics said they should have a voice in selecting their parish priests, and 62% believed they should take part in deciding whether women should be ordained to the priesthood.[114]

Meanwhile, the decline in the number (and many believe the quality) of priests led to the need for greater involvement of lay women and men in ministry.[115] We began to reimagine what Paul meant when he said, "There are different kinds of spiritual gifts but the same Spirit; there are different forms of service but the same Lord; there are different workings but the same God who produces all of them in everyone. To each individual the manifestation of the Spirit is given for some benefit." [116] Given that the common good was the building of the kingdom, how were we an active rather than a passive part of it?

COMMUNITIES OF DISCIPLESHIP AND SCRIPTURE ✪

**Being a Jesuit Volunteer (1977-78) really started me thinking differently about Church. It opened my eyes to the more activist nature of Church.

**Conversion to justice as a way of life changed me, as has seventeen years of working as a change agent.

**I studied theology, worked in renewal groups such as Marriage Encounter and the

Institute for Peace and Justice.

**My husband and I have spent years doing volunteer work in inner cities, and for the last several years I have worked with homeless women. We began to question this system that keeps people down, "in their place." Our ministries opened our eyes to the pain of what life is like for people who have little. This could not have been what Jesus wanted. I so often feel helpless because of a system that controls and impoverishes people. We find this as true in the Church as in the government.

**The authoritarian nature of church leadership led me to compare the present system to the Gospel and early church. Glaring differences abound.

Our church has a two-thousand-year history of caring for the wounded, based in Jesus' own tenderness. We perhaps have never imagined what the force of Jesus was in Roman Palestine, but Elisabeth Schüssler Fiorenza paints this picture:

"Sinners, prostitutes, beggars, tax collectors, the ritually polluted, the crippled, and the impoverished—in short, the scum of Palestinian society—constituted the majority of Jesus' followers. These are the last who have become the first, the starving who have been satisfied, the uninvited who have been invited."[117] Jesus offered the kingdom (basileia) now through bread and fish and healing. He offered the kingdom of future to the sorrowful, the poor, the meek, the hungry, those who suffer injustice. But these are not separate experiences, "This life and the life of the *basileia* are seen as a continuous whole. . . . The *basileia* vision of Jesus makes people whole, healthy, cleansed, and strong. It restores people's humanity and life. The salvation of the *basileia* is not confined to the soul but spells wholeness for the total person. . . ."[118]

Telling the good news and tending were two sides of the same coin. And the good news was (and is) that there is hope for now, you need not wait. God is on your side and cares when injustice is done to you. You (poor, sick, degraded, unclean, women) are favored by God. You have a right to food, to clothing, to dignity, to a voice. These are not favors granted by society, they are God's will. The community of Jesus not only told the story, they lived the deed, they shared what they had (which was sometimes, no doubt, perilous little) with whomever had need. The various roles of ministry arose from the talents and willingness and love of the community. Since there was no hierarchical institution, the community looked to its own for supplying its needs.

The basis for community rests in discipleship. Discipleship means turning to God and seeking forgiveness, seeking Baptism as a sign of conversion and then turning to others and sharing the good news by word and act.[119] The model for this discipleship is Jesus. "Jesus summoned them and said to them, 'You know that those who are recognized as rulers over the Gentiles lord it over them, and their great ones make their authority over them felt. But it shall not be so among you. Rather, whoever wishes to be great among you will be your servant; whoever wishes to be first among you will be the slave of all. For the Son of Man did not come to be served but to serve and to give his life in ransom for the many.'" [120] This is the mission: to be like Jesus.

Again and again Jesus shares the ways of discipleship and the good news of the kingdom with everyone, even the tax collectors. "Afterward he journeyed from one town and village to another, preaching and proclaiming the good news of the kingdom of God. Accompanying him were the Twelve and some women who had been cured of evil spirits and infirmities, Mary, called Magdalene, from whom seven demons had gone out, Joanna, the wife of Herod's steward Chuza, Susanna, and many others who provided for them out of their resources." [121] And "meanwhile, so many people were crowding together that they were trampling one another underfoot." [122] It is to the "great crowds from Galilee, the Decapolis, Jerusalem, and Judea, and from beyond the Jordan," [123] women and men alike that the Sermon on the Mount, that portrait of ideal discipleship, is directed. A good disciple must be poor in spirit, lowly, hungry for holiness, merciful, suffering for justice, forgiving and non-violent, prayerful and trusting, sharing possessions. All this is modeled in Jesus and it opens the kingdom of now and future. Elisabeth Schüssler Fiorenza, whose work on women and scripture is basic, tells us that it is the very inclusivity of the Jesus movement that called women, and that women are recognized in all the Gospels as disciples who shared fellowship with Jesus. [124]

Kenan Osborne says of the New Testament, "We are presented again and again and again with the meaning of discipleship. Only here and there are we presented with small windows of church leadership. . . . Even in these few places on leadership, however, one does not find that there are two ways of discipleship: one for leaders and one for followers. . . . The New Testament could be described in contemporary language as 'the people's book,' not the 'hierarchy's book.'"[125]

There is, to be sure, leadership in the New Testament; Jesus often used examples of negative leadership to tell the disciples how not to behave. The positive example is always a leadership of service, patience, inclusion. It is leadership based in the needs of the community. The concept of an ordained class appeared slowly in the centuries following.

Osborne maintains that ordination in the New Testament is a difficult matter to prove and that many biblical theologians have worked on the presupposition that an ordained vs. non-ordained ministry status was proclaimed by Jesus. On the contrary, in all of the New Testament:

"a. Nowhere are the twelve ordained.

b. Nowhere are the apostles ordained.

c. Nowhere are the apostles or the twelve described as ordaining.

d. Nowhere is there a command of Jesus to ordain.

e. Nowhere are episkopoi (bishops) ordained.

f. Nowhere are episkopoi described as ordaining."[126]

In fact the word *priest* represented the sacrificial priesthood of the temple, not the discipleship of Jesus-infused ministry. Jesus himself is called priest in Paul's letter to the Hebrews, though Paul says, "it was not Christ who glorified himself in becoming high priest; . . ."[127]

Peter himself sees the priesthood as embedded in the discipleship of Jesus. "But you are 'a chosen race, a royal priesthood, a holy nation, a people of his own, so that you may announce the praises' of him who called you out of darkness into his wonderful light."[128] Isn't that a wonderful thing to announce?

"Th(e) historical record requires some modification of the traditional Catholic notion that Jesus directly and explicitly instituted the Catholic priesthood at the Last Supper. . . . Jesus' institution of the sacraments is implied and/or included in his proclamation cf the Kingdom of God, in his gathering of disciples, and in the special significance he accorded the Last Supper which he ate with his disciples. . . . The priesthood as we have come to know it represents a fusion of different roles and ministries which are to be found in the New Testament churches. It is not even clear, for example, that anyone in particular was commissioned to preside over the Eucharist in the beginning. . . . There is no explic't mention that any of the Apostles presided over the Eucharist. Indeed, there is no compelling evidence that they presided when they were present, or that a chain of ordination from

Apostle to bishop was required for presiding. Someone must have presided, of course, and those who did so presided with the approval of the community.

"We simply do not know how a certain individual came to preside and whether it came to be a permanent or regular function for that person. . . . The most that can be said is that those who presided did so with the consent of the local church and that this consent was tantamount, but not always equivalent, to ordination. . . . Significantly, not until the year 1208 is there an official declaration that priestly ordination is necessary to celebrate the Eucharist." [129]

Instead, what was probably understood was a ministry of function; that is, based in the discipleship of Jesus, the community looked to its own charisms, or talents, and the specific ministries of the believers sprang from that discernment. Charisms are not extraordinary. Everyone possesses one or more. They are gifts of the Spirit, the likeness of God in us. The acting out of them in the service of community is our returning of these gifts to God. In communities of the people of God, the charism is a given; how it is put to use is discerned by the community.

Those who caught this spirit and discerned these gifts gathered in prayer and work for the kingdom. Out of this an institution developed, especially after the destruction of the Temple in 70 AD. "Once the separation from the rabbinical Jewish religion began to take place, the Christian dependence on the structures of Judaism was gradually abandoned, and in their place the Christian community began to form its own institutional structures. . . . from the beginning of the third century onward we find, sporadically at first, and then as the years go by more commonly, the use of the term *kleros* referring to an established group of Christian leaders, i.e. the 'clergy,' while those in the Christian community who were not of this leadership group were increasingly referred to as *laos* or 'laity.'" [130] By this time the active leadership of faithful women in the communities had disappeared as societal structures, which disempower females, began to reimpose themselves. What followed was an accretion of theology to support a separate sacral character, rooted more in the Old Testament priesthood than in the discipleship of Jesus.

Gradually that separate naming was accompanied by a defined and hardened separation of ministries. The clergy had begun to take on a special character, which ever so slightly set them apart from the community. The ministry firmly embedded in the need and discernment of the believers began to shift to a power over the community. It was with this shift that clericalism began.

By the early part of the third century the writings of North African theologian Tertulian already imply a hardening of roles and a distinct dignity that belonged to the priest. "It is ecclesiastical authority which distinguishes clergy from laity, this and the dignity which sets a man apart by reason of membership in the hierarchy." [131] And yet, the right to gather and celebrate could still be held by the community, "Where there is no such hierarchy, you yourself offer sacrifice, you baptize, and you are your own priest. Obviously, where there are three gathered together, even though they are lay persons, there is a Church." [132]

The supper community of Eucharist began to be superseded by the sacrificial understanding, and the Eucharist became more ritualized. The canonization of Latin in the liturgy, a language which most no longer spoke, isolated the people more and encouraged a mute witness to a cultic rite, rather than a full, deep and joyous sharing in the meal of the Lord. [133]

Gradually, a young man put forward for the priesthood no longer had to be sent by a discerning Christian community (in earlier times young men were not allowed to present themselves separate from a supporting community). [134] The discernment began to fall to the established hierarchy, removing it from those Christians who knew him best, and eventually he could be ordained without a community to which he would return.

The centuries since have witnessed an ebb and flow in the understanding of discipleship and its place in the community, and the function of leadership and its role among the priestly people. Such tension continues today.

Scripture research burgeoned in the half century which preceded Vatican II. New methods of understanding and criticism, especially the historical-critical method, came into use. The stories of the early Jesus community were examined for content, language, literary integrity, as well as history of the life and social customs of the society in which the scriptures are based. All of this work flowered in the lives of non-scholars as a reintroduction to the radical freedom from oppression promised by Jesus. It announced to Catholics the very words on which our faith is based, material which had transformed the lives of the first disciples.

The Whiteheads give these insights:

"As the results of this historical study were more widely shared, an important realization dawned: our liturgical practice and other religious customs were not eternal! . . . Among Christians in the first century th(e) liturgy was celebrated more as a communal meal than as a ritual sacrifice. It was celebrated in believers' homes rather than in churches, at tables instead of altars, in the local language rather than in a universally shared tongue. . . . The historical uncovering of the lives of earliest Christians also revealed a very different world of ministry. Many members of a community participated in this service — preaching the word, caring for those in need, managing the group's resources. Women and men were both active in these ministries . . . these initial communities were actively involved in selecting and evaluating their own leaders." [135]

This embrace of Scripture and its study were echoed in the Council.

A generation began to meet the scriptures through bible study groups and classes, in universities and parish halls, and in parishioners' homes, in addition to any exposure from the pulpit. Though some in the Vatican worried publicly that the new methods which explored the history of scripture might lead to uncertainties on the part of the faithful, there was no way to reprivatize that which had been opened. The attempt to vet biblical scholarship through the editorial process of the magisterium has often been ineffective.

For many men and women a balancing act began in which the tradition of the institution was weighed against the revelations of the Scripture. How was the community of Jesus like or unlike the church of the mid-twentieth century? How much could a twentieth-century church resemble the group of women and men who gathered with Jesus in Roman Palestine? Did the call of the scripture resonate in the dailiness of parish and in the church at large? How did the authority of the "people of God," "faithful of Christ," "priesthood of all believers," relate to the authority of the institutional hierarchy? Those names for the initiated assembly, gifts from scripture, were the ones used most frequently in the documents of Vatican II. What did they call forth? If there is no priesthood attached to the apostles mentioned in the gospels, and yet we are all a priesthood of believers, then what is the authority of the priest?

Pierre Hegy points out that we have, in America, moved away from framing the questions about belief and practice as "What does the church teach?" to "What would Jesus do? (This movement) emphasizes the *empowerment* of all through Scripture. . . ." which along with our baptisms carries us "beyond the traditional definition of a 'good Catholic' as one who accepts official church beliefs and practices. Empowerment leads to the praxis of liberation theology, the commitment to social justice for all and the end of limiting gender roles in church and society. Empowerment is not a 'liberal' agenda for church reform from the top down, but the hope for a life in the Spirit from the bottom up. . . . Time has now come to ask about new beginnings."[136]

It was in this environment that Catholics began to experiment with small community Eucharists.

**Folk masses and home liturgies. . . .

**When I was young (12 years old in 1973) a small group of people split off from my parish and held folk masses down the street in the K of C hall. I truly felt like these people cared about what they were doing. (I) had good spiritual experiences with small group liturgies in retreat programs in colleges.

**I remember my first hearing a shared homily in a small evening mass group. It was astounding to hear people be asked for their insights by the priest.

**Cursillo masses were so personal.

**A year in the Jesuit volunteers exposed me to alternate/progressive liturgies. Wonderful!

**I came to know my religion as an adult and participated in liturgies outside the traditional parish routine.

**Communion services in my previous religious community were more meaningful than traditional Mass.

**We came into group liturgy gradually. Once we became familiar and comfortable, we began to talk about all sorts of issues surrounding Church. We weren't in protest originally, that came slowly and in very small steps.

**If I evaluate the experience of "here" as opposed to the parish, I found this to be more genuinely religious.

The late sixties and early seventies still boasted a host of priests, young, full of the documents and a wish for intense community, and many of us baked bread, made banners, learned the profane guitar, sang the music of the St. Louis Jesuits, prepared the readings, spoke in the homily time, sat on the floor and began to "become church" in our celebrations.

Rigid, watchful silence gave way to noisy involvement; small numbers of men and women started feeling proprietorship over their worship. The question of whose Eucharist was it anyway? and Why can't our parish have a little more of this? grew more frequent.

Women included themselves (they were often the organizers, in the ongoing tradition of the Pentecost church) in preparing, hosting and sharing Scripture, which made the non-inclusion in many parishes more chafing. Families found their children willing to go to Mass, which was fun. Parents didn't need to silence their children, the bane of Sunday Mass.

The names of certain celebrants who were open to experimenting, flexible and committed to justice issues became familiar. Groups discovered that they could invite a specific priest to lead the Eucharist. Priests who were lonely had the warmth of sacramental community and often shared in the privacy of homes ideas and beliefs which they were cautious about in the rectory and the pulpit.

College campus liturgies began to reflect the new-within-the-old. Liturgy schedules grew more sensitive to the odd-hours lives of the student population. Young men and women, going to Mass outside of their own parishes, were excited by the relaxed nature of the services which often gave them roles in preparing and celebrating. The homilies were often dialogue and directed to their concerns and for many the personal possibilities of liturgy became apparent. What was other became own.

Interest groups, especially ones united around justice questions, celebrated with sympathetic priests, choosing their own scriptures, often those that speak eloquently about Jesus' stand with the poor and oppressed. Homily time lasted an hour and no one complained.

As priests resigned in huge numbers, groups found fewer available, amenable celebrants. Some groups dissolved, with many not returning to the parish. Those who did return tried to share their understandings, sometimes successfully, sometimes not. Others went parish-shopping. Which church had a liturgy which included, uplifted? Blinders came off as different liturgies were compared. Parish loyalty for many became less sacred then vivid worship. Some groups were fortunate enough to keep their "good" priest but knew that there were fewer and fewer from whom to choose. Some groups continued as scripture study groups, or remained together in other non-sacramental ways. All carried with them the precious memory of the personalism of Jesus in small community.

One gathering lost several celebrants and, after mighty discernment, asked a married priest to be their leader in liturgy and eventually examined at great length the nature of priesthood and ordained one of their own, who remains as their celebrant.

All in all, there was a general move away from what Father said, into a concern about the many opinions and experience which the individuals in a community expressed.

**Our group allows plurality to exist and a statement of our variety in God. We fall in line with a long and healthy tradition.

Communities encourage active participation; women, men found their names known and their talents employed. Small groups have very few passive observers. Diversity is encouraged.

**I married— three pregnancies before the third anniversary because we were trying to use rhythm. In 1968 Humanae Vitae came out and I gave up and started using birth control and little by little gave up church teachings.

Into the midst of this experimentation detonated the warhead of *Humanae vitae*, in which Pope Paul VI rejected the majority recommendations of his own advisory commission. The expectation of a moderation of birth control strictures was dealt a heavy blow. With a swiftness only possible in a media age, hundreds of theologians dissented, and loudly. Women and men who had begun to formulate mature consciences while struggling with pregnancy, debated endlessly the morality of contraception. Mass attendance fell significantly as Catholics thought they had to decide between the magisterium and personal behavior. Thousands read it as an either/or position. Years passed before a significant number of the baptized elected to see that their choice for birth control did not preclude their choice for the sacraments. (In 1987, 66% believed that one could be a good Catholic without obeying the church's teaching regarding birth control; that number rose to 73% in 1993.)[137]

The *sensum fidei* was rejecting an encyclical, signaling a new era in which a teaching, delivered with the weight of papal authority, was tested and found wanting. It was a teaching not received.

Simultaneously, divorce rates among Catholics were rising rapidly, and contemporary psychology had much to say about the damage of remaining in unworkable relationships. The stigma of remarriage lessened, and if one could still not seek the sacrament again in one's parish, return to the Eucharist became a matter of personal conscience.[138] Many parish priests who felt the weight of pain and opinion encouraged people to act in good conscience and didn't worry about who lined up for communion.

**I needed to decide at age 33 to marry a divorced man and on faith in Christ as primary, let go of guilt about laws, same with birth control, a matter of the mind of Christ over the Law.

In private discernment and public debate people asked whether Jesus would have rejected his friends at such a painful time. Biblical theologians who examine the creation story of Genesis and the divorce readings of Matthew, Mark, Luke and Paul, came forward with divergent opinions, some holding that Jesus' intentions on divorce and remarriage are not sufficiently clear to make an absolute proclamation in all times and in all situations possible. [139] Many families witnessed one of their own whose divorce from a spouse also meant divorce from the Church. At a time when people most need the comfort and grace of the Eucharist they were effectively excommunicated. Though the prohibitions drove many from the church, there were also many who remained or returned, having found that Eucharist was more compelling than the force of law.

Queries about proper exercise of authority continued to be raised in both secular and sacral matters. The war in Vietnam was rejected as unjust by senators and students. "Hell no, we won't go!" reverberated through the cities of America and conscientious objection or a flight to Canada became serious considerations.

Many Catholics sensed that the institutional Church was addicted to law and its enforcement, which obscured the gospel. Retrenchment to pre-Vatican II theology stretched the chasm between liberal theologians (and those who read them) and Rome.

**With institutional Church attempts to subvert Vatican II there has got to be a ground swell of folks that bought Vatican II and will not be silenced. Granted what happened to Leonardo Boff, despite his 29 years of trying to "get along" and move valiantly ahead at the same time, should discourage most of us. However, those of us who have not yet reached our maximum of tolerance of the system must continue the resistance and fight for justice. It is the only way worthy of us, with Boff as our model.

In 1977 Joseph Fichter observed "American Catholicism is experiencing adaptation at the grass roots. The most significant aspect of this change is the switch of emphasis in the basis of moral and religious guidance. Dependence on legislation from above has largely switched to dependence on the conscience of the people."[140]

The institutional Church had begun to be seen as adversarial by many, leading all statements and encyclicals to be viewed with a somewhat jaundiced eye. If the documents resonated with personal and community conscience they found favor in the hearts of Americans. If they were viewed as repressive or insensitive they were rejected. Tremendous teaching opportunities were lost as congregations resented papal positions which seemed to be power-preserving. The democratic principles of (if not election) free and open discussion, a right to a fair hearing, negotiation and conciliation were not a part of the Curial thought process.

Hermann Pottmeyer, a professor of fundamental theology calls this position *tradition-alism*: "any attempt to limit improperly the common search of God's people for the binding tradition and its necessary current expression. (Traditionalists) also set themselves up against the dynamic of God's ordained economy of salvation. To the extent that people become aware of their own personal worth, freedom, conscience and responsibility . . . their claim to be taken seriously as responsible and faithful member of the church grows. *But the demands on the people also grow, to assume this responsibility and to become true servants of the word of God"*(my italics).[141]

Assuming mushrooming responsibility for themselves, groups of women and men launched a new wave of small communities, many of them energized by the network of Central America. Frequently parish-based, they do not necessarily see themselves as replacements of the institution, rather as a living source of renewal within it. Centered in personal recognition, love and faith sharing, and scripture, Leonardo Boff says, "The base community constitutes . . . a bountiful wellspring of renewal for the tissues of the body ecclesial, and a call and a demand for the evangelical authenticity of ecclesial institutions, so that they may come more closely to approximate the utopian community ideal."[142]

The American church changed phenomenally in just the thirty years since Pope John

XXIII convened the bishops of the world, and thousands of lay people claimed the church as their own, naming themselves "center," refusing to leave and denying the hierarchy's right to throw them out, while disagreeing often and loudly with the pronouncements of the papacy.

How have you encountered discipleship and scripture in the embrace of faith community? How has it shaped you?

COMMUNITIES OF VOWED WOMEN ⊕

**After Vatican II my religious community began to reexamine our mission statement, and our ministry outside the community began to grow.

**Being a part of a women's community for 26 years taught me to value women and to count on women; we learned to live independently of male structures and relationships, being scandalized by the hierarchical church's treatment of women, as a religious community of women, especially as issues of power come to the public arena.

**30 plus years as a woman religious have led me to seek community wherever I go.

**My membership in a religious community led me to social justice concerns and actions in behalf of minority groups.

**My religious community is a small grass roots segment of the world.

**I was a Papal Volunteer for Latin America where we all together *were* the church and then I returned to the US church where our education and experience are ignored because we are not clerics.

**I spent nine years in a really progressive canonical religious community where I learned about feminist, Marxist class analysis and community organizing and the need to be with others on the journey.

**I was a nun for seven years. After that I retained a deep need for prayer and a prayer-filled community.

The decades which redefined the experience of church for lay men and women found women religious coping also with tremendous change. The nuns of our past, often mysterious and other-worldly in their life styles, began to emerge from behind the walls of their convents, and enter with gusto into ministry to the secular world.

Women's religious orders have also participated in the myth of possibility, the American opportunity for change and accomplishment. Many European-based orders had answered the call to ministry by sending large numbers of their women here in response to the invitations of bishops to staff schools and open hospitals. How brave those women must have been, and adventurous, to forsake their ordered lives for the uncertainties of the America!

These women ministered to the families of immigrants like themselves, staffing hospitals, orphanages and schools, sometimes with only slightly more education than the children in front of them. They graduated young men and women with sturdy skills to meet their needs and the requirements of society.

The early 1950's saw the Vatican encourage reexamination of religious constitutions, rules, customs and practice in a move toward modernization. This move was coupled with a dramatic rise in the educational level of women religious in the United States, brought about, in part, by the vision of such women as Sr. Madeleva Wolff[143] and Sr. Bertrande Meyers, who saw the need for young nuns to increase their formal knowledge in response to the challenges of the modern world, while resisting haste and making certain to educate the whole Sister.[144] (The establishment of the Sister Formation Conference in 1954 sparked an explosion of systematic pre-service learning which prepared sisters spiritually and professionally for their mission.)

Vatican II brought, not only all the documents on liturgy and the modern world, but also one aimed at their specific lives of prayer and ministry, "Decree on the Up-To-Date Renewal of Religious Life" (*Perfectae Caritatis*). It called for a significant renewal and rebirth which will only happen with the cooperation of all the members.[145] Reminded to follow Christ in everything, sisters were encouraged to adapt their lives to contemporary society.[146] Seeking to accommodate religious institutes to the people of God, the document said they should be educated concerning the behaviors, emotions and thought processes of the secular world[147] and amend their ministries to fit the needs of contemporary society.[148] In addition, major superiors were invited to form conferences which would enable cooperation and deal with problems common to various orders.

A significant step forward in understanding the impact of the Council was Sr. Marie Augusta Neal's National Sister's Survey, which found "that those sisters who preferred older theologies also tended to perceive their own goals as adjusting to existing conditions within church and society, whereas those sisters who read postconciliar theologians and imbibed the spirit of Vatican II were more likely to aim at the transformation of society."[149]

The swelling sense of community understanding of shared power was reflected in the name change of the Conference of Major Superiors of Women to the Leadership Conference of Women Religious in 1971. It was a move not readily accepted by the Vatican. In the document issued in the same year, Apostolic Exhortation on the Renewal of Religious Life, there was still a reinforcement of the need for adaptation, but with what some heard as a veiled threat that this experimentation was proceeding "sometimes too hardily . . . We know well and we are following with attention this effort. . . ."[150]

Women in religious life became more deeply engaged in social justice issues as their educations and their jobs opened understanding of institutional misuse of power. Community prayer and study reinforced the Biblical call to stand with the poor and the tyrannized.

In response to the call of the bishops, nuns by the thousands went to Central America where, while serving the poor, they witnessed the growth in the base community movement. Blossoming in part from the desperate shortage of priests, this exciting new grassroots action is the place in which "The laity carry forward the cause of the gospel . . . and are the vessels, the vehicles of ecclesial reality even on the level of direction and decision-making."[151] The nuns found what Leonardo Boff calls "one of the great principles of church renewal worldwide (which is) building a living church rather than multiplying material structures."[152] The base communities are "characterized by the absence of alienating structures, by direct relationships, by reciprocity, by a deep communion, by mutual assistance, by communality of gospel ideals, by equality among members."[153] Spirit-filled and centered among the poor, it is exciting, it is joyous, it is power-with, not power-over.

Many sisters were overwhelmed by the passion of people who felt the ". . . rejuvenating leaven of the gospel ideals of communion, in a community of sisters and brothers simply living one and the same faith in the spontaneous worship of Christ in the midst of humanity."[154] Missioners were filled up with the excitement of this abiding leaven rising in the people, the yeast of faith, and they brought it home with them. For many orders, their own fermentation, already in process, was hastened by this authorizing encounter. The question was, how do we bring this miracle alive in our own convents, and in our parishes?

Simultaneously, confrontation of the greatly declining numbers in vowed orders, called forth first fear of the death of religious life as we know it, then a search for ways of adapting religious life to the contemporary scene and dreaming the future. "Indeed, our communities will be smaller in the future than in the past. . . . But size is no measure of the vibrancy of the ministry. Religious life is called to be a leaven in the world, not a labor force. It is what we are about, not how many of us who are about it that will be the measure of our meaning."[155]

**As a member of a progressive religious community I was called and challenged in that community to determine my charisms. There was a lot of discernment. I saw the scripture base for ministry to the people of God. It changed my life. It also brought me, and my community, smack up against the institutional Church as one of the places where injustice happens often.

Enlarging their sphere of understanding through education, prayer and action, many women ached with the knowledge that their own Church had responsibility for a part of the pain that they saw on the streets of the world, whether because some bishops sided with the entrenched powers against the needs of the people, or because the papal institution denied the equal participation of women in sacramental and policy roles.

Increasing activism and criticism by American nuns (most visibly, Sr. Theresa Kane and her address to Pope John Paul II in Washington DC) was ignored by the Vatican or attempts were launched to rein those women in. Hierarchical authority butted heads with liberating agents for change.[156] Many nuns see this struggle in terms of faithful dissent which is marked by a need for open, honorable, moral dialogue without fear in which all are recognized as morally mature, each in image of God.

Honoring their common discernments many women religious agree with Sr. Rose Tilleman's statement, "I believe our greatest strength as religious women has not been in our vows, but in our bondedness as women. With our collective power drawn from our common roots and history and our current strength, we could be part of enormous growth and change in church and society if we focused mainly on justice and peace."[157]

Experiencing what could be thought of as a Vatican practice of the theology of anxiety and threat, and also the loss of daily Eucharist in convents because of the shortage of priests, they "found themselves relating to each other for spiritual direction, theological insights, and liturgical celebration, thus displacing 'father' as a central authority figure."[158]

As the 1980s progressed this breach widened,[159] especially on gender analysis of structure and power to self-determine. Requests for dialogue with Rome were often met with denial or silence. Many nuns feel pulled apart by their loyalty to the Church which is home to generations of faith and indeed site not only of baptism but of mature vowed commitment on one hand, and the call of the future nurtured in the liberating radicalism of Jesus on the other. "Indeed, when the Church and its documents and its structures and its symbols and its language and its laws and its liturgies forgets or foregoes or forswears the place of women in the Christian dispensation, there in its Scriptures, the vision of Jesus with women stays vibrant and vital and unable to be forgotten." [160]

**Belonging to a community of religious women led me to celebration of Eucharist. We worked hard on reimagining our mission in the world based on the principles of our founder, and we tried to be faithful to the call of the Gospels. Eventually we saw that we must stand with the poor and the disaffiliated and that meant standing with Jesus. Eventually we came to understand that "do this in memory of Me" meant to do not only Eucharist but all He commanded, to break the bonds of oppression, to minister to the sorrowful and the needy, and most of all to ask why they are as they are. Questioning the institutional structures of the secular world led us to see that the same repressive structures were in place in the Church.

At the same time, the decline of the number of men in the priesthood, led many women who had embraced hospitals, prisons and the streets to begin to redefine sacrament as they found themselves hearing the sorry confidences of the sick, the incarcerated, the homeless. When someone came and poured out a confession of guilt and sin and wanted peace, how was this like Reconciliation? When people broke bread and prayed together behind bars how was this Eucharist? When a dying indigent asked to pray together and be blessed, was this the Sacrament of the Sick? Is all this work-love the basis for sacrament? "Women have initiated children into the Christian experience at every level; they have heard the anguished avowals of the guilty and loved them to reconciliation; they have made mealtimes experiences of Christian unity; they have consoled the sick and assisted the dying into the arms of God. None of this ministerial activity, even though it is the substance of the sacraments, is ritualized when carried out by women.[161]

Ruth Wallace, in a study of twenty Catholic parishes administered by women, many of them nuns, points out the real, everyday confrontation with matters sacramental. She reports numbers of encounters in which women pastors heard confessions "informally." One such woman explained: "I have found when people are sick that they are really confessing a lot of the time. I had one person say to me, 'I have told you, and God is listening, and that's enough.' I agreed."[162]

She also shares stories of baptisms and sacraments of the sick which occur when no priest is available. Women pastors have had to regularly confront the situation of the no-show or almost-no-show priest on Sunday morning. One priest who is involved in such a situation recalls: "Many times because of the schedule, they (the woman pastor and her congregation) would start and I would come in after the start. Many times I would leave before Communion would start because I would have another Mass to go to."[163] Do those assembled for the Eucharist have a right to it? And what does Eucharist mean if it is held captive to such situations?

Women religious have simultaneously pushed and been called out of the security of the set routines of the past, and continue to look to their own traditions and the Gospels for guidance while affirming the power of vowed community engagement with the call of the Spirit for the future.

How has vowed sisterhood engaged your sense of the divine in your life?

COMMUNITIES OF FRIENDSHIP ✪

**Personal prayer and friendships with other women have changed me.

**My delight in women's groups and the at-home feeling when I work, pray, play with women and men who are at-one-ment with women.

**Relationships brought me here.

** When I first joined the group I joined to be in solidarity with my friends.

**I came and I stay because of my interdependent relationships among women.

**I started in the group and stayed in the group because of my friends. They have showed me the face of God in ways I never knew or expected.

**Friendships here are sacred. In the Eucharist we see and remember Jesus' ultimate act of friendship. He taught us how to live, gave his life for us and shared with us a way, a real way, to have him present for all time.

**I am in a loving committed relationship with a woman. It is beautiful and blessed. Same-gender relationships can be celebrated in this group. In the traditional Catholic Church one must either lie or be ostracized. Certainly we could not celebrate the joy in our lives.

**I'm here because of friendships.

**I was fortunate enough to have a friend who was starting a group and invited me to participate. This became a turning point in my life.

**I have come because I am in spiritual direction with a trained woman who very much affirms me and is a real close companion on my journey.

**My deepest human relationships are with women. It is only natural that I would wish to celebrate Eucharist with them.

**I have been known to treat friends poorly in the past. When I was invited to be part of a WomenChurch group I began to reassess my relationships and to behave as a better friend.

**A special and treasured friendship is the major reason my spiritual journey has even found this path. God has truly blessed me. I couldn't make this journey alone; I've often prayed that God allow me the gift of awareness. This gift has allowed me the opportunity to recognize those who would help me in my struggles to that perfect relationship with the Lord.

**I simply have a need to celebrate with other women; to share my story, to bring all of my experiences, joys, difficulties, sorrows to the liturgical celebrations.

**I began because a friend asked me if I was interested.

**I have been searching for a liturgy that would include me and my friend told me about this.

**If it weren't for friends I wouldn't be here now.

The most frequently named response to the question, "What experiences in your life led you to be a part of this group?" is friendship. Those who understand us, embrace us, laugh with us, and accept us also pray with us.

These wonderful people who share our vision of the world's struggles, who have heard the depth of our pains and joined in our rejoicings, who have put up with us when we are boring, are the ones with whom we celebrate.

Is this not the model that Jesus gave us? Jesus made friends. The scriptures imply a lord-disciple relationship, but if we are to know him as truly human it must follow that he needed, wanted, treasured friends and in the daily life of that small company we see friendship. They hung out together, went to the same parties, shared their food and their lives with each other. Jesus heard them squabble, they heard his fears. They loved him. He loved them. It was friendship so great that they left their work and families to join him on his rambles through the countryside. In the garden, he asked them, begged them to stay up with him. Peter denied him, Judas betrayed him in a couple of fine examples of the sometimes pain of friendship. Mary and John stayed with him in disaster.

While we theologize about many types of human relationships it is rare to do so about that most basic of all: non-controlling, equality-based sharing of our lives intimately with another. One of the deepest of human longings is to be known and accepted by others. The facades we erect are for fear of judgment.

If we ask women to describe their best friends, words like accepting, loving, embracing, non-critical are used. Phrases such as, always there for me, takes my side, picks me up when I'm down, makes me laugh, forgives me, are common. Sentences like, I know I can trust her; We can tell each other everything; She has gone through so much with me, resound.

Women's friendships have not received their due in the work of theology. Women themselves have often undervalued them. When marriage is the expectation in a dominant heterosexual society, women's deep relationships with other women are often seen as temporary or second-best. Many women have seen friendships die on the altar of marriage, as husbands take first place. We often see these relationships in an either/or mode, while then expecting a spouse to be all things in marriage.

Shifting family models, however, with many single parent families, women-identified women, a reunderstanding of women as religious community, women single by choice, and with the explosion of printed material by and about women, provide a growth in the public acknowledgment of the importance of women's friendships.

I suspect that friendship, genuine, voluntary, non-hierarchical embrace of another, is the core of most Women's Eucharist groups. Friends begin groups, friends bring other friends, friends of one person become friends of another. This is easy. By WE's most frequent model, people have no control over another, nor wish it. Women attend to each other's stories, lifting them up, recognizing their importance. Women do not remain mute in the assembly, but have holy interchange. Women see the sacred in each life tale and do not dismiss each other. As we begin to value ourselves highly, we also lean towards giving higher intentional value to our friendships. Those characteristics which have been unappreciated often in a masculine world are respected and admired.

Mary Daly calls this activity Be-Friending, which "involves Weaving a context in which women can Realize our Self-transforming, metapatterning (changepatterning) participation in Be-ing. Therefore it implies the creation of an atmosphere in which women are enabled to be friends. Every woman who contributes to the creation of this atmosphere functions as a catalyst for the evolution of other women and for the forming and unfolding of genuine friendships."[164]

One thing that women discover is that in good friendship we intend each other toward God. This is especially true if we have come to recognize our friendships as formed on an elevated model, the model of Jesus' relationship to his friends, God's relationship to us.

If friends are good they lead each other to the Divine friendliness of Jesus. They accept us, forgive us, help us to forgive ourselves and others, share their food and drink, want justice for us, lift us up, aim us in the proper direction and remind us of the good things in life. Friendship immediately creates community. This paradigm of relationship comes from Jesus, and enlarges our understanding of love.

Mary Hunt, in her wonderful work on friendship, sees that "Divine attention is expressed not only in the fact of creation, but in the abiding presence that religious people experience God. The Goddess, the Holy, God/ess, et. al. can be conceived of as an attentive friend. This friend is waiting and cooperating creatively in the unfolding of history. This friend thinks of the smallest detail and permits the largest indiscretion without dominating or breaking the friendship. . . A divine friend keeps on generating without end, so history overtakes and pushes into the future without apology. People go with that energy trusting that a divine friend is leading the way. . . . People recognize common roots and celebrate the common condition as friends of the One who nurtures so many." [165]

The Gospel of John tells of the ultimate personal, political gift: "No one has greater love than this, to lay down one's life for one's friends." [166] Jesus does not couch this radical love in a transcendent, hierarchical relationship, but in one that is so deeply human that it is knowable by us all.

Does our experience of friendship help us to dare to call Jesus friend, soul-mate, lover? Does Eucharist in a friend-filled environment speak more profoundly to our souls?

COMMUNITIES AGAINST PATRIARCHY ✪

**The more feminist I became the less the institutional Church spoke to my experience. In fact, the church diminished it.

**(I) developed a critical consciousness about the sexism, racism and homophobia within the church.

**I'm married to a priest (and) have children, both daughters, and want them to be intelligent adults and not dumb sheep.

**(I was) tormented in my early years because of the dichotomy between rules and the human/spiritual experience. Oppressive actions by Church leaders toward those who sincerely wish to love one another and work together for the good of the kingdom.

**I do not like sexist language in liturgies and do not like the way women are treated in the traditional church. I also would like my children to see a different church than the one I experienced.

**The oppression and abuse of women by Church leaders and their teachings outrages me and I choose to act constructively to bring about change.

**The church doesn't accept women as equals and Dignity as a whole comes from the church though I see the church as emerging and transforming in small base communities as to what I believe Jesus was saying.

**The scandal of the patriarchy brought me here.

**My experience as an active professional in the Church made me aware of the unethical conduct of clergy; the inequality existing and dividing clergy and laity and dividing men and women.

**I have frustration with male power struggles in the institutional Church.

**I see the hierarchy fear the Spirit and feel called to have Christ's presence outside the oppressive structures of Church.

**I awakened to sexual and racial discrimination in our culture. Christianity as it is practiced in the Western world is very much a part of it.

**I joined the woman's movement and saw a glimmer of how the RC church oppressed women and found a group starting a WomanChurch and I joined. Little by little, I freed myself from oppression, of course, I didn't "free" myself, I had lots of help.

**The clergy do not a church make; what takes care of only its own is already dead.

**My hunger for God, my lesbian self, my feminism, my three daughters and a grand-daughter, frustration at sexist language and the limitations of women's roles drew me to (a women's Eucharist group).

**Disaffection with the Church; a need for deeper connection with God; a need to have a safe group to share with; a method of being change, led me to be here.

**Finding my own holiness, yet feeling unaccepted by the church by not even being allowed to consider the priesthood, having a daughter who can't be an altar server.[167]Needing to find a language which resounds in my body to talk about God-within-me.

**Feminist conversion touched my faith and prayer.

**I am scandalized that the present situation exists but even more so that the institutional Church would not work at the highest levels to reform, to apologize, to amend past (and I might say) present behavior. I cannot have any hope for my own future in the church and for the future of my daughter unless I pray, work and protest now.

**I came to a women's group in part because I see it as hope for the future as well as help for right now.

So much has been published about the problem of patriarchy that I refer readers to the wealth of material to be found elsewhere. [168] I will use the definition which Rosemary Radford Ruether puts forth in *Women-Church.*

"Patriarchy is named as a historically contrived social system by which the 'fathers'— that is, ruling-class males —have used power to establish themselves in a position of domi-nation over women and also over dependent classes in the family and society."[169] Features of patriarchy are the building and maintaining of social, economic, cultural and political systems which assure that males will continue generationally to monopolize control.

The words of my responders cry out the pain the patriarchal, institutional Church has inflicted. Would you go back and read them again? They speak of the hurt, of not one discriminating encounter but, of thousands of them couched in a religion which *sacramentalizes* discrimination.

Women Church and WomenEucharist rejects the idea that this could ever be the vision of Jesus friend, whose very name means Yahweh Frees.

The negative power of these encounters calls us together to bond in hope of both flee-ing the effects of patriarchy in our lives, and building up our imaginings of what it is, in fact, that Yahweh Frees has calls us to.

We sang "We Shall Overcome" in the streets and "Priestly People" in our churches and wondered how they connected one to the other. We marched for the liberation of others and realized gradually it was also for ourselves. We did not, do not compartmentalize the material of our lives and learning. We do not see experience as unconnected. We know our living, our actions reverberate in new situations, uncovering new understandings of old material,

Blacks behaved in ways which were condemned as uppity (a word also used against women who do not know "their place") and as unlawful, but the moral rightness of their actions was, in retrospect, unassailable, and if they had waited they would still be waiting.

Feminists and especially feminist spirituality groups are responsible for taking part in reclaiming the world from the destruction of patriarchy. Feminist spirituality can interconnect the web of life — human, non-human — with the vision of a loving, liberating, freeing Yahweh. We claim that this is what we are called to do now in this time.

God's intent for us as a world is continuously revealed, not in the abstract, but in the concrete events of life. The covenant with the exodus people of Israel to freedom was promised yet again in the covenanting of Jesus. We believe that this promise continues to be lived out now.

Our past is shaped by experience, and our future is imagined as what we hope will be. We cannot wait for the future to happen. It is happening as every moment comes into being. To change the future we must change the now and let the shape of our anticipations help to carve out our tomorrows. For those of us who are hopeful, that very hope of deliverance from war or emotional slavery, an unjust institution, helps to shape our understandings and our behavior and our orientations in the present, and that reshaping affects our lives to come.

Those of us who are hopeful treat our futures with great care. Those of us who celebrate now are "hoping" our future into our now. Matthew Fox calls this the Eternal Now. "By the choices we make now about what we birth, the past presses into the future. Whether the future presents itself as still more beauty or as still more pain depends upon our choices as we respond to our role as co-creators in an ever-unfolding creation." [170]

For many feminists this means gathering separately from men to articulate women's own reunderstanding of what the world holds for us all, men as well. "The need for a period of withdrawal from men and communication with each other is essential for the formation of the feminist community, because women, more than any other marginalized group, have lacked a critical culture of their own. . . . women need separate spaces and all-female gatherings to form the critical culture that can give them an autonomous ground from which to critique patriarchy." [171]

This does not mean permanent separation. Most of us work and live with and around men, and wish it so. However, our bonding, our comprehension of sharing experience, our healing begins in the circle of women. For most of us, this is a chapter, not a whole book.

Feminist spirituality groups are missioned to pray and imagine us all toward the future which will be as good or as terrible as we all make possible. It is to those who have suffered that the responsibility for framing the healing process belongs. Those who have been damaged by the patriarchy know what must be made new, and it is in the heart of such groups that, bathed in God's freeing love, all will be joined in the mending process.

How is it that you find the patriarchal church oppressing you?

COMMUNITIES OF SACRAMENT ✪

**Four years ago I made a "Creation Liturgy" retreat. I was deeply moved then by the daily liturgies because of inclusive language used and the participation of women present.

**We need a Eucharistic celebration that springs from all of us, not just from what some priest's ideas are. It is terrible to go to a parish liturgy and feel lonely because my presence is unimportant. I suspect that there are many other people who feel the same way.

**I learned that sacraments are signs of God present and interacting with all of the community but most places there is little community, just a group of people sitting in the same church, and little sign of God, since there is little reaction from anyone. How can this be sacrament?

** (I came) because I was angry and lonely but also because I am sacramental and ceremonial. I saw a documentary on *60 Minutes*, I think, about this. When I was called to help in a women's liturgy in the church proper, I asked if they knew of something like what I had seen, and was welcomed to the outside-the-church masses.

**The apprenticeship of 5 years with a priest at the Newman Center who lives out what a true liturgist is, an enabler, non-clerical, who shows how to be mystical and practical in worship (led me). My total love of the Eucharist from high school boarding school daily Mass, to the convent for 15 years, to active liturgy groups in 3 parishes.

**(I came) because of boring Masses, uninvolved crowds fulfilling an obligation, not being fed spiritually.

**I have been horrified when Mass was used to separate and divide people. When it is within the church itself that women learn every Sunday, year after year, that they are somehow inferior.

**You have only to go into most parish churches during liturgy to know that something is dreadfully wrong with how the church does sacraments. Look at the faces of the people past the first ten rows. Bored, don't sing, they're reading the bulletin and waiting for the hour to pass so they can get on with their "real" lives. Is the fault with them, or is it with a church that has withheld Eucharist from them? We're so used to it that we accept it, but it is really scandalous. The church is afraid to let Jesus loose, afraid that they would lose power. A terrible shame.

**We had a community which really dreamed beauty and meaning and transformation in our sacraments, then we lost the priest who made it all possible. Oh, it was a terrible loss. That was when I began to look for another place to be church which would continue this powerful experience.

**Our group liturgies treat Eucharist with such reverence, such tenderness. You can't imagine how wonderful it is to be part of a group that sees this action as truly sacred.

**Eucharist has been the center of my spiritual life for many years. I have had to wear blinders so often, make excuses for the poor liturgies so often. Now I am tired of that, and too old to care what the official church says about women. With my Women-Church group I had found a spiritual home, the Eucharists are blissful and encouraging and hopeful and true. Jesus is here with us and I am deeply filled.

**Eucharist is just too important to me to let it be held hostage by the institution.

**There is such a time of joy in our group.

**From month to month I can't wait to go. There is no other place I go that is so much fun. We love being together, and to think that we do this! Eucharist in this group takes on a much different, much deeper meaning for me.

What ardent responses! Joy, enthusiasm, fun, miracle. What a wonderful idea, that the Eucharist could be fun.

The coming together as community and for sacrament makes WE church by the earliest definition, and to be church is the fundamental sacrament. What we do exhibits belief in the risen Jesus and belief that Eucharist is the way in which we are deeply linked to Jesus, Christus, died and risen, and present with us today. In this action we are bound together in God's presence and in hope of metanoia.

Eucharist is identified as "the true center of the whole Christian life both for the universal church and for the local congregation." [172] Women, perhaps more than men, agree. Spend a moment in reality or memory. What gender is consistently more greatly represented at Mass?

And what happens for these women when Eucharist is more and more frequently unavailable? When parishes are closed, and consolidation removes Eucharist from the center of the community? When a shortage of priests promises that Eucharist will become increasingly rare? When education informs us that it is in the thanksgiving and will of intentional community that the seed of Eucharist is planted? When the sign value of Eucharist is perverted by the patriarchy? When the liberating nature of the Eucharist is denied by the very way in which it is performed?

The quotes tell us that groups see the act of celebration rooted in the community. That liturgy begins in the will of the community to place in the hands and heart of one or two at a time, the job of focusing the prayer of the group by planning the liturgy by which we act as church entering into sacrament. Rotation of that role calls us to remember that each person has a sacred interaction with the Spirit which can be called forth for all the community to share. If worship is truly praise, thanksgiving and transformation, then part of the liturgical function is to elicit from the community how that can and will take place. Having drawn from the ideas of the many, the planners can help to focus and fuse that impulse into collective prayer and action. We move away from a hierarchy of ministries, toward a coequality in which the community cannot be whole without the gifts of all.

We are excluded, women and men alike, even in the midst of many priests, if the sacraments are played out on the ordained's terms alone. When he sets the stage, chooses the language, selects the prayers and consecrates as if he were alone in the room, then we have been denied the Eucharist in its fullness.

"All the functions of church . . . are simply expressions of entering and developing a true human community of mutual love. The greatest possible distortion of church is to identify it with an ecclesiastical superstructure that distorts our true nature and has been created by competitive and oppressive hierarchicalism. The whole concept of ministry must be understood as the means by which the community itself symbolizes its common life to itself and articulates different aspects of its need to empower and express that common life."[173]

Do these Eucharists better symbolize (make sacrament) the life of the community? Are they signs of God's life among us, of a celebration of God's promise of freedom, and an intimation of the kingdom?

**I keep coming, in part, because when we celebrate together I have hope.
**Eucharist means more to me here. It is like a veil has been lifted and I can see more clearly that the words and actions are not just that, but that they have clearer meaning about what God wants.
**When I am with my group and we have Eucharist, it has much more significance to me.
**I go away glowing, doing this changes how I live my days.

Part of the ministry which WE is called upon to reclaim is the sign of Eucharist, through careful attention to the ministry of community (in which Jesus is present), the ministry of Word (in which Jesus is revealed) and the ministry of bread and wine (in which Jesus is embraced).

This calls for active participation, for it is those who celebrate who must search out how to make the sign clear.

"This communal activity recalls the original activity of Christ and his disciples which constituted the Church and the meaning of membership in the Church. Thereby it generates a new beginning of the community. But, as with all social groups, this effect is conditioned by the *active participation* of the believers who express the faith they live by daily life . . . . this activity is needed because the members of the Church exist in history and must continually celebrate their common faith lest they lose their identity as the Body of Christ"[174] (my italics).

How do we participate actively as disciples in this hour of creation so that our joined belief that we are the Body of Christ will not die? We can only assume that God is doing God's part, and that we are responsible for ours. What is the imperative, but to "Do this in memory of me"? To gather, discern, pray, eat, and go out as Christ to each other: that is the ancient and present command and that is our active part.

The Vatican II document *The Constitution of the Sacred Liturgy (Sacrosanctum Concilium)* says "Mother Church earnestly desires that all faithful should be led to that full, conscious, and active participation in liturgical celebration which is demanded by the very nature of the liturgy, and to which the Christian people, 'a chosen race, a royal priesthood, a holy nation, a redeemed people' (1 Pet. 2:9, 4-5) have a right and obligation by reason of their baptism."[175]

How does active participation happen in this time in history? How are we, the Body of Christ, bound to fulfill that full, conscious and active role in the dialogue between God and God's people? And how can it be an active dialogue if someone else writes all the parts without input from the community and no one is permitted to deviate from those words? "(The document) states: 'From the liturgy . . . grace is poured forth . . . and the sanctification of people and the glorification of God . . . are achieved with maximum effectiveness' consequently, the need for active participation so that believers will be open to engage in this dialogue and to cooperate in the goal of redemption, which corresponds to the goal of creation, becomes a major concern of this constitution."[176] And, increasingly, a major goal of the people of God.

Is this impulse so strong, so immediate, so intense, that we, in trembling should reject one set of human rules in order to enter into Divine command?

The answer is, slowly, yes. As we become involved, energetic participants in the community and take responsibility for our worship, we hear more clearly the words of Jesus, "Let me solemnly assure you, if you do not eat the flesh of the Son of Man and drink his blood, you have no life in you. The one who feeds on my flesh and drinks my blood has life eternal. . . ."[177]

The ordained priesthood is not nearly as important, as compelling as the call of Jesus. The call to praise, thank and understand is a part of the whole of human history. The command to take and eat predates the hierarchy, and in the hierarchy's efforts, or willingness, to limit access to the Eucharist the command of Jesus is held captive, perverted.

Doing now, preparing for the future. Practicing mentally, intellectually what sacrament means. The call to worship does not come from the institution, but from the Spirit, through and in the people of God, it is "practiced" and polished.

Rosemary Radford Ruether named this years ago. "Reappropriation theology (declericalizing the church) . . . facilitates the taking back of ministry, word, and sacrament by the people. . . .Eucharist is not an objectified piece of bread or cup of wine that is magically transformed into the body and blood of Christ. Rather it is the people, the ecclesia, who are being transformed into the body of the new humanity, infused with the blood of new life."[178]

Other theologians are beginning to cautiously move in this direction. The liberation theology work of Leonardo Boff raises the issue as a disputed question. "What is decisive for sacramental value lies in the acceptance of faith in the Lord present and living in the eucharistic celebration, and in the value of the eucharistic celebration as representation of Christ's sacrifice and not only of the Last Supper. In this view, the eucharist celebrated by ministers without any bond with the tradition of the laying-on of hands would be valid and sacramental in virtue of the apostolic doctrine of the real presence of Christ."[179]

Sacramental theologian Bernard Cooke edges toward the matter in a response to the issue of whether small groups can celebrate Eucharist: "Without question, there is a *gradation* in what happens in these various celebrations. There is more of the full symbolism of Eucharist in some, and less in others. How? It's very tricky. It's not just a question of the extent to which they are official, but the extent to which they are genuine for this particular group."[180]

In an article on the shortfall of priests to meet the sacramental needs of the baptized, William H. Shannon, a religious studies professor, commenting on the validity of a baptism performed when no priest is available, suggests that, because of the priest shortage, the same principle might be applied to Eucharist. "A fundamental principle of Roman Catholic theology is that the sacraments exist for people. . . . If the celebration of Eucharist is threatened, and the Eucharist is *that* necessary for the life of the church, can we not see this as a case of necessity in which we must do something similar to what we do with baptism? . . . Even granting that the hierarchical priesthood and the common priesthood of the baptized differ in essence, still every baptized person does share in the priesthood of Jesus Christ. And if it is clear that the priest does not have some magic power of changing bread and wine into the body and blood of Christ, but rather is deputed by his ordination to pray in the name of the church that the Holy Spirit will effect the change in the eucharistic element, then—I want to ask—is there any reason why a lay person who is a recognized leader in a particular ecclesial community might not *be deputed, in a case of necessity,* to do what is ordinarily done by the priest, but which cannot be done by a priest because one is not available? . . . History witnesses that the church's understanding of ministry has gone through many changes across the centuries. Perhaps the 'needs of the time' call us as church to a radical rethinking of the meaning of ministry and of how and by whom it should be exercised in the church." [181]

Necessity exists, especially for women who have been denied the right to the fullness of Eucharist because of their sex, for all people who are denied the fact of Eucharist because there is no one to celebrate their faith and belief.

We who long for a more *fully recognizable* Eucharist only dimly "remember" that of which we dream. We need bring that dream into daylight, not by hoping for it, praying for it alone. Sacraments are not an idea which exists mentally, they are an act and an interaction of love and liberation which we all perform. But with that hope, the prayer moves into action.

**I am very enthusiastic about the possibilities of small numbers of people joining for Eucharist. Jesus' presence is so deeply felt. We have a couple of children who come regularly and love being a part of this group. I look at them and see how they like to be included, and how they can talk freely and easily about Jesus because of this time we all have together. That is a miracle.

How do you move your dream of Eucharist into reality?

Grassroots to sacrament. The baptized communities which name themselves church are examining their needs and experience in the light of the Gospels and are struggling, rejoicing, discerning and celebrating their way to the future.

✪✪✪✪✪

GATHERING

FORETHOUGHT ✪

This chapter addresses who gathers and how we identify ourselves, as well as the characteristics and function of women's spirituality groups. We talk about the importance of shared experience, and discuss the planning, format and materials for WomenEucharist.

✪✪✪✪✪

*Catholicism is the tongue of my heart, and as the song says, "you can't take that away from me." Respondent.

*Something is happening that we dare not miss. In many places and circumstances, a new ecumenical community is emerging, radically rooted in faith and deeply committed to justice. People and groups from diverse traditions, who have not been connected before, are discovering how much they need each other. Together, they are forging a practice of faith in action that can genuinely be called prophetic; and, together, they are harbingers for a more prophetic church. [182]

*There are so many hungry people that God cannot appear to them except in the form of bread. [183]

*Free of patriarchal restrictions and the expectations of polity and canons, many feminist spirituality groups are experiencing a genuine koinonia, and on that basis are redefining "church." they are doing so within the Tradition, for many Christian traditions now teach and preach an ecclesiology based, not on hierarchical structures, but on the laos, the people of God. Christian feminists are rejoicing in their discovery of what it means to be church and re exploring the potential inherent in the realization, "We are the church!" [184]

**We're Catholic in heritage.

**We're catholic, with a small c.

**The group is Catholic but we welcome anybody and have members from other traditions.

**We're all Catholic in a broad sense.

**Many of us are Catholic-rooted but with several long-standing participants from other churches.

**We're United Church of Christ, a large proportion of participants are former Catholics, many former clergy.

**Initially the group was all Catholic. After meeting for about three years a Methodist woman joined with us and now our group regularly includes her and an Episcopalian.

**95% Catholic but open to others.

**Probably mostly Catholic but we don't ask a person's religion.

**The majority are Catholic and have varying relationships with the Church, from vowed religious women to those who no longer consider themselves a part of the Church, from those who regularly attend Eucharist in a parish to those who seldom or never attend.

**90% Catholic, a few Episcopal and United Church of Christ.

**We're Catholic but not intentionally so.

**We have Catholic roots. Anyone would be welcome but so far all are Catholic-rooted. Some of us are Catholic by culture only, and no longer participate at all in institutional Church activities except as a protest presence. Some of us find Jesus and the Bible important, some do not identify strictly as Christians.

**We are interdenominational.

**We're mostly Catholic, all Christian. One of the great things about our community is that we have several women who are former nuns, but are now married. They have a lot of training that has been a big help in forming and developing us as a group.

All together, 92 responders identified themselves as Catholic in some fashion (i.e., cultural Catholic, recovering Catholic, Catholic by birth). The remaining twelve either failed to answer the specific question on religious affiliation (though two identified themselves as Catholic in one or more of the other survey questions), or named themselves as Methodist (2), Episcopalian (2), "grew up Protestant" (1), unaffiliated (3), no answer (2).

What is most intriguing here is the loosening of the links of traditional church identification, not the denial of that affiliation, but as seeing it as only a *part* of the way in which responders see themselves. Their Catholicism is hemmed up with adjectives, mostly ones which reveal a much more tentative relationship with the institution than would have been imaginable two decades ago. Linked to this is the statement, repeated frequently that, while the WE groups may be in the majority Catholics, there is a tremendous friendliness to, inclusion of those who come from other traditions. As we shed our bonds to the institution we have begun to look abroad seeking new community.

**We're open to all who find the Eucharist important.

What we are seeing is groups which are based only partly in church affiliation and have some other components which draw them together.

From twelve step programs to bowling teams, we have been long involved in the making and nurturing of "affinitive groups," which meet for support and networking.[185] People are drawn by common interests, shared concerns, like desires. Some are short lived, de facto groups, others which touch deep ongoing needs or values may become so important that they survive all manner of obstacles.

When groups become deliberate in their understanding of why they gather, and self-reflective of how it affects their lives, they have intensified their bonds and take on more of the character of intentional community.

As authority structures in our society crumble and people grow in education and self-affirmation, they perceive a greater need for intentional community.

What we have in the past believed should come from experts we now often know must come from ourselves. We in the company of equals have the power to accomplish much. Subsidiarity has become both necessary and desirable.

Women have long sensed the strength that comes from shared experience.

What women have done is to continue to create community, for the purpose of solidarity and affirmation. Communities for women have a long tradition both within and without the Church. From the most casual community of the moment around the well in the town square, or the cups of coffee at a kitchen table with children on the floor, to consciousness-raising groups and Bible study, or salons for women in the 17th and 18th centuries in France and England, to the formally vowed communities of religious women, all are somewhere on the continuum from affinity spaces to intentional community. They provide time and space for affirmation, encouragement, shared interest. Some are extremely casual, meet irregularly and may have unspoken reasons for gathering ("I just feel great when we're all together"), or may be a flight from isolation. Some, such as orders of religious women, are extremely formalized in organization, shared work, common mission.

For women, such small deliberate gatherings have been traditionally and continue to be seriously important because the market place of ideas and exchange has often been denied them, and because they have often found their concerns to be devalued.

Women's gatherings provide time and social space which "has proven historically to be of particular importance in allowing women to move from one stage of consciousness to another. Whether this is so because of the pervasive effect of negative gender indoctrination on women's self-esteem and courage, which make a friendly environment a necessary precondition for their inner liberation, it is hard to say. Historically, men have also needed such social spaces to formulate liberating ideologies, but their institutionalization in universities, trade unions or political parties has been readily available. For women, confined by gender restriction to the domestic circle and discouraged from participation in the public sphere, such social spaces have had to be privately created."[186]

One of the important aspects of our circles is the need for time and social space. In other words, you get together with others in a safe place and try to free up who and what you are. This is hard work, full of stumblings, it's like practicing yourself into fullness. It is far easier to begin in private, and "try yourself out" with accepting others than to go public from the start.

We have learned much from the secular experience of intentional community and are beginning to carry that knowledge into the religious sphere. We are discovering that mutual life experience and values orientation can be as weighty as the denomination label. What we are envisioning is the difference between belonging to an institutional religion and being church to each other.

"Roman Catholic feminist theologians have begun to make it possible for Catholic women to reimagine the church on their own terms, and the Women-Church movement has begun to provide a setting in which Catholic women along with their Protestant sisters can experience the power of the Gospel in a new, self-created space. These women who describe themselves in exile from patriarchy deny the smothering misogyny of the traditions and texts in order to celebrate the stories that valorize women. Those who continue to be part of the institutional Church but long for some supplemental liturgies and alternative sources of spiritual support begin to get in touch with their own strengths and to feel the stirrings of the spirit in the collective voices of women. [187]

Theologians who have begun to recognize and validate the significance of the small feminist community have provided the push and the language to allow women to carry their needs and wishes into deeds. Recent work, *Defecting in Place,* an in-depth examination of feminist spirituality groups in a number of denominations, has shown that the words of Ruether in 1985 have taken flesh in groups nation-wide.

"The most prevalent form of feminist spirituality groups are those with members from diverse denominational and religious background. Feminist women concerned with spirituality find they have more in common with other women who share some of the same convictions about women and God, church and society, patriarchy and theology than women of their own denomination. *Feminist spirituality contributes to the blurring of denominational identities, . . . Among feminist spirituality groups, a plurality of the groups in the sample (45%) consist of women from a variety of religious traditions or none."* [188]

What are the characteristics of feminist spirituality groups?
The gathering, on average:
    "-arose out of a felt need
    -is fairly small and relatively stable
    -meets regularly, ordinarily in homes
    -compensates for what is lacking in institutional religion
    -contributes to the raising of feminist awareness
    -liberates individual women
    -deepens spiritual connections
    -results in group loyalty and bondedness
    -is feminist with or without the label
    -continues only for as long as it is meaningful
The following characteristics of feminist spirituality group meetings are representative of most groups in this study.
Meetings reflect:
    -flexible design and agenda
    -shared leadership
    -full participation
    -freedom of expression
    -decision by consensus
    -personal sharing and integration
    -acceptance and affirmation
    -nurture and empowerment
    -creativity and inventiveness
    -alternative worship experiences." [189]

These characteristics, this phenomenon is not the pattern of women's groups alone. It is happening in many spaces. Small intentional, denominationally-mixed community is seen by many to be the future of religious celebration.

" A new form of tribalism is growing. No longer do we cluster around such terms as *Baptist* or *Roman Catholic* or *Methodist*. Increasing numbers of men, women and children are shopping for spiritual home bases that have more to do with fundamental stance, with 'world view,' than other factors. . . . The most heartening development . . . is the growing spiritual hunger people have to connect their most deeply held values and their daily lives."[190]

The specific which makes WE circles different from other feminist spirituality groups is that we maintain deliberate active contact with our heritage of Eucharist. Believing that Jesus would keep no one from the table, we are delighted to break and share the loaf.

Those most "Catholic" of our sisters, women religious, have carried many WE groups into existence, offering their formal knowledge of and previous or current participation in intentional community. The work which many of them have done with marginalized groups, their experience with prayer in common and discernment within their vowed communities, and, in particular, their struggles with patriarchy as they have attempted to recast their mission in the contemporary world, has prepared them well to join in sisterhood with other women in order to pray.

"Their power . . . lies in their powerlessness and their outsider status in the hierarchical church gives them insider status in the women's movement. At the same time, sisters have some real power of their own: they are highly educated, committed, and bonded. . . . They are an existential manifestation of the connections between death and new life: the "dying" experienced by religious orders is happening at a time when sisters are growing closer to laity and when a new kind of bonding coupled with a post-Vatican II ecclesiology offers new possibilities for growth."[191]

As the number of women in religious life shrinks and as those still in community seek new ways to develop their ministries, more and more groups of companions, mixed groups of sisters and unvowed women, have united for prayer and work. For many lay women, this has been a gift beyond words. Sisters often bring a wealth of knowledge about scripture, forms of prayer, liturgy, experience in base communities, developed political and theological learning and a strong background in Church history. They also frequently yearn for new expressions of sisterhood, and are highly committed to WE groups as a part of their spiritual lives. The breaking down of barriers between religious and lay women has been one of the great gifts of the WomenChurch movement.

As we continue we will hear a range of voices of women, some of whom have remained quite traditional, while liberating the Eucharist into their own space and time, and others who have moved far from rubric worship. Nonetheless, they have *all* continued to find a home in the bread and wine tradition.

Women who are gathering to celebrate Eucharist seem to want to share their experience with whoever wishes to join them. We are no longer separated by the thick walls of theological haggling, wasting our breath, time and energy on the shape of the table when there are hungry people, hurting women, sisters and brothers who have strength to share their world view with each other. The desire to be, pray, do with others who take part in common values is more powerful than the party line, and we are crossing it with greater ease.

Joan Chittister says it so well, "The function of community life is for us to be and do together what we cannot possibly do nearly as well alone. Can you pray alone? Yes, you can. Can you pray better in a group that enhances and is a vehicle for your prayer? Yes, you can. Can you work alone? Of course you can. Will you work with more energy and probably more effectiveness if you're working with a group of similarly-committed people? Yes, I think you will.

"Will you be a sign of Christian presence and sense of community alone? Certainly. Will you be an even stronger, clearer, more capable sign of community if you're supported by people who think about community the way you do? Yes, you will."[192]

Letting go of human rules which inhibit community, seeking the signs of the Spirit in our lives, recognizing our alone-ness which needs others, we know that we are more than the sum of our parts when we gather. We were raised in churches which, by their very nature knew community to be foundational to prayer and work, but allowed suspicion, prohibition, fences, to repress our sharing of the Gospels. We believed that huge numbers of bodies assembled together were a sign of success, but we lost much of the personal encounter which allows us to be Christ to each other.

Leonardo Boff spelled out the vision in his wonderful book, *Ecclesiogenesis,*

"Christian life in basic communities is characterized by the absence of alienating structures, by direct relationships, by reciprocity, by a deep communion, by mutual assistance, by communality of gospel ideals, by equality among members."[193]

All groups, by their very nature, are about relatedness, about facing, interacting, being interconnected. The paradigm of all relationships we know is the Trinity, the Power, Presence and Wisdom, separate, yet so deeply in relationship that somehow they are one. Some of us have flickers of that in blessed, sacred moments of WomenEucharist. Sometimes as a group of pray-ers (when the word, action, symbol becomes the people doing, being it) the people become one in the prayer. Those intentional moments are graced, God life moments. These moments are the New Renewed Creation, when what we know dimly, what we forget and relearn (if we are lucky), when we as a group act out again, seek out again the relationship of selves to God, selves to each other, we take part again in the Creator's act of relationship, creating us and all that surrounds us.

This is tentative, this is new and we are growing, making the circle larger, as we see our primary rootedness in shared womanhood.

PLANNING⊕

Given that we now recognize how important the return to small community is, what do we do in order to develop a Eucharistic liturgy for one which is gathering?

**Every woman in our gathering has a gift to give in planning, even if she has never done it. We have women who have been very shy in the past about volunteering. They say, "I've never done it before" or "I don't know how," and we don't push, but we do reassure that they can. We always team up, so no one has to plan alone. We try to pair a new planner with one who has done it before and feels comfortable. We encourage each other by planning together, we usually "pray" a theme before we begin to plan, so that we can hear how the Spirit is moving. It is a wonderful activity, really special, and it gives two people some intimate time together as they prepare the liturgy.

**Someone signs up to plan each month.

**The leadership passes around the group on a volunteer basis, someone offers to host the liturgy and someone else to host the meal which follows.

**We have one group planning session carried out collegially, setting an agenda gleaned from each member's input. Apparently this is how a community of women religious plans and many of our group are former women religious.

**Individual members plan the liturgy.

**Planning rotates through the group on a volunteer basis. We choose topics ahead of time by a consensus model.

**We allow each liturgy to be a reflection of the women who plan it.

**Someone volunteers to facilitate and someone else to plan the ritual. Usually the group gathered decides about agenda or theme for the next gathering.

**I do most of the planning, choosing scriptures and songs. Then I share out the responsibilities in the group. I have had years of liturgical planning in a parish before I came to this group and feel comfortable in planning.

**Each person takes a turn in planning the ritual.

**People (usually two) share the planning on a revolving basis.

**The planning is done by a liturgically gifted member of our group.

**At the end of each Eucharist we plan the next one.

**The planning is done by a leader who agrees to that position. The membership feels free to interject suggestions. We're more relaxed than rigid.

**We schedule "presiders" every four months. The presider(s) plans, facilitates and hosts the liturgy and provides refreshments.

**In the discussion each time, we set the theme or topic for next time and someone volunteers to lead prayer, someone to send an article for preparation before the discussion and someone to host the covered dish supper.

**A person volunteers to plan the liturgy for the next week.

**Two women at a time work on preparing the liturgy. They decide on the theme, readings, etc. They contact other group members by letter, explaining the theme so that the women can make preparation.

Three themes are implicit in the comments about planning: mutual empowerment, openness and trust.

We believe we are peers, that within our gatherings there are no experts who have, by their knowledge or experience a lock on leadership. There is no secret lore which divides the group into the cognoscenti and those waiting to be told. Everyone is free to enter into the task of preparation, in fact, is called to by being a part of the group. Many newcomers find this strange though wonderful, since we have been enculturated to depend upon the expertise of the specialist. This is not a sign of casualness about the importance of what we do, quite the contrary, it is an awareness of the sacred speaking out of the mouths of each of us. The ways of charting a worship are quickly learned. Any one person could choose or be assigned the task, and some groups choose that method, but what is almost universal is that the voices of individuals are a constant; even if there is one final planner, the community has consistent input. The assumption is that the God-spark in each woman is waiting to be heard.

"No single leader in the community is responsible for creating worship. Not only worshipping, but also planning, are corporate acts, so there is a fluidity of leadership. In practice this means that a different core group of women is intentionally brought together to plan each gathering."[194]

This fluidity also encourages freshness. With no single planner, the problem of developing a case of boredom, or going through a dry spell is limited. The sharing of responsibility develops expertise in many members, and saves the group from being "plannerless" if the woman who has been so entrusted moves away or is unavailable.

Women are empowered by others, and then begin to empower themselves and they come to see through planning that they do have a great deal to offer the community.

**Seeing a liturgy from the "inside" was a whole new experience for me. I have really gained confidence as I have taken part in planning. Ideas that I contributed were well received and I have begun to believe that I can trust my own life-path as one of the sources that can be translated into prayer and will have meaning for others.

This woman is developing assurance in her equal gift for the ministry of the table. "Ministry should draw out the unique gifts of each person in the community and give each person the confidence and skills to develop these gifts for the sake of others." [195]

Even when women choose not to be part of the planning team, or as that ministry is rotated, their input is regularly sought, so that the liturgy which is celebrated reflects the hearts of many.

One of the gifts of WE is the opportunity to select thematic approaches to Eucharist. Selection of topics such as giving thanks, justice, the waters of baptism, courage, forgiveness, call us to focus on a specific part of our own journeys. For the planners the theme is a call to be open to how they as individuals have given thanks, or failed to, have had courage, or been cowardly. Where have they been able to forgive and where have they clutched anger to themselves? How has God been present in those moments? The very nakedness of taking a chance on sharing who we are is an act of trust. We have been taught not to air our dirty laundry, to mind our tongues. It is an act of courage to try and tell our truth. This sometimes faltering openness calls forth trust. How can you plan a liturgy based on brokenness unless you are willing to name your own, and believe that others can accept your experience? How can you participate in a worship dealing with the topic of joy and not acknowledge as valid the reasons for joy in other lives? WE is remarkably free of "If you think you have it bad, let me tell you . . ." language, which discourages trust by minimizing the stories of others. There tends to be a great deal of time given to being present to each other. This is "holy listening" and it calls for patience and attention. [196] It is the ultimate act of hospitality, when we listen actively and deeply, without rushing in, accepting people as they are. As trust grows, so does the willingness to self-disclose more deeply in reply. An underlying certainty is that this circle, this time, these hesitant words are sacred. I break open myself to you and you will not betray me. Openness and trust are sisters, and they constantly shore up each other.

Gradually, with our stories set in sacred context, our respect for each other grows. WE trust that our sisters can, will hear us without judgment, and have confidence that God is present in all the steps of our journeys. It is in this self-actualizing confidence that we are able to see the transcendence of our own stories, how they first find resonance around the circle and then in the world which struggles to be free. This is "the personal is political" translated into prayer.

FORMAT ✪

**When we began we wanted to stay close to the liturgical format of Eucharist but adapt it to a feminine style. As time goes by we've tended to follow our own spiritual style.
1. There is always some kind of gathering, usually in a circle. 2. there is always some passage from scripture used, in line with the theme. 3. there is always the blessing and sharing of bread and wine. 4. There is always some kind of faith sharing.
**Most of the time we use traditional liturgical format, taking the basics from the Sunday

missalette. 20% of the time we depart from this because the liturgy is being led by those who do not like being so structured.

**It is always a Eucharistic model. The liturgical tradition is our guide. Our general format is: Song, opening prayer, readings, perhaps a responsorial prayer or litany, shared reflection, Eucharistic prayer, sharing of bread and wine, closing prayer, song.

**We always have a liturgy of the word and of blessing and breaking and sharing bread, but how that is done is up to the person planning. We don't follow the sacramentary. Faith sharing is of great importance.

**We use the traditional liturgical format, minus the patriarchal emphasis.

**There is a sharing of readings, a discussion which relates to them and a personal response, and a sharing of Eucharist.

**The only guideline is that the liturgy include a eucharistic celebration with bread and wine.

**We use a traditional liturgical format: readings, discussion, intercessory and thanksgiving prayers, Eucharistic prayer, the Lord's prayer, communion, sign of peace and closing prayer.

**Each woman does it differently. I use the traditional consecration prayers as the heart of my liturgy but the rest change the prayers to fit the season.

**We begin our gathering with a "go-around" in which everyone shares what has been happening the past month and how it relates to her presence on this night. We always have an opening prayer, a few readings, a meditation and time for group reflection. Then we have the eucharistic prayers, sign of peace, the Lord's prayer and communion.

**Our liturgies are usually original compositions, usually following a theme with segments freely borrowed from authors as well as original prayers and meditations. We have a Eucharist service using bread and wine (or grape juice), peace greeting, and Lord's prayer.

**We always use a traditional structure but our reading come from a variety of sources. We always begin by asking each woman to share how her last month's journey has been.

**I look to each Eucharistic prayer for its essence which I outline and we pray from the heart with that essence in mind. We begin with music and centering, then reading followed by a sharing of the Gospel's meaning, followed by intentions to be prayed for, next the Eucharistic prayers, sharing of bread and wine, then silence and the final prayer followed by music.

**The guidelines are that we are a Eucharistic people. There are almost always a thematic symbol, readings which reflect that theme, a time of sharing, blessing and sharing of bread and wine.

**For the most part we are very flexible, using music, readings, discussion, the sharing of bread and wine.

**Besides bread and wine blessed and shared we break the bread of our common experience.

**Our format is somewhat traditional: opening prayer, liturgy of the Word, shared homily, consecration, distribution, closing prayer.

**We generally use the Sunday readings but sometimes use substitutes to fit the theme.

**When I lead I use Scripture reading used in the parish churches. I use this for two purposes: 1. our union with the larger church and 2. I believe God continues to reveal God's-self through these readings even though we recognize the patriarchal stance in which they were written. We take bread and wine and use the same words as are used at a traditional Mass.

**By custom we pray, ritualize, share readings, and the blessing of bread and wine. We excluded use of the roman canon, using instead materials for women's liturgies or we create our own.

** We always bless and share bread and wine and this follows some sort of readings, reflection/sharing, communal prayer and song. Sometimes we use scripture and sometimes not. Sometimes we follow the sacramentary and sometimes not.

**Oh we have great liturgies. We're Eucharistic, and that is a lovely form on which we can drape a complete liturgical experience. We use water and LOTS of it, not little dribbles, and we let it flow. We use fire and not just one little candle. We use rocks, and sand and feathers. We use big beautiful loaves of bread which are a mouthful, real sustaining, and good wine and we drink it, not just little sips. We honor the meal and the symbols of our lives and our world and we listen to the Word and the words of others and we weave them together, and we listen to each other tell about how that weaving seems to them. We laugh and sometimes we are sad, but mostly we know that Jesus is with us and so, at least for this moment, we are all right.

**We have readings, response, prayers for others and a liturgy of Eucharist.

**We share the bread and drink of life. We sing and sometimes dance.

**We have a growing number of books containing prayers, stories from Scripture which we use in formulating our liturgy. We have discovered a wealth of very excellent material prepared by other women's groups or by one or two women. We also write some of our own original material. We use scripture appropriate to the theme we have chosen.

**I have an overwhelming sense of gratefulness, of the sacred in my life as I plan a liturgy. A sense of what a tremendous privilege it is to have these books, these symbols, to be part of the journey of many people, those who came before us and all who are with us now. People come so hungry to the table, and I am hungry too, hungry for God. I come to be fed. So when I have the honor of being a planner, I do it with reverence and awe. I feel like the cook at a banquet for very special people. I want it to be as perfect as it can be, every ingredient carefully chosen, the seasonings just right, a mix of sweet and salt, some things light and others dense, but that they will all come together just right, so that all will be happy they came and go away satisfied.

Eucharist, bread and wine, are obviously the heart of the matter. WE has at its core the belief that Jesus and his sacrament of presence and unity cannot be held captive by an institution. Jesus' life spirit is readily and freely available to us when two or more are gathered in his name. Believing that this is so sacred and so certain we, now are called to liberate Eucharist for ourselves (and by extension for everyone), so that we can participate in this life-giving, hope-producing, justice-promising encounter.

We believe that our eagerness to share in the preparation and celebration of the liturgy is a sign of the Spirit present among us. We believe that the Eucharist is a sacrament of true reunion with Jesus, and that it is our tradition, which by our baptisms we have the right and honor to embrace.

"Over the centuries the sacraments had come to be seen as specific rituals that only official ministers were empowered to perform. This led to a fascination with the 'matter and form' of these rituals: a concentration on the exact words and precise gestures that constituted sacramental formulas. . . . A reversal of this individualized vision of the sacraments is under way in the church today. We are recognizing . . . that the church itself, and particular communities of faith, are the sacrament of Christ in the world. Christ's presence—his hopes and values and mission—become palpable and believable in the daily activities of dioceses and parishes, ministry networks and other groups of Christians. Each maturing group of believers *is* a sacrament: ''Where two or three are gathered in my name, there am I in their midst.'" [197]

WE is the maturing community of believers and remembers the words of Vatican II which call for our intense participation in the message of Jesus. "No less fervent a zeal on the part of lay people is called for today: present circumstances, in fact, demand from them an apostolate infinitely broader and more intense. . . . The need for this urgent and many-sided apostolate is shown by the manifest action of the Holy Spirit moving laymen (sic) today to a deeper and deeper awareness of their responsibility and urging them on everywhere to the service of Christ and the Church."[198]

Though, no doubt, the particular vision of the Council did not include women gathering to celebrate Eucharist, their words have a prophetic ring that has been validated in our time as the body of priests shrinks and so many are alienated. We have listened to the call of the Spirit and found ways to make the salvific Jesus present through the Eucharist.

"When we talk about the saving work effected by Jesus as the Christ, we must not lose sight of the fact that he does not accomplish this as an isolated historical individual. Rather, his saving work is carried on in relation to others and through their cooperation, i.e., their discipleship. . . . Thus, 'Christ as savior' refers to what sometimes is called `the whole Christ,' the risen Jesus and those who with him make up one body which is Church. The implication . . . is that women members as well as men share in the salvation being accomplished by `the whole Christ;"what they sacramentalize as women Christians is intrinsic to Christ's sacramentalizing a non-patriarchal God."[199]

One thing which should be noted is that no one calls this gathering *Mass*, which has come to be viewed as the rite which designates an exact rubric or conduct of the sacrament, and implies the strict control by the ordained. *Eucharist* has gained favor as the term that speaks our thanksgiving and desire to enter into the intimacy of Jesus and be changed by that embrace.

"Inasmuch as a sacrament is not merely the sign of the gospel but is itself a transformative act, its form is less important than its willingness to be guided by the spirit of God."[200] Nonetheless, we embrace the form which we believe comes directly from Jesus, though we do not believe that there is "magic" in specific word formulae. Rather it is intent, hospitality to Jesus, genuinely inviting his presence that makes the difference.

Readings from outside the canon of scripture are frequently used. Perhaps a poem by a woman from Hungary, or a diary entry from a pioneer woman, will be used in concert with a Gospel from Luke. Many WE, growing comfortable in planning, go farther afield in their search for material. Everything brought to the assembly is brought into the realm of the sacred.

This is not to say that scripture is not important, however there is growing cognizance in many groups about its misuse in the subjugation of women. WomenEucharist is, at base, implicitly scriptural, in the replication of the paschal meal. Beyond that, we wrestle with the usability of texts, many of which are intrinsically oppressive to women, if only by our very exclusion from them. Can we find a way to reinsert ourselves into the scriptures by peeling back the layers and exerting historical imagination? Or shall we pick our way through the minefield of androcentric texts, or must we turn away completely from materials which have been used against us, concretizing our oppression by patriarchy for millennia?

". . . women, whose number is increasing, have examined the biblical material and, having found overwhelming evidence of its androcentric, patriarchal, and sexist charac-ter, have concluded that the biblical text is so totally and irredeemably oppressive of women . . . that it cannot possibly proclaim the true God or function as word of God for self-respecting women.

". . . there are some women who have neither agreed to a seemingly biblically man-dated inferiority nor found a way to avoid the problematic conclusions of sound exegesis. And yet, leaving Christianity behind is not a viable option for them. These are women who recognize not only the damage that Christianity has inflicted on women but also its posi-tive effects. . . . Their spirituality is profoundly christocentric and the roots of their identity and personal history are deep in the soil of Christianity. It is these women who continue to struggle with the question, both theological and exegetical, of the Bible and its role in Christian faith."[201]

Most planners use it, alert to how it has been employed in the past, while including material from a variety of sources. "Even though there is no canon of an alternative femi-nist religion of ancient times, we are not left without sources for our own experience in the past. We can read between the lines of patriarchal texts and find fragments of our own experience that were not completely erased. . . . We can resurrect them, gather them together and begin to glimpse the larger story of our own experience."[202]

We can take back the Scriptures, reopening them as a new dynamic guide to our own freedom and salvation and that of our sisters and brothers. Elisabeth Schüssler Fiorenza calls this "not so much rediscovering new sources as rereading the available sources in a different key."[203] And she encourages us to do the work. "Western women are not able to discard completely and forget our personal, cultural or religious Christian history. We will either transform it into a new liberating future or continue to be subject to its tyranny whether we recognize its power or not."[204]

I think of mines which have been abandoned because they no longer seem to have enough ore. But if you were to go in there with a head lamp and a pick and look very carefully, you would find the gleam of gold, a bit here, a bit there. looking carefully, digging deep, being patient.

**If Scripture is used we do our own "de-sexing" of the text. We often use other readings, women's poetry, prose, material from women of other ethnic, racial, class backgrounds.

**I use now mainly *The Book,* published by Tyndale House in 1985. It is ultra-modern English and what it sacrifices in beauty and poetry it makes up in clarity.

**We aren't fussy about which translation of Scripture we use because we have to do adaptation usually anyway.

**I am still looking for a Scripture translation I can live with. We've used the RSV but need a more inclusive translation, more than the NSRV. We use a lot of outside material, prayers, reflections.

**We make the Jerusalem and New American editions inclusive. We use some Native American readings.

**We use the Scripture readings prescribed by the church, usually the Jerusalem Bible.

**We use the New American Bible, liturgies and prayers developed by the lesbian community, the music of Michael J. Porier.

**We use The New American or Jerusalem Bible, *Liberating Liturgies* from WOC, *More Than Words* (J. Schaffran & P. Kozak), *The Risk of the Cross, Prayers for the Earth,* the writings of Dorothy Day, Meister Eckhart, and Hildegard of Bingen, writings of Rosemary Ruether and Joan Chittister. We have used lyrics to popular songs, Native American prayers, prayer and meditations from Eastern religions, writings from Merton, Berrigan and Boff, the list seems endless, even to including T. S. Eliot, Kurt Vonnegut and Walt Whitman.

**We are free to use music and readings which are spiritual but not necessarily "religious." We use poetry, songs celebrating women and justice themes. There is no shortage of material because of all the creativity out there.

**We often use the RSV, changing the language. I borrow prayers (and rituals) from *More Than Words, Liberating Liturgies, Prayers for a Planetary Pilgrim, Peace Prayers,*

Peacemaking Day by Day (from Pax Christi).

**We use music from Carolyn McDade, Marsie Silvestro, D. Nieratka and Kathy Sherman. We love *Birthings and Blessings* and *Cries of the Spirit*.

**I personally have found several books by Christian feminists helpful. Some I'd recommend to others are *Image Breaking Image Building; A Handbook for Creative Worship with Women of Christian Tradition* by Clark, Ronan and Walker; *Foremothers; Women of the Bible* by Nunally-Cox; *Womenprayer Womensong* by M.T. Winter and the books of Ann Johnson.

**We use a lot of materials from our respective religious communities. Most women's religious communities send such materials to members with some regularity. It is a way we share in each other's community of origin, Franciscans, Mercies, Notre Dames. Very enriching. We're not particular about our Scripture translation since all in the group are quite adept at "cleaning up" the gendered language.

**Our resources are varied and I look at what materials we choose and use as a part of our struggle and search to be Church to ourselves and each other in a real way.

**The group uses anything but Scripture. We feel that women need to rescript since the patriarchal pattern is so limited.

**The liturgy of the Word often does not use the scriptural texts of the day, or for that matter, scripture at all. The liturgical prayers used come from a variety of sources: Catholic "approved" texts adapted for inclusive language, a book of texts, and other sources members have found. I usually start with the texts of the day. I then add prayers or readings from many sources. Ed Hays' work, items found in newsletters, readings I have come across. All Scripture is made inclusive.

**We use readings centered around social justice issues.

**We use women's poetry and music and the psalms.

**As we've grown I think the whole experience has become less word-heavy. We tend to take something short and simple and "break it open."

**Jerusalem Bible, modified for gender. Everything from *The Nation* to the Bible. Miriam Therese Winter's book. The WATER things are good, so is Pete Seeger. We tend to use whatever we're reading, i.e., Matthew Fox's *Original Blessing, Chalice and Blade, Gnostic Gospels*.

**WOC's *Liberating Liturgies,* Miriam Therese Winter's things, Native American prayers and blessings, *Moon at Hand* readings. WATER resources. We also use the writings of contemporary writers such as Chris Glaser, Mary Hunt, Rosemary Radford Ruether.

**We use women's spirituality resources such as *Women Wisdom*, the Miryam series and the music of Miriam Therese Winter, Carolyn McDade and Marsie Silvestro. Any Scripture must be adapted to be inclusive and non-sexist.

**The work of Carter Heywood, *Cries of the Spirit,* edited by Marilyn Sewell.

**The world is full of writing, music and art into which God has entered. We feel that much can be gathered in and used to show how God is here in the world and in our lives. More often than not we do not use Scripture because many of us have had the painful experience of it being used against us, used to justify injustice. We need materials which can challenge, call forth, comfort and heal. Many of us do not go to scriptures for that material. God is present in the materials we use.

** A major source of material is each other's lives and the events of our world.

The wealth gathered in for our reflection and celebration is a splendid sign of a basic fact of feminist spirituality: we do not dichotomize between the sacred and the secular. Believing that all of God's creation is good, we can use the Scriptures as a jumping off point, or not use them at all, and find a great deal of written and sung material that is food for our hunger. Scripture is not devalued, but other writings are raised up as source material. Groups find that the writings of women and men of ethnic and racial backgrounds other than our own, of various sexual orientations encourage understanding of their prayer and struggle, and ally it to our own. Those words encourage us to see that we are more alike than different, and that we embrace a common humanity. For white women to read the words of African American or Hispanic women, for straights to read the words of lesbians, encourages an acknowledgment and acceptance of shared sisterhood.

The importance of our own personal stories as material in our gatherings cannot be overstated. We have been kept silent for so long and we have been bursting to tell of our lives. We are beginning to honor their content as part of the ongoing story of creation history.

"Why must only past experience be considered authoritative? We who live with the Holy Spirit as inspiration within and among us surely have every right to add our piece to the deposit of faith." [205]

We need to recognize the sacred in our own personal histories and reverence it in others, in order to see our bit part in the salvation story which is not at all finished. The separation of any bit of our experience from theology is a false and dangerous dichotomy.

Every attempt to see our lives and the lives of others as the work of God returns us to the reality that there is nothing too unimportant to pray about, nothing too piddling for God's concern. The stuff of our lives: our families, our work, our money, or lack of it, our play, our loves, broken and whole, that is where we begin.

This is the raw material for shaping our theology. We do not so much passively receive theology as *do* it based on our understanding of this earthy dance. We cannot be Christ to each other unless we can understand what that means based on deeply felt personal experience. When we understand that we are involved in a process that begins within and expands out to others in the context of God we are "doing theology."

"To *do* theology is to free theology from the exclusive hold of academia. . . . To do theology is to recognize that the source of theology is human existence, its questions and concerns as well as its beliefs. To do theology is to validate and uphold the lived experience of the oppressed, since the dominant cultures and countries not only deny its validity, but even question its very existence."[206]

Isn't that an absolutely revolutionary concept? We are accustomed to accepting from the institutional Church a theology which we could not necessarily validate by our own experience. We need to try on over and over the image of ourselves, our stories as important, as the stuff of theology.

Women who gather help each other to tell our tales, to place them in the circle of the Divine, to see self as unique, so that the whole story is not complete without the telling of each one, and yet as part of the greater, universal saga of the love affair between God and human.

"In finding peace and recognizing the light in yourself, we say there's a hearth in your heart where the Creator has given you something very sacred, a special gift, a special duty, an understanding. And now is the time for us to clean out those hearths, to let that inner light glow."[207]

We are greatly gifted by women who have prayed their lives into rituals and published them to be shared. They go ahead through what is largely uncharted land, making a path, cutting back the undergrowth, blazing the trees, dropping crumbs. Why do we need rituals created specifically by feminists? "We are searching for the right words to match our ritual behavior to the content of our beliefs. The recent insights of feminist theology the power of shared experience, and the witness of so many dedicated lives have led to a hunger for new worship language and new worship images, new songs and new celebrations that will be for us appropriate prayer and praise."[208]

The work of the women of WATER and WOC, the songs and liturgies of Miriam Therese Winter, the ceremonies of Rosemary Radford Ruether are seminal work. They plant the seeds of ways to worship which are faithful to feminism, recovering women of the past from Scripture. Faith traditions and secular life are sign lights, shaping their thoughts and dreams into celebrations. I am delighted by their willingness to make their work available. It is rare to find prohibitions. *Woman's Song*, a resource published by National Sisters Vocation Conference begins "Please use this material, but in its use kindly give credit accordingly."[209] What a gentle and gracious way to not only offer us their own experiences but also call us to join them publicly by acknowledgment.

Many liturgy sources also call us to adapt the material to our own lives, rather than looking upon them as set in stone. There is an implicit trust that we know our own needs and that these are resources, not rubrics. "We encourage the creative adaptation of these prayers to the needs, time constraints and diverse background of those who gather to pray."[210]

Exposure to Catholic ritual has taught us the power of symbols. Those of us over the age of forty grew up in a cloud of incense. We all know intimately the meanings of water and fire, darkness and light, and now we affirm them by our appropriation, and we claim them in their fullness: not a dribble of baptismal water, but a full splashing tub with rose petals floating, not one little candle but a leaping fire. Our symbols are worth intentionality, not just a polite nod for they speak to us in ways which words cannot. If they are good symbols they touch memory chords which are buried deep in our personal histories, and are also a gathering up of mutual understanding. They sign what has gone before and what is still unfolding. The cathedrals of Chartres and Notre Dame and St John the Divine and the Immaculate Conception, by their immensity signed our smallness in relationship to God. The very removal of their altars to dim distance signaled God's transcendence and untouchability. The locations of people during worship taught of our relative nearness to God, priests close to the altar, laity greatly separated. And woe to the woman who passed into the sanctuary, except to clean it. Yes, we understand deeply our worth by what has been signed to us. Some symbols we take back, some we discard, and some we embrace deeply.

WE most often uses the home as a symbol of our connection to the house churches of the early Christian communities, and as a remembrance of the daily presence of God among us, making all things holy. [211] We sit in a circle, representing our belief that all are equal, and that our lives are not linear but spirals of experience.

Every woman has put in her time as table setter for her family or community or guests. We deeply know the unstated message of sloppy place settings. WE tables are usually arranged with reverence. One group always uses a beautiful old lace tablecloth, the heirloom possession of one of its members, which belonged to an aunt who had struggled for women's suffrage. Another group lights one candle for any member who is not able to be present that night.

A bowl of rough stones, which we are encouraged to pick up and handle might represent our sinfulness, a scattering of autumn leaves on the cloth can remind us of the death of seasons of our lives. Wrapped packages can call up the gift that Jesus is to us and that we are to each other.

We do not recognize a line between that which is thought to be holy and that thought to be profane. By our very use of symbols from outside of standard institutional worships we reclaim all creation as sacred. For a liturgy which recalls the brokenness and rejection of females, a bowl of tampons on the table returns what we have been taught is unclean and shameful to the realm of the sacred as we reunite women's bodies to the God who chose to create them.

Women need to take back and reinvent the word "lady." It is a term so weighed down with the accretions of time, and has been used to control our behavior for so long that we have forgotten its marvelous meaning. A lady is a loaf maker, or loaf giver. We who measure the flour and mix in the yeast and warm the milk and knead the dough are ladies, at the heart of the meal, at the heart of the Eucharist.

"Bread as symbol. Not those horrible bits of white paste; big brown loaves, fresh tortillas, Portuguese flat bread, long crisp baguettes, chewy whole wheat. Signs of the fullness of Jesus. How nutritionless, how vapid is what pretends to be bread in our churches. Jesus was not insipid and neither should be what symbols him in our worship. Only a church which has lost its compass could continue to insist that those zestless wafers are the bread of life. They are not the staff of life, but a crooked crutch. We need to remember the goodness of bread and how it fills us up, and how we can work all morning on a couple of good slices. That is what the symbol calls forth; we need to remember that it is a universal symbol, shared by nearly every culture on earth; we need to remember the land from which it comes and be rejoined with that land as a gift of God now in our hands.

"Then God, gathering up her courage in love, said,
Let there be bread!
And God's sisters, her friends and lovers, knelt on the earth
planted the seeds
prayed for the rain
sang for the grain
made the harvest
cracked the wheat
pounded the corn
kneaded the dough
kindled the fire
filled the air with the smell of fresh bread
And there was bread!
And it was good!" [212]

As the primary food preparers for our families and communities, we know that all those meals reported on in the Gospels did not appear magically. The water into wine of Cana may have been a miracle but the food that the guests ate came straight from the hands of women. Peter's mother-in-law, good hostess that she was, immediately got up and began to serve them, no doubt food she had put by before being taken ill. Poor Martha got stuck in the kitchen while the party went on elsewhere.

WE most often does not end with the closing song. Respondents testify that most groups keep on eating. Pot luck suppers, fruit and cheese, bowls of soup, delivered pizza, cookies and tea. This is the continuation of the banquet, and provides a space for us to keep on being community to each other. We know deep in our bones, deep in our stomachs that this is good. We do not fast while the bridegroom is present.

"It is dusk on a spring evening in 45CE in Thessalonika in the province of Macedonia. Inside a shop along a street lined with crumbling tenements, the shoemaker and his apprentices clear aside their tools in the failing light, making room for the daily meal. Here fifteen or twenty believers in Jesus will crowd around the rough worktable to break bread together. A single lamp is lit.

"Each person or family must bring food—a loaf of bread, a jar of wine diluted with three parts of water, some olives or raisins—so there will be enough. Those unable to work bring a few crusts they have begged. This meal is the high point of their day, for it sustains them physically and spiritually. Together they share food, remembering the broken body of their now-exalted Lord. A matronly woman who has brought a bowl of cabbage soup in which to dip their bread leads in the prayers. A psalm is sung. A hymn is taught to the newest members. A story from Jesus' life is retold. This common meal is an everyday supper for the Thessalonian Christians. It is also Eucharist where Christ is present." [213]

This tradition of tablesharing is common to us all in its grounding in every day and in its holiness. We need to celebrate our hunger as well as our fullness, and see that as a sign of the interconnectedness of our table and the world.[214]

So we gather together our bread and our wine and our readings and our rocks and flowers and shells and voices and we practice ourselves into life. The feminist cannot read or intellectually learn this community. We must "do" and "be" it into existence. This is not theory, though when we read we may affirm, even become excited by the ideas present-ed, but until we sit in the circle, try, praxis, learn by doing what works and what doesn't we cannot know what it is we are about. This calls for intellectual and emotional honesty, such as was not asked of us within the walls of the Church, where we were offered the plat du jour but never the menu. We were expected to accept, never to choose.

"The rituals and ritual components of women-church type groups illustrate what is meant by feminist spirituality. In these groups, language, God-images, symbols, content, rit-ual elements and orientation, the role of women and essential attitudes toward women differ starkly from what happens in traditional patriarchal liturgy and worship. These decid-edly feminist celebrations are the locus of what radical feminism is about. In fact, the alter-native liturgies and innovative rituals of Christian feminists are at the heart of women's ambivalence about remaining in the institutional Church. More often then not they reflect the integration of those alternative biblical, theological, eccelesiological, social, psycho-logical, and cultural perspectives foundational to the feminist movement in the church." [215]

This is an exciting experience.

✪✪✪✪✪

REALLY PRESENT

FORETHOUGHT ✛

A central concern of Christians through the centuries is how Jesus is present in the sacrament of Eucharist. Theologians have struggled with the question. Some positions have been declared heretical, others have been officially embraced. Some explanations have faded from grace, their places taken by new understandings.

Those who answered my questionnaire had various responses to the ways in which they found Jesus present in WomenEucharist. (As one respondent points out, "just as you would find in any pew in any parish.")

For the purpose of order, this chapter is divided into three areas in which our theology claims Jesus is present: commemoration in community, in word and in the elements of bread and wine.[216] However, you will note that the responses of the participants cannot be nearly so neatly divided, a fact that is always true within celebration, because there is a constant interweaving of one element with another throughout ritual. Therefore, we will discover elements of the community in responses about scripture, responses which speak about bread and wine and the people all in one sentence.

You might wish to be aware in this chapter of how WE continues to fulfill the original Jesus command to do this in his memory, since this commemoration is at the heart of all eucharistic liturgies.

Through these sections please note the four factors which traditionally make up eucharistic practice: along with *remembrance* (do we remember him and if so, how?), there is *ritual* (do we put that memory into prayer and celebration?), the relationship of these to our own *ethical behavior* (does this acted-out memory change us?) and eucharistic *theology* (how do we spell out what happens in celebration and in us when we gather?). [217]

These are elements which have been present in eucharistic rituals. How do WomenEucharist communities meet these traditions? These facets of ritual will give us some idea of how WE in the present converses with the community of church in the past.

✪✪✪✪✪✪

JESUS PRESENT IN COMMUNITY ◑

✳*In the midst of this community . . . all of a sudden I knew that — here, now — I had entered the Kingdom of God. Or, more precisely, that the Kingdom of God had slipped in and settled around me.* [218]

✳*There is a range of divergent celebrations going from the retrieval of the Latin Mass to feminist liturgies, from large-scale papal rites to small-group gatherings that foster a more ready face-to-face interaction. . . . None of the elements in the situation can be neglected, none of the ritually expressed aspirations rejected out of hand as inappropriate or inauthentic. . . . The question (is) whether the process of liturgical change ought to be called accommodation, adaptation, inculturation, or even fresh incarnation.* [219]

✳*So he went in to stay with them. And it happened that, while he was with them at table, he took bread, said the blessing, broke it, and gave it to them. With that their eyes were opened, and they recognized him . . .* [220]

**Jesus is present in the use of bread and wine, in the use of reenactment in various forms and words of Jesus' last supper, and in the care and love evident in our gatherings.

**We break bread together. My best understanding is that the sacrament of Eucharist happens in the context of the believing community.

**Jesus is present where two or three are gathered in His name.

**I believe that Jesus joins us because we as community ask him to do so.

**We always remember Jesus' sharing bread and wine with his friends and note that we are doing this in his name and at his invitation and that he is therefore present with us.

**We all need to keep on remembering that what we celebrate, the radical transforming love of Jesus, is based in history, in an historical moment, and that it was in his *community of friends* that he asked to be remembered. That is what we, now and as friends, try to do also. When we remember, and when he joins us, we can more intensely use him as a pattern for our lives.

**When we get together each month we are reminded of, and participate in, the sacramental (and by extension the historical) community in which Jesus ate and drank and taught. We are eager as a group for the intimacy, the memory and the strength which comes from these encounters.

**This community gathering for, with and around Jesus, Christed, is for me a visible sign of the invisible but extremely palpable presence of Jesus.

**We feel that, when we celebrate eucharistically, Christ empowers us by saying, "Whenever two or more are gathered in my name, there I am."

**We simply share bread together. God is with us.

**Eucharist affirms the presence of the Sacred in our midst and in each other. It is in the sharing and eating that we proclaim oneness in and with God.

**The longer I participate in my women-church group, the more genuinely, the more I *really* feel the presence of Jesus. I have been going to church all my life and I have never felt so close to God in the community. I see Jesus in the faces of my friends as they try to work out the struggles of life in the context of how Jesus would do it. When we get together I know that those around me have "put on Christ" and I am growingly encouraged to do the same.

Not an accidental band of individuals, these are gatherings of believers, bonded by faith. The responses demonstrate this: "God is with us," an act of faith; "The presence of the sacred in our midst," an act of faith; "Jesus is present," an act of faith. These are women joined not in a secular manner, nor solely as an affinity group; rather they unite intentionally because they share belief in the importance of Jesus' supper command. Here we see a group of people who find Jesus present, teaching, loving, not dimly known but ever more vivid. Many respondents find Jesus quite clearly experienced in the intentional community of WE.

Intentional communities are characterized by deliberateness. People choose to be together on a regular basis. They exhibit depth; the involvement of community members moves beyond surface concerns. This depth encourages cohesion as members see and feel the common bonds which they share. This cohesion encourages intimacy and empathy, in which the recognition of mutuality is felt on a personal and deepening level. This empathy increases duration as the members wish to spend time together frequently because they perceive their continued (and growing) acceptance and welcoming. Likeness rather than disparity is the focus of intentional community, not cookies cut out with a stamp, but human similarity. (In the case of WE, the similarity is a growing surety that we are each imaged in God and that Godself is present with us, an often difficult concept for women.)

In this recognition of likeness, people tend to wish well for each other: my interests and your interests coincide. Because each person's individual gifts are sought, shared strength, rather than authority-over, is a goal. Intentional communities tend toward the non-hierarchical model, and can be viewed more as a web of interrelationships than as a chain in which a person is closely linked to only one or two others. (WE assumes that it is seeking wholeness/holiness/Jesusness which is our shared goal and that in the gifts of all we are more likely to discover it.)

When intimacy and shared stance are united, intentional communities tend to act out the sharing. This happens privately when by ritual they affirm to themselves and each other what they are together. This happens publicly when they demonstrate to the larger society how they have grown and changed by being members of this intentional community.

And yet such groups only hint at the depth of meaning which surges in groups with God-focus.[221] The Jesus/Eucharist-centered community can easily fit the concept of sociologist Ferdinand Tonnies.[222] "*Gemeinschaft* (relationships in which there is a degree of commonality) is founded upon direct relationships . . . it is characterized by a high degree of cohesion, communality, and duration in time. The most obvious and historically persistent examples are kinship groups, castes, and small village communities, and guilds. The family is the archetype for this form . . . *Gemeinschaft* relationships involve our total personalities and focus on every aspect of our lives. Intimacy and the sharing of emotion in depth are encouraged. . . . One gives whatever love demands, and the basis of a person's worth is founded solely on their being."[223]

Are women more *gemeinschaft*? Is the intimacy of community easier for women? Perhaps. If males have been reared to value (and therefore, practice) the skills which move them toward autonomy, while neglecting and even disliking the skills of relationality, they are more apt to regard with suspicion the intimacy skills which lead to deep community interaction. The responders here use the words "us," "together," "we," "oneness with," "community," "friendship," frequently and easily. A growing understanding of women's maturation process indicates that interconnection, rather than total autonomy, is basic to feminine maturity. It is also basic to a greater discovery of God, as the ultimate relater and friend, who desired interconnection so greatly that we, God-images, were created.

**Jesus is the one who teaches us how to be Christian and in relationship with God. Jesus said he would be in the midst of us, where ever two or more gather in His name. He has given us freedom.

Mary Hunt names this as the friendship model, a non-hierarchical deliberate joining which leads to powerful religious agency. "Women's friendships contain previously unexplored and unappreciated elements that reveal something about the human condition. . . . . Friendship, especially within the Christian tradition, is often based on the mutual search for justice. The Christian tradition began with the disciples and members of the Jesus movement who were, if nothing else, friends seeking ways to express their faith in a hostile environment."[224]

It is in this kind of friendship, which was perhaps too lowly, too ordinary, too much a part of dailyness in the past to have caught the attention and imagination of theologians, that many women find Jesus. "Imagining the divine as a friend is quite easy and rather pleasing," says Mary Hunt, "More than parent, spirit, and force, friend has the advantage of being widely available as a positive relationship, as one that is personal without being intrusive, powerful without being mystical."[225]

A masculinized world which honors individualism and personal achievement as the pinnacle of maturity has a hard time seeing interconnection and responsibility as maturation also. Women practice relationship all their lives.

The work of Carol Gilligan supports this concept of men's and women's significantly different views of social maturity. "Men see . . . danger more often in close personal affiliation than in achievement and constru(e) danger to arise from intimacy, women perceive(e) danger in impersonal achievement situations and constru(e) danger to result from competitive success."[226]

In the non-affiliated model, the estranged, competitive winner/loser model, we have slipped dangerously away from the friendly, freeing Jesus known by his companions. In

WE we yearn toward, ache toward, share toward that Jesus companion who knew he was leaving but promised to always be with us when we gather. And when we see this Jesus friend in the faces of those around our own tables we know that Jesus is present.

I would suggest that intentional communities more genuinely image the Body of Christ, than impersonal hierarchical groups.[227] In 1 Corinthians, Paul uses the physical body to suggest how close and cooperative we should be with each other. If you break an arm, not only are you inconvenienced for several weeks, you also are reminded regularly during that period of how many different ways that arm functioned for the whole body. Stomach flu shuts down practically everything but breathing and heartbeat and causes us all to reflect on how much we take our digestive processes for granted. Every limb and organ is important to the whole, and must be friendly to the whole. This is an intimate and non-hierarchical image in which the function of the whole is dependent on the well-being of each part. In healthy bodies, the individual organs are boon companions to each other.

Good Christian communities behave in the same fashion. There, concerns and actions are based in understanding of the needs and wishes of each God-sparked individual, not in a set of arbitrary rules which were codified elsewhere.

WE participants do not see this friendship community as existing only in the now. They reference and commemorate the historical community of Jesus and his friends.

** I always remember Jesus sharing bread and wine with his disciples.
**The gospels record the historic event of the supper where Jesus blessed and shared food and asked his friends to remember him in this way. We can only do the same.
**Jesus came as a human and he entered into human community. Though he has left and gone to heaven he has most surely been here and through his interaction with people like us he changed the world. We are as called to be part of this as Peter and John and Mary Magdelene were.

WE respondents indicate that time folds inward, telescoping the now into the then, as the experience of Jesus' community is not just remembered but also re-presented. In Jesus' community his friends, mostly poor and marginalized, gathered around him because he clearly offered something different from, in definite contrast to, the ethos of the culture of his time. WE attempts to uncover that contrast, to make visible for self and community how Jesus' difference is needed desperately in the historical community of today. Women are often greatly attracted not only to Jesus, but to the Jesus-centered historical community because that community and his message made possible a whole new life-experience for women bound to inappropriate and limited roles. It made possible the verbalization and the acting out of personal liberation within the embracing arms of a loving, forgiving God. The God-centered community offered support for seekers after justice and liberation and continues to do so.[228] Jesus as center, Jesus as model, Jesus in the community, Jesus in me.

In the voices of the respondents, rings belief in the willingness of Jesus, perhaps even the eager friendliness of Jesus, to be where WE gathers.

A theology of greater immanence develops when participants speak not of a transcendent JesusGod who deigns to be with the community fleetingly, but of a loving God, passionately in relationship, whose desire it is to be part of us. When cohesion, durability, depth, intimacy and well-wishing are rooted in the desire to express and experience God's presence and love, we have a faith community. When we choose to respond ritually to Jesus' request to bless and break and share, we have a sacramental faith community in which the very people are the sacrament of Jesus' presence.

The participants of WE seem to be ever so gradually recognizing, experiencing Jesus' very real presence in our community when we gather.

In an encounter with his friends, Jesus walked and shared with the disciples on the road to Emmaus, filling their hearts with excitement. They, however, could not envision this stranger as Jesus; their imaginations could not yet carry them in the leap through death to new life. It took a meal, a blessing, breaking and sharing, for the eyes of their imaginations to fly open, for them to see beyond the rules of life. This was Jesus with them and they hadn't even known!

WE participants testify to the same wonderful experience. For so very long, women have known the "facts" of sacramental life: the real presence was not possible in a community of women without the power of the ordained male. (If it is certainly not possible, then there is no point in gathering, no point in looking for that real presence without a priest.)[229] How is it then that WE experiences the powerful permeation of the friendship of Jesus when we dare to invite him and recognize him when he comes?

"Faith is an exercise of the imagination—not inventing a fictitious pattern or distorting reality's painful patterns but recognizing barely visible patterns of power. . . . (T)he imagination is indispensable to faith: God's saving patterns of power are finally and practically revealed only when we recognize them, when we assertively seize the hints and clues strewn in our path and make of them a personal vocation of purpose and direction."[230]

Our religious imaginations have finally slipped the bonds which tied us to one painful experience and have allowed us to see Jesus here in each other and with us all. The mystery and miracle of Godhuman present with us has confounded and amazed and succored us for centuries. How possible that the Maker of all wonders should deign to come and walk among us in our skin, would choose to die and rise for us? How possible that Godhuman would choose to keep on being flesh of our flesh, love of our love even though we so often profane and wound that very flesh, when we profaned and wounded his on the cross? Nowhere in scripture does Jesus promise to be among us if we are male or if we are selected, tested by our institutions. No, so simple. Ask and I will be with you. That is what WE confesses and celebrates, say the respondents.

Women finding Jesus in the table-sharing community stand in the long line of Christian tradition. Not only did Jesus dine often with his friends (acceptable and unacceptable to the established order), but in his post- Resurrection days, he again joins them in food-sharing, a bit of bread, a bite of fish, a picnic on the beach. They knew him in this way and so do we.

One would imagine that the physical presence of Jesus was cause for tremendous excitement, his charism so great that his friends risked life and comfort to be around him. They had not only external witness, but internal response. "Were not our hearts burning inside of us?" they asked each other in the ah ha moment of recognition at Emmaus. Even following Jesus' return to heaven, it is that ah ha, Spirit-infused moment within the community, that Pentecost moment, which is the guide to the presence of Jesus. "It is the experience of Christians that when their faith in Jesus is fully engaged by the sacred symbols of his Supper, e.g. the reading and preaching of the Good News, the faith and fellowship of Jesus' assembled community, the eucharistic bread and wine, their faith is confirmed by an inner communication of God's Spirit. . . . This *inner communication*, which is God's way of confirming our faith in the Risen Jesus, has been conferred on the faith community of Jesus from the very beginning."[231]

The Constitution on the Sacred Liturgy of Vatican II stresses the point that Jesus is present in the faith community. "In order that they should achieve a deeper understanding of the mystery of the Eucharist, the faithful gathered should be instructed in the principal ways in which the Lord is present to his Church in liturgical celebrations. He is always present in a body of the faithful gathered in his name."[232] Even in fragmentation Christ is present, Christ is friend in large groups and small, in diaspora and basilica. In uncertainty and in sureness.

**I came very cautiously to my group, in fact, only because a friend invited me and I didn't know how to say no. I have been here for three years. My friend moved to Texas. I plan liturgy, I sing, I bake, and all because I know that Jesus is here. It took me a while, but I was converted. That just amazes me, that after being a Catholic for 51 years, I am a convert to a loving warm community in which God is present.

This woman voices the slow process of unveiling, seeing really, the presence of God in her little band of women. She came cautiously, she listened, prayed, learned and gradually saw church, was church to others. She has experienced that *inner communication* of which we spoke earlier. We continue to need to attend respectfully to what she (and others) see from her place on the circle.

As in that little community of three on the road to Emmaus, as in the upper room, the Spirit of Jesus transformed people only when *they* recognized that the Spirit was present with them. That inner fire, that Godspark felt, led them to confirm in those little communities the presence of the Spirit of Jesus. That presence is spelled out, not only through inner confirmation, but also through the actions of others in the circle. Letty Russell points to the fact that "It would seem that wherever Christians gather, the presence of Spirit of Christ is made known by the simple acts of shared word, liturgy, service and community."[233]

JESUS PRESENT IN THE WORD ✪

✳*And the Word became flesh and made his dwelling among us* . . .[234]

✳*Mountains and meadows and free-flowing streams,
gardens and ghettoes and poor people's dreams,
down through the ages the good news is heard.*

each of life's pages expresses the Word.
love that engages enfleshes the Word.[235]

✱*The tax collectors and sinners were all drawing near to listen to him, but the Pharisees and scribes began to complain, saying,"This man welcomes sinners and eats with them."*[236]

**Some people use Scripture when they plan liturgy, some do not. The ones who don't are women who do not trust Scripture much because of the way it has been used to mislead and control us.

**Jesus is often left out of our celebration except for the consecration. We have a number of women who have been confused and discouraged by the Church and who are reevaluating their spirituality. They tend to avoid traditional references to God/Jesus. However, we do have as central the issues of justice, and have Jesus' ministry as a central model for our lives.

**We, our group, went through a long time when we almost didn't use the Bible at all, except for the story of the last supper as used in the prayers of consecration. It finally seemed that this was throwing the baby out with the bath water, so now we try to use the scripture more but we are very cautious about how we use it. Some of our women have had such bad experiences.

**Though I use the Bible when I plan a liturgy for my group, not every planner does. Some women have felt that as they grew up the scriptures were used as a tool to "keep us in our place." That is so sad.

**There are certain scripture passages which are flash points for women, and lots of women just prefer not to embrace a book which has so often been used against us.

**I find "His Church" (RC and others) a tragedy and a disaster for humankind, since they so often share a distortion of his teaching.

The field of scripture has become a bloody battleground on which the body of Christ, and the perceived will of God, has been terribly rent. Did a male God create women not quite human, and by His will and by gender affiliation, wish them subjugated to the will of fully human men? Or is liberation of all from oppression the passionate desire of an embracing God? Did Jesus come primarily as a man who would genuinely speak only to other men, or did he come as a human being, incidentally male, whose call to freedom flows out to all of us?

Elisabeth Schüssler Fiorenza says, "The Bible is not only written in the words of men but also serves to legitimate patriarchal power and oppression insofar as it 'renders God' male and determines ultimate reality in male terms, which make women invisible or marginal."[237]

Andro-focused biblical Christianity has concretized itself in the symbols, social structures and the courts of law of Christian nations. It has canonized the subjugation of women to fathers, husbands, sons, even men whom they have never met. It has denied us the right to inherit, the right to a voice in the physical and religious control of our lives, to even protect ourselves from physical abuse. Church and state have conspired in the deaths of countless women by reinforcing the rights of even a vicious man over his spouse.

The Genesis story of creation and fall, and the Pauline texts on the role of women, among others, have been used to absolutize power in the hands of men for over a thousand years. These sit like monstrous boulders in the road with which women who hope for equality must contend. Many women have turned and fled. They view the misuse of the Bible as so perverted that it is unredeemable. Sandra Schneiders observes that the issue of Scripture and its tradition "raises questions of whether the God of the Judeo-Christian tradition can be God for a self-respecting woman; whether Jesus is a savior or an oppressor of women."[238] Many Christian feminists find the use of scripture so deeply entangled with a repressive hierarchical society that rejection of the entire Bible is mandated.

An attempt to reorient the understanding of Scripture away from misogyny has been going on for centuries. Unfortunately, the majority of this work was attempted by women who were marginalized in church, academy and publication, so that their work often went unheard while the Biblical interpretations of Augustine and Aquinas were inscribed in granite.[239]

Women have been out there smashing stones for centuries. Hildegard of Bingen (12th century), Christine de Pizan (14th century), Isotta Nogarola (15th century), Anne Askew (burned at the stake as a heretic, 16th century), down through Julia Smith (who translated the Bible five times, 18th century). Elizabeth Cady Stanton and Sarah Grimké (19th century) studied and argued for understandings of Scripture which reflected a view of equality before God.[240]

The work goes on with vigor in the writings of Elisabeth Schüssler Fiorenza, Elaine Pagels, Letty Russell and a blossoming of others.

What is the point of all this work if scripture, as Elisabeth Schüssler Florenza asks, is "not retrievable for women, since it ignores women's experience, speaks of the godhead in male terms, legitimizes women's subordinate positions of powerlessness, and promote male dominance"?[241] Responding to her own question, and helping us to address ours, she points out, "Western women are not able to discard completely and forget our personal, cultural, or religious Christian history. We will either transform it into a new liberating future or continue to be subject to its tyranny whether we recognize its power or not."[242] (And sad as it seems, we not only battle the past, we battle the present. Two newsworthy examples are the official rejection of the inclusive language lectionary in 1994 and the ongoing selective reading or omission of scripture texts which name women as disciples of Jesus, as prophets and as missioners. By such exclusivity, omissions and selectivity, congregations are denied the chance to hear about women in their roles in salvation history. It is one thing never to have heard from the ambo of the work of Joanna, Susanna or Lydia, but a tragic omission never to hear Mary Magdalene (whom all four gospels name as first at the tomb} in an Easter Sunday reading while Peter and John make a yearly appearance).[243]

Trying to transform misused tools by reclaiming and trumpeting the texts of liberation is swords into plowshares in its finest hour. It is hard work, too, and only now being recognized as a mainstream discipline.

Some scripture scholars, and many respondents, have picked and chosen among the texts of Old and New Testament, searching for those which whisper liberation, while ignoring or downgrading those which are repressive. Others respond that only in confronting the sin of patriarchy in scripture can the texts in any way be redeemed.

Rosemary Radford Ruether points out, "(B)oth Testaments contain resources for the critique of patriarchy and of the religious sanctification of patriarchy. We make it clear from the start that feminism must not use the critical prophetic principles in Biblical religion to apologize for or cover up patriarchal ideology. Rather, the prophetic-liberating traditions can be appropriated by feminism only as normative principals of Biblical faith, which, in turn, criticize and reject patriarchal ideology . . . it is to be denounced, not cleaned up or explained away."[244]

**We are a small group. We meet every Sunday evening for liturgy and we always use the readings of the day. Sometimes this is very painful, since we feel that the selections are sometimes exclusionary, but we decided to confront them, to seek in them what is good, and to denounce what is patriarchal. I have been able myself to grow a lot and see our own power and Jesus' power of healing as we do this.

Respondents did not indicate any particular desire to clean up or explain away offensive texts. The two methods of approach which were most often endorsed and employed were ignoring texts which cause pain and concentrating attention on those which are rich in community, women and justice material. The great majority of respondents indicated an ability and desire to use scripture, though some in the minimalist way of only within the eucharistic commemoration. Others, as we shall see, are far more embracing.

**Jesus is very present, especially as he relates to women and to feminist concerns.

**(Jesus) is included in scripture and in prayers, our communion is a sacramental representation of Him.

**Jesus as historical figure is important as discussed in scripture as a model for us in terms of loving community, commitment to justice. Jesus the Christ is important for me in terms of my relationship to Him as God. The human person of Jesus has been particularly meaningful for me as I struggle and evolve in my faith and understanding. I believe Jesus also struggled.

**I am a part of a scripture sharing group which evolved into a Woman-Church group, so scripture is a major part of our time together. Sometimes we spend a hour working on the selections for the day. The scripture is more powerful in my life because we go on to celebrate with bread and wine. It is a far more complete experience.

**Jesus is present in the Word and in the sacrament and in each one of us as baptized Christians.

**Our group is trying to work to uncover the women of the Old Testament as the predecessors of Jesus. Where would Abraham have been without Sarah who bore the promised child in her old age? What is the role of poor Hagar who was a slave and yet the mother of a nation? We have studied Rebecca, who carried two nations in her womb. We try to see how they took part in the covenant and so led to the New Covenant of Jesus. We're trying to transform "faith of our fathers" into "faith of our parents."

**We see Jesus in Scripture, in presence, in the breaking of the bread and in the others present.

**I believe Jesus was a great prophet, I follow his teaching.

**He is usually seen as one of the great prophets and models for life.

**We see Jesus as avatar, as brother, as mystery, as embodied Spirit whom we can relate to and who can identify with us.

**We try to live as Jesus would live if he were here. We don't always have the courage but we try to do the best we can where we are.

**It is in Jesus' love for us which I discover in the Bible that I have the power to be strong in belief, in life. I believe that he expects much of me, not just in how I live personally, but in what he expects when I deal with others. I know he wants me to act justly and fairly and expects me to want the world to act the same.

Why is it that women persist? After all, the effort is like trying to pick apart an old and matted close-woven rug, thread by thread. It calls for superhuman patience, excellent eyesight and the conviction that the those yarns can be rewoven into beautiful and usable cloth.

Persistence flows from hope, hope that the words used for oppression are side by side with those which promise freedom from all unjust bondage, and that those emancipating words, released, believed, can redeem us all.

How shall we reclaim Sarah, who was called to a faith perhaps greater than Abraham's? Who shall announce Miriam, savior of Moses, and co-leader of the exodus people? Or Ruth and Naomi, who give us a model of powerful friendship like the one offered by Jesus? Or Judith, a widow who, with God's help, saved her people from slaughter and pillage? Or Deborah, prophet and judge, whom "God and people trusted . . . as one of their own?"[245]

Mary provides a challenge. How can we resurrect her from the silent, self-effacing ideal used to teach us the false femininity of submission and obedience? How do we unwrap the layers of Mariology to find what Joan Chittister does in Mary: "The power of the icon and the power of the rebel brought to white heat."[246]

As we search for Mary how do we unite with her son Jesus in liturgy? How do we redeem him from the generations in which his banner was flown by an oppressive force?

How does he become the Word made flesh for us as women?

The responders name him often as the person-God they have discovered in Scripture: in loving community, a model, a human/divine person who struggled and developed, a teacher, in relationship with the creator, a justice-seeker and freedom-giver, a prophet, brother and friend, a healer who is respectful of women. Why do they choose these descriptions if not because these are the places in which they can find meaning?

WE finds shared ground with the Jesus of suffering, of friendship, of community. We invest in him the hope of freedom and healing, who will lead us to our creator. We particularly find encouragement in the boundary-breaking dealings of Jesus with women.

It is obvious from the Gospels that women had great meaning for Jesus. He broke the rules to be with them. They traveled with him, they often paid the bills, they fed him and anointed him. "Far from keeping women in subservient positions, Jesus took every opportunity to treat them with sympathy and respect, and to place them on an equal basis with men. Most miracles were performed for them, or at their request. . . . He sided with women against men in every dispute. . . . He conversed about philosophy and history with the woman at the well . . . he let Mary of Bethany sit with the men listening to his teaching. . . ."[247]

Let us remember for a moment what was said about visions and values in Chapter One. Women have permitted others to name what is valuable, or been forced to submit to someone else's definition. The canon of scripture has been named as having primary value, as being the sacred vision and the canon makes women almost invisible in salvation history.

That canon of scripture has also been taught as the inspired word of God and doubly sanctified by its ritual use within liturgy. The texts were chosen by men and their value or meaning is preached by men. Large numbers of women are only beginning to seek their own import in scripture. They speak in the above responses. Many do approach scripture with the hermeneutic of suspicion, taking what is valuable, challenging and setting aside those portions which imply subjugation.

While we affirm that the gospels call out to us today, we recognize that they came into being in a time and a place far different from our own. We acknowledge that they were written in an androcentric, patriarchal culture, and we need to recover women's part in them. "Both Christian feminist theology and biblical interpretation are in the process of rediscovering that the Christian gospel cannot be proclaimed if the women disciples and what they have done are not remembered."[248]

We make a serious mistake when we enshrine the books only as having come down from on high. These books belong to us, as they have belonged to every generation, and not just to the historical moment in which they took place. The only way in which they can have significance for us is if we are willing to enter into them, metaphorically tearing them apart in search of the secrets meant to be announced in our time and place.

This is how Miriam Therese Winter describes scripture: "God's word is essentially event, continually contemporary, open to everyone. . . . God's word is far more than words recorded in ancient books, even those that are canonical. Before there were words, the Word was God, and God spoke and there was life. Women are searching among the words for the Word of God, a word of life."[249]

This is where we bring our stories into play. How does your experience, specific and real, merge with the stories of Jesus? The Word, truly embraced, calls forth a response. We are invited to embrace in return. Bernard Lee says, "The Word of God is not primarily a voice speaking from an ancient text about a past time. True the sacred text is a voice uttered once upon a time, but it is also a voice that has been turned loose from its original speaker and its original time. When the Word is heard again—really heard—it levies a new claim now upon immediate lived experience. Whatever levies a new claim now on behalf of a better tomorrow puts today at risk. Did it not do that, it would not yet be God's Word but only a voice from the past."[250]

It is wonderful to become aware of how many groups of people world-wide, how many WE circles, are discovering the living Jesus through the scriptures, rather than seeing him only through the often dusty filter of tradition.

The living Jesus is named as a man who loved and had friendship with women, a Godhuman who can be a model, teacher, friend, lover. WE participants find power for moral agency in the love and recognition that Jesus gave to women. If we were important to him, then we must have a role to play, and not a derivative one, in bringing the kingdom of heaven into being.

**We frequently refer to the values of Jesus (as spelled out in the Gospels), caring, equality, peace. We see his teaching as a source of our belief in love and how we are able to love in this world, sometimes in terrible circumstances.

**We believe that the sacramental Jesus is present in our Eucharist and that the historical (and perhaps the sacramental Jesus) is present in the liturgy of the Word.

**We only use the stories of the New Testament which refer to how Jesus confronted injustice and how he provided a new vision of how life can be.

**Jesus' life stories have wonderful meaning for women in relationship to justice issues and our group tries to uncover how those stories are deeply meaningful and instructive in our lives.

**We don't discuss the historical Jesus, except in the context of his treatment of women and his passion for Justice. He isn't approached in academic terms. The historical Jesus doesn't reflect the status quo.

**I am, and my group is not just interested in what we read, but in how we read it. Does the Word, either scripture or the writings of someone contemporary, have an impact on our lives? How do we hear the readings? Do we feel, experience ourselves changed because of this ongoing conversation with the Word? Our homilies are shared time in which we try to find the ways in which we are made new because of how the Word has entered into us.

**Jesus is brother and friend. I feel that he affirms what we are doing, helping us to birth a new church modeled after him. He was not a political leader. He was a healer and reconciler, willing to suffer, anxious to forgive. He did not institute a power structure and he treated women with respect, as equals, as he did men. He is central to what we do.

Choosing to examine the gospels as a call to minorities and the oppressed, we have heard it as genuinely good news for us. The base communities of Latin America, deprived of Eucharist by the priest shortage, are scriptural. [251] Often, not having a priest available to provide sacramental access, they choose the stories of Jesus, who does not leave them. In the embrace of the scripture, people find good news for them, a call for transformation, in self and in society, not a maintenance of the status quo.

Leonardo Boff comments, "One is often struck by the acute social awareness prevailing in the (base) communities. . . . This 'raised consciousness' is not the fruit of some leftist ideological infiltration, but of the reading of the handbook of the faith, the Bible, and of an attempt to understand it in the context in which it was written. The Bible was written in communities of poor people, nearly always under the domination of foreign powers and yearning for integral liberation."[252]

The women of WE testify that it is the justice and freedom-based message of Jesus which calls us forth. By daring to read scripture in a sacramental setting, with an ear cocked for freedom and responsibility, WE can hear Jesus really present, par excellence, in the Word.

"Like other communities of faith and struggle, they practice the presence and connection to God and to the people on the margins of society through the study of the Bible and its interpretation and celebration in the round table community of Christ." [253]

WE provides yet another forum for women to hear each other into consciousness and into understanding, this time in the context of scripture.

Sharing Jesus through scripture, WE can begin to take fuller responsibility for our lives. The model is less filtered through male voices. Women circled for scripture have the opportunity to rehearse ourselves, to practice justice on ourselves, and imagine what that means in our lives and how the Word can be enfleshed in our society and our world.

This tremendously important feature of such sacramental Scripture study encourages self-authorization. This can be best described as being able to name where authority exists in one's own life and then being able to act from that authority. Women who gather for Eucharist claim the sacrament's having spiritual authority. Many women cautiously also name scripture as a source of authority on how we believe and live. "Authority is the explicit *understanding* of power that stands behind and supports the everyday structures of the group's life, those regular patterns that shape relationships among members. . . . (It) is the explicit face of social power in a group. To 'have' authority means to be acknowledged as having the right to be heard and heeded, the right to make demands on others."[254]

The respondents are able to verbalize the power they find in scripture. It is, no doubt, a different kind of power from that experienced in the childhood and young womanhood of many, when scripture was used to control and channel behavior. The scriptures, liberated from such interpretations, can be given a new and legitimate authority by women. The admission that Jesus is with us in scripture is dangerous. This admission calls us to minister, challenge the status quo, champion those unjustly treated. Self-authorizing through scripture, we can and must call ourselves and others to action.

The respondents consistently express their preference for the life and ministry scriptures, as opposed to the death and resurrection ones. [255] It is not primarily to the end time of Jesus' life that WE groups look when selecting scripture, rather to the scriptures in which on a daily basis the kingdom of God is made known. How do we heal, bind up wounds both mental and social, calm storms, feed many, dry tears? The expression of respondents is that Jesus can and will guide us on how to live justly, and that is our present need. Model, teacher, doer of justice.

Sr. Francis Bernard O'Connor, who studied the deprivations of Catholic women of Brazil, Bangladesh, Uganda and the United States says this, "How is it that women in such disparate cultures, races and language groups, thousands of miles apart on four different continents could have identical questions about their church and envision similar solutions? Their questions along with their proposed solutions seek to remedy injustice and are grounded in the gospel. . . . An overwhelming 94% of the women polled in my research indicated their belief that Jesus Christ wants women to be treated equally in the church. Is it possible or even probable that so many women in so many different countries are wrong? Whatever happened to the *sensum fidelium?*"[256]

When we look back to the people of Judea as the message of Jesus began to flow, we see the leper, the beggar, the woman make up much of his audience. Now, we hear the same. This dangerous message, of freedom and healing for all, unites WE with the church universal, the hungry and hurting on every continent, as we drink together at that well where we will never be thirsty again.

Rosemary Radford Ruether comments, "Feminist theology that draws on Biblical principles is possible only if the prophetic principles, more fully understood, imply a rejection of every elevation of one social group against others as image and agent of God, every use of God to justify social domination and subjugation."[257]

This should mean, and means more audibly every day, that blacks in inner cities, lesbians in France, farm workers in California, handicapped people in Belgium, Chinese students, become united with middle-class women of cities and towns in the United States. Our pain is their pain and their struggle ours.[258]

**I have never had the gospels so fully in my life. Being able to talk with others about them, I see how they not only have deep meaning in my life, but also in the lives of people everywhere. Now, when I see on television, or read in the paper about a group of poor people calling for jobs or just wages, when I see the blacks in South Africa wanting the vote, I see Jesus with them, urging them on, and I feel as if I am with them, too. I think study of the gospels, seeing Jesus break unjust and foolish laws to serve people, has encouraged our whole group to be more active for others. I believe that we recognize this because of the presence of Jesus' spirit in our midst as we break open the word and listen to it and share it. I believe that Spirit of Jesus can and will speak to us through the scripture and expects us to listen and to be transformed.

"The Spirit of God, dwelling in any genuine and maturing community of faith, constantly stirs such a group with insights, charisms and courage. This Spirit authorizes the group to actively express its faith. We recognize the authenticity of the Spirit in this group when its actions are both faithful to its shared past and prophetic of a purified future."[259]

In growing numbers, women slowly pull aside the veil which hid or distorted or downplayed the stories of Scripture in which Jesus came to visit and be friends with women. He did not employ an interpreter or interlocutor, even when the law and custom of the time forbade it. Think of that woman at the well. As she left him, her future purified, and went back to her people, she had already become a sign of him. He was already living and visible in her, just as women gathered now become increasingly a sign of him and he becomes more visible in them.

The last words of the Gospel of Matthew are Jesus' final promise, on which he makes good constantly, "And behold that I am with you always, until the end of the age." [260] Not, "I am with you as the institution permits." Not, "I am with you within a strict rubric." I am with you *always*.

The words of the scripture have the possibility of coming alive now in our living rooms, on the front lawn, in the meeting room. They should change our lives.

**I see Jesus with all of us in the Word (I have always loved the idea of Word made flesh). It seems that more and more we only use Scripture at the Gospel time. Our first reading and sometimes a second or third one is from some other place, almost always from a woman writer. We try to find contemporary women's poetry or journalling which fits with the Gospel.

**The world is full of the Word if we believe that Jesus is present in the life and experience of each of us. We try to hear the Word enfleshed through the words of many different people whose writings we use in our liturgies.

**Every planner is able to choose what is meant by "scripture." Sometimes she finds it in the newspapers, sometimes in poetry, sometimes in the writings of a woman of a Third World country.

**We include writings from other women, contemporary people often. These words which we often link with a Gospel with the same theme, help us to see Jesus in our time.

In seeing Jesus Word as the way in which we are drawn together, we also see Jesus present in the uncanonized word, the writings of many who came after Jesus and attempted to make sense of life. Numerous groups testify that they use other writings than the Testaments to open their eyes to God's presence.

In this the writings of women are often used, writings whose sacred character we recognize when we bring them across the threshold into our worship circle, and "canonize" them by giving them prayerful attention, both with ear and tongue. WE gives voice to the expression of joy and struggle of women worldwide, and encourages us to make Jesus-sense of it all, to hear the call to justice in it, to transform ourselves by our knowledge of it so that we can be bearers of goodness, so that we too can be made new. Miriam Therese Winter asks, " Why must only past experience be considered authoritative? We who live with the Holy Spirit as inspiration within and among us surely have every right to add our piece to the deposit of faith."[261]

The choice of new texts, and naming them as inspirited is yet another example of women finding their own religious agency. It is a sacred activity to name the place where we find God present and to share that with each other. There is always far more to God than we are aware of, more to be revealed than has been enshrined in the past. In any event, all texts are only dry crusts of words unless we can bring our own heart, conscience and intention to bear upon them. Rosemary Radford Ruether, in commenting on the use of a variety of texts during liturgy, says, "When a text is read in liturgy it becomes more than an inspirational reading. It becomes a paradigmatic text. It becomes a place where we expect to encounter the transforming Spirit speaking to our own lives."[262]

Naming where we find Jesus, celebrating it, is a sign that we claim him present for us, in us. It is tremendously intimate and inturning first, and then tremendously outgoing in service of others.

"Blow through me, Breath of God,
blow through me,
like a pipe, like a flute, like a reed,
making melody,
the cosmic song in me,
Breath of God."[263]

It is a woman who gives us this image of ourselves as cosmic song.

Following are some selections which respondents have shared as powerful.

LITURGY

"All the way to Elizabeth
and in the months afterward,
she wove him, pondering,
'This is my body, my blood!'

Beneath the watching eye
of donkey, ox and sheep
she rocked him, crooning,
'This is my body, my blood!'

In the moonless desert flight
and the Egypt-days of his growing
she nourished him, singing,
'This is my body, my blood!'

In the search for her young lost boy
and the foreboding day of his leaving
she let him go, knowing,
'This is my body, my blood!'

Under the blood-smeared cross
she rocked his mangled bones,
re-membering him, moaning,
'This is my body, my blood!'

When darkness, stones, and tomb
bloomed to Easter morning,
she ran to him shouting,
'This is my body, my blood!'

And no one thought to tell her,
'Woman, it is not fitting
for you to say those words.
You don't resemble him.'"[264]
(Used in a liturgy in which the Gospel was
Mark 14: 22-25, the story of the last supper.)

"No one asked us to do this work. The mayor of the city did not come along and ask us to run a bread line or a hospice to supplement the municipal lodging house. Nor did the Bishop or Cardinal ask that we help out the Catholic Charities in their endeavor to help the poor. No one asked us to start an agency or an institution of any kind. On our responsibility, because we are our brother's keeper, because of a sense of personal responsibility, we began to try to see Christ in each one that came to us. If a man came in hungry, there was always something in the icebox. If he needed a bed and we were crowded, there was always a quarter around to buy a bed on the Bowery. If he needed clothes, there were our friends to be appealed to, after we had taken the extra coat out of the closet first, of course. It might be someone else's coat but that was all right too."265 (Employed with Matthew 25: 31-45, using the theme of employing our gifts in the service of God and each other.)

"Count them, my spirit, and be grateful.
Count the wonders one by one.
 Each drop of rain, each kiss,
Each kindly word, each rose and garlic bud.

Observe them all, my soul, and give thanks.
How many times have you been redeemed?
How many breezes blew the clouds away?
How many seeds burst into life?" [266]
(First reading of a liturgy with the theme "In Gratitude," followed by Luke 1; 39-49 as the Gospel.)

JESUS PRESENT IN THE ELEMENTS OF BREAD AND WINE ⊙

*This is done by Divine power in this sacrament; for the whole substance of the bread is changed into the whole substance of Christ's body, and the whole substance of the wine into the whole substance of Christ's blood. Hence this is not a formal, but a substantial conversion; nor is it a kind of natural movement: but, with a name of its own, it can be called transubstantiation." [267]
*Jesus said to them, 'I am the bread of life. Whoever comes to me will never be hungry, and whoever believes in me will never be thirsty. But I said to you that you have seen me and yet do not believe. Everything that the Father gives me will come to me, and anyone who comes to me I will never drive away. [268]

*Baking your own bread may not be an economic saving anymore, but it still satisfies as a powerful rite and expression of yeasty growth and conversion. [269]

*For what matters in eucharistic belief is what has always mattered, namely that the reality of what we receive is the Risen Lord; and what matters in the belief is not constricted by the categories of obsolete modes of thought. . . . The imagery of one age can prove an encumbrance for the next. "[270]

*to look rather than to say what it must be. [271]

**Personally, I view transubstantiation at our liturgies the same way I do at traditional Roman Catholic Mass. What makes Christ really present is not magic but what happens within the communal celebration and in many ways. For me, the bread and wine are truly and mysteriously the body and blood of Jesus.

**I believe that when we have Mass and participate in Eucharist we are eating and drinking the body and blood of Christ.

**I hold our Eucharist as valid, the true presence of Jesus, the Body and Blood of Jesus.

**I believe that transubstantiation happens here as at the traditional Mass.

**We consider Eucharist here as legitimate as Mass in a church.

**Transubstantiation remembers Jesus and makes Jesus present to each of us, not different from the institutional Church.

**Jesus is more present to me, and to our community here. First, we have no division in which we are left to feel less equal in our baptisms. Second, we try to be more present to him here. Our community worship is lived out more fully and faithfully as we try to live what we celebrate. This does not feel like empty ritual which makes no impact. This experience is changing the way I live. This signs to me that we have Jesus truly really present with us.

**There is such power in our group, an adult, spirit-filled power, to invite, to welcome, to converse with Jesus, who is *truly present* here, but not just in the bread and wine as we understood as children. Also he is present in us and in the readings.

The people of God alive now have had more opportunity than any generation in history to study Eucharistic theology. Vatican II broadened our understanding of the sacramental encounter of God and God's people. In the classroom, in the church hall, in print, the teachings on Christ's presence and our call have been available to us. By discernment and participation the community has greater intimacy with Eucharist. So in this Eucharistic conversation with the past about the present what have we learned? What has been affirmed and reacknowledged and what has been discarded or demoted in importance?

Most responses profess belief that Jesus, died and risen, has real presence in the elements of bread and wine during WomenEucharist. Of 104 respondents, 102 responded to the question, "How does the group view transubstantiation?" in a chartable way. Of the 102 responses, 57 (56%) answered in ways which indicated positive belief that at WomenEucharist the bread and wine becomes the body and blood of Christ. [272] Only 5 (4.5%) respondents indicated that at WE Jesus was fairly certainly not fully present. One answered "It makes no difference what form the bread and wine take." The remaining 40 (39.5%) use phraseology which shows that *transubstantiation* is a term which they no longer employ or which does not adequately express the experience of Jesus present in WomenEucharist: "Present in a special way. . . . Our lives are transignified. . . . When we celebrate eucharistically, Christ empowers us by saying, 'Whenever two or more are gathered together, there I am'. They refer to WE as being as valid as the "traditional Mass" or that of the "institutional Church." There is no sense of separation from the parish in terms of what occurs during the consecration of bread and wine. Only one responder indicated that she was fairly certain that Eucharistic presence happened with an ordained priest but not at her women's group.

There is the inner confirmation, Spirit-sparked, that Jesus is substantially present in the bread and wine. [273] What do we have to say about these affirmations?

The sacraments do not stand separate from the people of God. Jesus requests in Luke, " 'This is my body, which will be given for you; do this in memory of me.' And likewise the cup after they had eaten, saying, 'This cup is the new covenant in my blood, which will be shed for you.' " [274] The *active role* to which we are called is reaffirmed in the Gospels of Matthew and Mark. [275] It will be remembered from chapter 3 that there is no indication that Jesus established a cultic priesthood, and it was to his friends that he put the request that these actions be taken in his name, along with the promise that when we gather he will be with us.

Paul affirms the role of the people in the recognition of Jesus *completely present* in these ritual actions:

"I am speaking as to sensible people; judge for yourselves what I am saying. The cup of blessing that we bless, is it not a participation in the blood of Christ? The bread that we break, is it not a participation in the body of Christ? Because the loaf of bread is one, we, though many, are one body, for we all partake of the one loaf." [276]

The scripture names the active ("we bless . . . we break") role which sensible humans take in joining Jesus in a specific, aware moment in time. It is through our own blessing and breaking that we become actively involved in the genuine presence of God in our midst.

When the believing community reassumes its rightful place, we become more aware that the will to celebrate is largely based here, rather than solely in the hands of an ordained priest. [277] Jesus is no longer seen as the possession of the clergy. Rather, he is understood to be freely, willingly and ardently present to those who gather and ask him to be with them.

Our awareness of this free offering of Jesus can galvanize communities' deliberate prayer, moving it from dependence to dynamic action. Perhaps the sacrament of Eucharist as celebrated in intentional groups has a greater clarity and inner confirmation for most participants, because it is entered into freely and deliberately, rather than because of some notion of fear or obligation which may have been part of the experience of sacrament in other circumstances.

"The authorizing of the sacraments . . . is rooted in the shared memory of Jesus' recognition of certain patterns of power in life. This authorizing was and *is still performed* by various communities as they seek to safeguard and revitalize Jesus' revelation of these rhythms of power. We participate in this authorizing process when we reenact the sacraments: our faithful revision of these rites both purifies and reauthorizes these rhythms of grace in human life.

"But over the centuries this continual process of authorizing the sacraments receded from view. The sacraments came to be pictured as eternal, unchangeable rituals. They also came to be imagined as the sole province of the priest. . . . Today we are recovering a 'forgotten' aspect of the sacraments: that each involves a process as well as a ritual; that each is performed by a community as surely as by an individual minister." [278] (italics mine).

As we have seen earlier, most groups have a celebrant or leader or convener, but, as has been noted, the role is voluntary and switches from one Eucharist to the next. (I deliberately do not use the word *priest* because the respondents do not use it, no doubt because it is weighed down with enormous impedimenta. Nonetheless, there is frequent acknowledgment in other chapters of the priesthood of the baptized, an area which needs much greater study.) That person is deemed to be one who carries out the will of the whole community to ask God's presence. Thus the leader acts on the desire of the celebrants by putting their prayer, their desire for unity with Christ, into action. This more clearly reflects the position of the early church than the system of separation and elevation long in favor. *This is ancient ecclesiology.*

Rosemary Radford Ruether points out, "The actual sacramental actions of the Eucharist are rather simple, and anyone could learn to do them in an hour, this is obviously not a matter of special skills or expertise." [279] Those who have taken the part of leader can attest to this fact. The weight of the invitation to God to make God-self truly present, the responsibility to cross the threshold into sacred space and time, lies with the assembled. The gift of faith we share, that Jesus cared enough to come once, to make his saving presence known, and that he willingly truly comes again in the bread and wine, has been rewarded again and again, by the sense of his confirming spirit among us as we pray.

Our respondents speak of their growing participation in the action which is Eucharist, very much in line with the call to the people of God expressed by Vatican II.[280] They also see, as they recognize the authorization of the Spirit, that the celebrant is one of and one with the community, taking away from the actions the implications of the magical which for so long have hung over the rite. And in the midst of this WE respondents find Jesus wonderfully present in the celebration.

This is a return to an earlier experience of Christ in community, in which we did not have to look to official rules of celebration, to exact rubrics, to find out if he was with us. This is a return of that affirmation to the gathered believers.

As the following quotations will indicate, many WE participants, while confessing the validity or legitimacy in both parish- and home-based celebrations, do not become involved in the struggle of who has the real presence to the exclusion of others. This is a far more feminist position, a non-divisive position, for the heart of WE is the affirmation that Jesus is really available to *all* who ask, and that when he commanded, "Do this in memory of me," he meant exactly that. In line with redeveloping Eucharistic theology, the mystery of Christ really present is no longer seen only in the elements but also in the community and in the Word.[281]

The greater wonder in many parish churches is whether the people are really present. For it takes the real presence, the deliberate determined committed believing presence of the community, to enter into sacramental encounter. Edward Kilmartin says, "The central issue of eucharistic theology is not 'how does Christ become present to us?' but 'how do we become present to Christ?' . . . In short, the basic eucharistic question is not 'who is *on* the table?' but 'who is *at* the table and how did we get there?'"[282] The answers in this chapter and in the ones which came before indicate that these people who respond know that they are at this table, much more fully than in a parish, and they know many of the reasons why they come and why they stay.

Ritual has often been experienced as an escape from real presence. It can easily devolve into a set of assumed meanings which relieve us of the responsibility to be a part of the possibilities of change and growth in God's covenant, relieve us of the need to really be at the table. Regis Duffy puts it this way: "Just as a family can have a meal that is replete with rituals of love and shared commitment but fail to actualize those meanings, so too may the Christian community evade the needed intentions and crucial meanings of the Eucharist and settle for the comfort of familiar rituals."[283] The routines of our lives let us slip easily into rituals which have surface meaning but no recognized depth.

Think of how often we say to someone, "How are you?" using it as a polite ritual greeting, but with no particular wish to hear an answer which deviates from the standard, "Fine. How about you?" It is startling when someone unexpectedly takes our ritual question seriously. They have missed our intention. We may not wish to be nearly so present to this person as the ensuing monologue will require. We may not wish to enter into and perhaps be changed by this encounter. Eucharist requests that we be really present to the community, to the Word, to the bread and wine. "Eucharist will not allow us to remain indifferent disciples. Real presence, then, is a question of mutual presence and communication that permits us to see the need of God's people with the eyes of the Master."[284]

Previous and following responders tell us that they are experiencing over and over the change which Eucharist calls us to, a sign that the Jesus Spirit is really present.

**My view is that the presence of God becomes known again between us as we break bread and share wine. We are invited to see the presence of God that is already here. The power of women together being intentional about sharing the presence of God in their lives does this. Bread and wine symbolize this experience. We all become the loving body of Christ, not just the bread and wine (become the body of Christ).

**Transubstantiation is not a term that is used. What is sacramental is the gathering in love at the table, where Christ is host and invites us all. The bread came from the earth to which billions of people have returned following lives on this planet. I shall, too. My descendants will partake of me in that bread. Perhaps we are all divine. Bread connects us, at the Eucharist table and at the table at home when we eat with people we love.

**We have the ritual of breaking bread and sharing it and wine in His memory which is very central to us.

**Symbolically he is present in the bread and wine as a mystery that we cherish.

**We do not try to explain how or exactly what happens. We know when we are spiritually moved but we go easy on our judgments.

**We hold varying opinions on transubstantiation and that is fine. If you went into any Catholic Church on Sunday morning and could get worshippers to tell you what they thought really happened there would be a tremendous variety of opinion, as there is among theologians.

**Transubstantiation is left to the understanding of each participant. I could not presume to speak for the others.

**We probably have a variety of understandings. We gather to celebrate the Christian message and we use the words "Body and Blood of Christ."

**I believe when I consecrate the bread it is transubstantiated. Some women are not as comfortable and so seem to symbolize rather than consecrate.

**There are those who use the traditional Eucharistic prayers and see their priestly work as transubstantiating the elements. There are non-Catholics in the group who do not feel transubstantiation as a necessary process, as all is in God and all is God.

**I view transubstantiation as the recognition of Jesus' presence among us to be taken and internalized by us and to be given out to everyone we encounter.

Though a large number of respondents used, apparently comfortably, the term *transubstantiation,* there were others who used it gingerly, or who recognized that everyone in their WE group would not be entirely comfortable with the term. This falls into line with the thinking of a number of contemporary theologians, who while affirming our heritage of belief in the genuine presence of Jesus, suggest other terminology.[285] We need recall that Aquinas did not formulate the definition of transubstantiation until the 1200s. Prior to that, the people of God believed in Jesus present in the Eucharist. The term itself, somehow has been almost as sanctified as the Eucharistic meal. (P.J. Fitzpatrick comments that distance in time and in whole ways of thinking have isolated the term. He calls it a "marooned survivor." It has been isolated, and its use has become a matter of discipline rather than of theological reflexion.")[286]

In any event, the responses show that terminology as paramount is being replaced by event and experience. In recent years some theologians have favored more the term *transignification,* which "teaches that it is not the 'substance' of the bread and wine which is transformed at the Lord's Supper. Rather, it is the 'significance' of the bread and wine which is changed. When the bread and wine are placed on the table of the Lord's supper and sacred words which recall the memory of Jesus are recited over them, their 'meaning' is profoundly altered for the Christian faith community. They are no longer merely bread and wine, but have become sacramental signs which can mediate a faith encounter with the Risen Jesus. They now signify the life-giving (i.e. Spirit-mediating) presence of the Risen Jesus at his Supper."[287]

Some respondents make it clear that terminology is not nearly as important as the experience, the inner confirmation of the external ritual.

**I believe the sacramental Jesus, though not always explicitly named, is very present within our liturgies because: 1) we as Catholics bring that understanding even if it is not explicitly named, and 2) the Jesus I believe in reveals, becomes alive again in the circle of women who nurture and strengthen themselves and the world in their worship.

**I think Jesus is here with us as the messenger and model of our chosen lifestyles.

**We do not limit ourselves to the sacramental Jesus but we do what we do centered around Him.

**The historical and sacramental Jesus has played a radical part in shaping the spirituality of each person present and we still hold the belief that the Risen Jesus meets and nourishes and prays through us as we gather in one body.

**I see Jesus in our celebrations as a transcendent force which keeps moving us as a song, a hope and a pressing to the future.

**He is here as the touchstone of our lives. We are all explicit Christians.

**My personal view is that Jesus *is* present, "where ever two or more are gathered," whatever form the bread is in is of no interest to me.

**Transubstantiation is not a concern. I look for experiences which nourish my spirit.

**We believe that metaphysically or symbolically the Lord Christ is present in a special way in the bread and wine as Christ transforms it. But with the words of consecration, we all, the whole world is His Body, His Blood.

Powerfilled, aren't they? These testaments signify our gradual reclamation of our power to believe in our own experience. The inner communication of the Spirit of Jesus can lead us to give such declarations of belief. What are we to make of such statements as these from women nation-wide? The way they speak, the language they use is potent as they identify Jesus really present in their celebrations of Eucharist.

The statements are reminiscent of the recognitions of Jesus by his friends in the post-resurrection stories. He came to them in a locked house and said, "'Peace be with you . . .' The disciples rejoiced when they saw the Lord. (Jesus) said to them again, 'Peace be with you. As the Father has sent me, so I send you.' And when he had said this, he breathed on them and said to them, 'Receive the Holy Spirit.'" [288] The responses are spirited indeed, with no sense of hesitancy or uncertainty. These women have faith that Jesus is with them in celebration. [289]

The disciples continued to be convinced that Jesus remained with them even after the resurrection. The women who speak mirror that experience. "As they prayed, the place where they were gathered shook, and they were all filled with the holy Spirit and continued to speak the word of God with boldness." [290] Even within the experimental church of this decade these are bold words.

Yet these are not the only reactions which WE participants have. Some women put other names on the experience or struggle with just which ways the experience can be named at all.

**Transubstantiation appears to be an individual thing. I still struggle with the idea that it can occur outside the RC church, outside the priest-conducted Mass in a church.
**We haven't discussed transubstantiation. We use the model of communion, first blessing the offering of the food gifts, but I don't know if anyone believes she is consecrating.
**Belief depends on the individual, but there seems to be an unspoken belief that the bread and wine are changed.
**We have Christ in us, and we are able to share in His life, body and blood, by asking Him, and by remembering Him. We believe that what we share is holy and Christ is in it. For me, it doesn't matter if the bread and wine turn into the body and blood of Christ. He *is* here. We are sharing Him.
**I think transubstantiation is an internal and private belief, yet I believe we all think something has changed because of our mutual support for one another.
**We probably have a variety of understandings. We gather to celebrate the Christian message and we use the words "Body and Blood of Christ."

**The substance of Jesus is personally embraced but each person in our community is responsible for her/his reactions and beliefs.

**For some of us this is Eucharist. Others see it as a paraliturgy or agape. Interestingly, more women are moving into believing our liturgies are Eucharist.

For those of us who believe that in this commemoration Jesus is really present we cannot go away unchanged. In the community, in the Word and in the elements, we are called to put on Christ. If Jesus is more meaningfully present, then how are we to respond?

**Our Eucharist is a sharing and a symbol. We view Eucharist as Jesus viewed it, as change when we grow in the challenge and love of Jesus present.

**We try to live as Jesus would live if he were here. We don't always have the courage but we try to do the best we can where we are.

**Jesus is present as a great teacher.

**We have all grown in sensitivity as we have heard each other speak, shared Jesus in the word and in the bread and wine made flesh.

**Our lives are transignified.

**With women celebrating liturgy together we are able to see clearly ourselves as good, as powerful and important in the life of the world. This is new for me, and for lots of us. Gradually I can see that believing that Jesus is with us has changed our behavior and made us much more aware of justice issues.

** Rosemary Ruether and lots of other feminist theologians have helped us to see and name what we are experiencing. We see the Presence of Jesus in the readings and in the bread and wine and we talk about how we are being changed for justice by this presence.

** I go to our liturgies and I see us all changing, becoming more radical as we read and believe what we hear. Then I go home and read feminist theologians and I say "yes!" to their ideas and expressions. This is the first time in my entire life that I have had my understanding of God spelled out so clearly by someone else. It is wonderful to see myself in print!

**If we don't experience some sort of transformation then our liturgies do not signify Jesus with us.

In poetry Fr. Ed Hays helps us to pray that "I may see myself as another Word of Yours made flesh, to your glory and honor." [291] If this ritual of Eucharist encourages the preservation of our old selves, if it tells us that nothing can change, if it signs that the status quo remains, then it has failed us. All ritual is a pathway of growth, tending toward the One who made us, that we may be another Word enfleshed. [292] Through this entire chapter, through this entire book women speak of a need for change, in themselves, in the church, in the world. This is the call to justice which is potent in our reading of Jesus' teaching and in the sharing of his body and blood. For many of us it is more clearly visible that the awareness of need and the desire to make change happen are spirit-driven. Shared Eucharist is not a whisper anymore, but a shout that healing, peacemaking, justice can and will happen because the spirit of Jesus unites with us as we pray and celebrate.

Driver calls this "God together with the people of God, ritually perform(ing) to celebrate freedom and to hasten the liberation of the whole world." [293] The freedom of which Driver speaks, and the change which respondents hope for are not distant, not potential, but actual right now. The gospels call for it and our ritual celebrates it. Go back and read the words of the respondents from the beginning of this chapter. WE has begun to realize that change is possible, not in the far off time of eternal reward; our heaven, the heaven of all humanity, is creeping upon us now if we, united in the presence of Jesus, begin to act as ordained agents of change. Diann Neu says, "Feminist liturgy provides a place where we are filled with real love of ourselves that engages us in the justice issues of our day. In liturgy we get in touch with fundamental experiences of justice or the lack of them. . . . The liturgical assembly is not gathered for itself only, but for the world also." [294]

This is the relational characteristic of feminine community sacralized. This is the *gemeinschaft* relationship which calls us to be intimate with the whole community of God. The pain which we have known because we are women leads us to be present to the pain of the world, and that understanding is sacramentalized as we hear the Word and consume the body of Christ broken long ago and broken again for us.

We are called again to be ladies (for we recall that the word means "loaf-giver") of justice in Jesus.

"Begin to bake the new bread of life now. We must do more than protest against the old. We must begin to live the new humanity now. We must begin to incarnate the community of faith in the liberation of humanity from patriarchy in words and deed, in new words, new prayers, new symbols, and new praxis." [295]

What is it that we can conclude is happening among these WE groups?

The gatherings of women mirror the rule-breaking meals Jesus shared in his own time. Matthew records grain snacking on the Sabbath which brought the rebuke of the Pharisees. Jesus reminds them that David and his friends broke the law by entering the house of God and eating holy bread reserved for the priests because they were hungry.[296] Jesus sits down with tax collectors and sinners who follow him, and goes to a sinner's house as a guest as he breaks bread in the hospitable home of Zacchaeus. [297]

The WE groups gather because we too are hungry and our hunger for the Risen Jesus in community, word and bread and wine has grown greater than a law of assembly which most have followed for generations.

Edward Schillebeeckx speaks in this way about Jesus' eating habits, "Jesus makes the reality of the kingdom of God imaginable in terms of a common participation in a festive and splendid banquet in which cripples, the poor and the social outcasts can share. Clearly connected with this is the fact that he ate illegally (in religious terms) with people from his own environment and specifically also with outcasts from the society of the time. Here Jesus radicalizes and transcends the Pharisaic notion of table fellowship. In the communal eating together Jesus implements by his own concern for his fellow Jews something of the coming reality and thus anticipates the kingdom of God which begins to exist where under the spell of Jesus people themselves become new."[298]

The testimony of respondents is that in these gatherings which are deemed illegal by institutional standards, WomenEucharist remembers and experiences Jesus to be really present as WE gathers and ritualizes. The testimony is that Jesus is really present in those in the circle. He is truly available in the words read in sacred space. For most people he is here in the mystery of bread and wine enfleshed. In these sacred gatherings WE are challenged to put on Christ and become, individually and in community, new creations. We are worthy of justice and called to do justice for and with others. Some of the respondents try to spell out what happens in these thanksgiving celebrations, and many of them turn to feminist and liberation theologians to put meaningful words to this life-giving-changing encounter with the friendship of Jesus.

This is an awesome and power-filled encounter.

✪✪✪✪✪✪

SPEAKING OF GOD

FORETHOUGHT ✪

Must we call God He? Is it heresy to call God She? How can female be seen in the image of God? In this chapter we explore who does naming, how we absorb what words mean, how and why we may challenge those meanings when certain words stop working, and why we even bother. For those who are conversant with the control exacted by language I suggest that you skip the material from WHO DOES THE NAMING up to WHAT IS RIGHT SPEECH TOWARD GOD? There we examine the ways WE members are expanding, relating and healing their God images.

✪✪✪✪✪

＊*Sophia wished that Florence would not talk about the Almighty as if his real name was Godfrey, and God was just Florence's nickname for him.* [299]

＊*Our savior is our true Mother, in whom we are endlessly born and out of whom we shall never come.* [300]

＊*O Guardian of galaxies,
Mother of the cosmos and
Father of stars beyond counting.
may I sleep in you tonight.* [301]

＊*the utterly helpless God.* [302]

＊*Ts'its'tsi'nako, Thought-Woman
is sitting in her room
and whatever she thinks about
appears.* [303]

＊*I am the Alpha and the Omega, the first and the last, the beginning and the end!* [304]

＊*Oh our Mother the Earth, oh our Father the Sky,
Your children are we.* [305]

＊*God of our fathers, known of old*

Lord of our far-flung battle-line —
Beneath whose awful Hand we hold
Dominion over palm and pine. [306]

✳Hold hands and crack the whip, and yank the Absolute out of there and into the light,
God pale and astounded, spraying a spiral of salts and earths, God footloose and flung.
And cry down the line to his passing white ear, 'Old Sir! Do you hold space from buckling
by a finger in its hole? O Old! where is your other hand?' His right hand is clenching, calm,
round the exploding left hand of Holy the Firm. "[307]

✳The Great Mystery, sometimes called Great Spirit, was the all-powerful being for many
of the Plains Indians. The Sioux called this being Wakan Tanka. These words actually mean
'mysterious' and 'great.' . . . All tribes had names for this power. The Omaha called it
Wakonda; the Pawnee name was Kawaharu. The Iroquois wordorenda is associated with
a universal indwelling spirit. [308]

✳A mighty fortress is our God, a bulwark never failing. [309]

✳O Lord Almighty,
God of our ancestors,
of Abraham and Isaac and Jacob
and of their righteous offspring;. . .
you are the Lord Most High,
of great compassion. [310]

✳Sinners in the Hands of an Angry God [311]

✳Oh, that you may suck fully
 of the milk of her comfort,
That you may nurse with delight
 at her abundant breasts!
 For thus says the LORD:
Lo, I will spread prosperity over her like a river,
 and the wealth of the nations like
 an overflowing torrent.
As nurslings, you shall be carried in her arms,
 and fondled in her lap;
As a mother comforts her son,,
 so will I comfort you [312]

✳Beloved, do not look for revenge but leave room for the wrath; for it is written,
"Vengeance is mine; I will repay, says the Lord." [313]

✳The LORD goes forth like a hero,
 like a warrior he stirs up his ardor;
He shouts out his battle cry,
 against his enemies he shows his might. [314]

WHO DOES THE NAMING?✪

**There is a strong anti-masculine feeling for God based on group anger at the male,

hierarchical, power-centered model of church.

**The institution really limits the names we can use for God, nouns and pronouns. Try sometime saying "she" in the responses everytime there is usually a "he." You really get weird, judgmental looks.

At the outset of the book of Genesis we find God creating up a world. God imagines into being each new object and *only after the naming* does God look upon this fresh creation and find it good. The satisfaction of creation seems to be not only in the fashioning, but also in the labeling of day and night, sky and earth and sea.

In the second account of the creation, God shares the naming with the human creature whom God has brought into being. "So the LORD God formed out of the ground various wild animals and various birds of the air, and he brought them to the man to see what he would call them; whatever the man called each of them would be its name," and when these creations were not partners to the man, God constructed a helpmate and let the man name her. " When he brought her to the man, the man said: . . . 'This one shall be called woman.'" [315] It has been the experience that men have continued to do the naming, almost as an exclusive right given to the male sex by God.

The job of naming frequently is extended to include not only the collection of letters which shall from this time forward signify the object, but also what implied meanings shall be understood when this name is used, that is, what is in the allowable *symbol sack* for this word. By the inclusion of some images and the disinclusion of others the subconscious understanding of a word is far greater than the original single meaning. The ones who do the naming and who claim the right to name (and deny that right to others) have extensive but not exclusive power to shape perception.

Labeling is a power-packed experience, for in it we have the capability of shaping the understanding not only for ourselves, but for those around us. The US Defense Department knows this. They call blatantly aggressive missions such names as "Operation PeaceKeeper" or "Operation Safety Net." African Americans know this, and have fought to name themselves. Gays have struggled with the desire of others to demean them with queer and faggot. Spic, slant, slope, bitch.

Some words on the surface are innocent factual labels, but have at the subsurface level collected such a tremendous negative baggage that the conscious level and the subconscious level are constantly at war.

I was again made conscious of this fact recently when I overheard an eight- year-old boy taunt his clumsy, learning-disabled brother, "You're a girl, David, you're just a girl." Though he is only eight, he has already learned the use of the feminine as derogatory. [316]

WITH OUR MOTHER'S MILK WE ABSORB NAMES AND THE SYMBOLS THEY REPRESENT ✪

From the moment of birth girls and boys are perceived differently and in a tremendous number of cultures that perception is made clear immediately.

Compare the Egyptian "Lullaby for a Son" which contains these lines:

"After our enemies had rejoiced at her pain
and said, 'There is a stone in her belly!' . . .
Go! O bearer of the news! Kiss them and
tell them, 'She has borne a son!'"[317]

with these in "Lullaby for a Newborn Girl:"

When they said, 'It's a girl!' —that was
a horrible moment.
The honey pudding turned to ashes and the
dates became scorpions.
When they said, 'It's a girl!' the cornerstone
of the house crumbled."[318]

Lullaby language tells a child that she is less treasured, less welcome. She is named from the moment of her birth (and now by amniocentesis before birth) as female and that will influence almost every aspect of her existence (frequently negatively). Anthropologists are coming to understand that there is virtually no area of existence, from the colors we wear to the words we speak, and how we speak them, the educations we absorb and the job functions we perform, our own capabilities and how we value ourselves, which will not be culturally inflected because of our sex. Any aspect of life which has so much importance is deeply entwined with all areas of language usage and speech patterns.

"Being inculturated in a thousand subtle ways through familial socialization, education, the media, and religious practice to the idea that women are not as capable as men, nor are they expected to be, leads to an internalized sense of powerlessness. . . . This process is strongly aided and abetted by male-centered language and symbol systems, key reflections of the dominant group's power to define reality in its own terms and a powerful tool of its rule. Women have been robbed of the power of naming, of naming themselves, the world, and ultimate holy mystery, having instead to receive the names given by those who rule over them. Since language not only expresses the world but helps to shape and create it, learning to speak a language where the female is subsumed grammatically under the male gives girl children from the beginning the experience of a world where the male is the norm from which her own self deviates."[319]

It is worthwhile to spend a moment on remembering how language becomes a part of our lives.

There is a study which indicate that children are already beginning to respond to speech variants by the age of nine weeks.[320] Our first language experiences introduce us to naming. A child begins to braid herself into the human community by learning and using the labels for the people and objects around her. Watch a parent's delight when the baby learns to say "mama" or "doggie." The child who is immediately and consistently affirmed in this function discovers it is a means of gathering favor from those around her, and also of grasping the "whatness" of the world. A tremendous part of early life is spent correlating words to objects, individuals, experiences. She "creates" her world through naming.

To learn the name of an object is to in some way possess the object. To learn and use the name of an object is to also agree with the linguistic culture on the "whatness" of the object. (This is important in our future discussion about naming, and more importantly, understanding what the word *God* means in our speech.) Children are early and often rewarded for that agreement, by a smile or by verbal encouragement.

Language is most easily learned in the give and take of daily life at an early age and in a social context. The language lab of the child is the kitchen, the bedroom, the playground and, very importantly, the television. It is in the interaction of human with human that the concept of language moves into the reality of speech. (There is an academic field which examines this interrelationship of language and community: sociolinguistics recognizes that speech is a almost always a social event and not an abstract concept.[321] Feminist sociolinguistics studies how women are affected by their social milieu in the learning of speech.)

Furthermore, mastering[322] language in a social context means that we not only grasp what word names or identifies an object. Also, by continuous exposure to the cultural biases of the teacher (parent, sibling, tv star) we learn the emotional and symbol content of a word.

The word has a *symbol sack*; besides its literal meaning it also contains possibilities for simile and metaphor. Its usage over a period of time loads it with shades of meaning which have suggestive power. It is almost impossible to underestimate the might which naming has in our unconscious as well as our conscious lives.

I have a friend who as a child was terrorized by seeing a pack of wild dogs attack a friend. His children not only learn that the word "dog" identifies a four legged canine, but also that dogs are vicious and to be avoided at all costs. That event forged the primary emotional content of the word "dog" for those children. It will eventually be in conflict with other experiences which the children have from movies in which the faithful pet saves the family from disaster, or from personal contact with dogs in which initial fear is (partially) overcome by alternative experience. This does not usually erase the previous image; rather it moderates it. This fact is a sign of the *plasticity* of language, in which meaning can be moderated by varied experience. (This plasticity will be an important concept when we discuss God-speech.)

To comprehend something's "whatness" is also to begin to grasp its "what-not-ness." A name not only identifies what something is, say "ball." A child also learns from repetition the object's characteristics, such as roundness, or usefulness for play. As children grow, their knowledge of what may be contained within the meaning of the word enlarges, so that they may discover that balls can come in many densities from nerf to bowling, and in many sizes from pingpong to basket. Ball holds many associations of what is appropriate to being a ball. Experience even allows a football (which does not have the complete character of roundness) to be included in the definition. The symbol sack can continue to expand as curiosity and discovery give enlarged understanding to the word *ball*. By the age of four, a child in our ball-conscious society will understand when the earth is compared to a ball. A little boy will understand the usage of "balls" in relationship to his testicles.

One of the functions of the authority figure is to discourage the misuse or misalignment of words. When a word is misapplied the possibility of confusion arises and a child who consistently calls a bicycle a ball will probably be shunned or ridiculed by her social group. Even the adult who has little understanding of how language works knows it is her job to encourage correct speech. (Correct here implies language which will help the child to fit in with the social circle.)

One of the perceived responsibilities of the authority figure is to guide children away from inappropriate gender statements. A little girl who wants to be a fireman or a policeman finds that "she" does not fit with the material in the symbol sack for those jobs. A sign of the plasticity of language is that as young women file suit to be hired onto a police force, or pass the tests to become "firemen," our sense of language expands, our unconscious symbol sacks expand to hold new images (which really only chafe temporarily) and we suddenly have firefighters and police officers. There are many professions which do not have gender specific words, such as lawyer, doctor, psychiatrist, priest, but long usage of them always coupled with the pronoun "he" makes the symbol sack bulge with masculine reference.[323] It takes years to realign the images. The courts and television have been helpful in beginning to grasp those and other culturally masculine words as being neutral rather than sex-specific.

One way that we know a statement is grammatically correct is that it "sounds" correct, that is, we have practiced it that way many times without correction by the authority figure. We have accustomed our tongues to the use of the pronoun "he" to always refer to empowered people. We are habituated to the sound and accept it as proper.

Miriam Therese Winter makes this point, "When referring to God, Christianity uses exclusively male pronouns, thereby assuming and imaging a masculine God. If you want to test the validity of anyone's claim to inclusivity, try referring to God as She. . . . A colleague, male, unwilling to call God Mother because it would be exclusive, said, 'Let's just call Him It."[324]

That imprinting of what is correct is difficult to break, and cannot be erased; rather, it will be modified or inflected by varied experience.

CHALLENGING THE NAMING ✪

How does our experience begin to vary? Among other things we grow up. One of the signs of the child moving away from adult control is the use of and development of teenage slang which the adult frequently finds incomprehensible, but which bonds the teenager to her peer group. An unspoken message from child to adult is "I will use language as I wish. I will determine meanings which flow out of my own experience. I know your language but I choose to speak my own (at least part of the time)."

Women also declare themselves at odds with the male-controlled speech and symbol system by beginning to approach all speech with the hermeneutic of suspicion, first working to change their own understanding and use of language, and simultaneously challenging the use of sexist language by others. During the 1970's and 1980's many meetings in the public and private sectors were disrupted regularly by women who would interrupt any sentence in which there was sexist use of pronouns and nouns. In the beginning, men met these disruptions with patronization of the "little ladies," then by explanation, "It's just easier to use 'he' to cover all of us," then by anger. When none of this worked and as more women gathered for support, public and private meetings and correspondence began to be marked by the uncomfortable business of modulating a deeply embedded language pattern. It is like learning to talk again.

What began in the secular world would flow into the spiritual world as women began to publicly challenge the practice of male-centered God talk and to name their own experience of God.

DO WE SPEAK A COMPLETELY DIFFERENT LANGUAGE? DO WOMEN BELONG TO THE LINGUISTIC BROTHERHOOD OF ALL MANKIND? ✪

It should not surprise us that within our spoken experience there is both High and Low language. (The very terminology used in the study of linguistics itself embodies a gender bias. You may wish to guess at this point who speaks High and who speaks Low.)

High Language can be described as that which is formally recognized as "proper" by those who control the media (mostly educated white males) and that which the major social group (mostly educated white males) would use in formal conversation or writing. It is often considered to be the educated way to speak. It is androcentric language and represents and embodies androcentric thought patterns.

Some examples of high language are: sermons (still mostly male), speeches in parliament or Congress (still mostly male), university lectures (still mostly male), news broadcasts, (getting closer to evenly female and male) and poetry (more male than female but improving as women gain more access to the print medium). [325]

Changes in High language are often demeaned as destructive to good language usage. *The New York Times* is considered to be a major definer of High language usage.

On the other hand, Prince Charles, in March, 1995, claimed higher ground by accusing Americans of contributing to the ruination of the English language. The French Academy chooses the role of language guardian in France. The ongoing implication is that there is a right way to express oneself, and if that means is not used, the speaker is self-identifying as less educated and lower on the social ladder.

This demeaning of alternate usage (Low language) is meant in part to keep people in line in language usage. Low language is considered to be colloquial, and therefore not appropriate to formal or "real" speech (men wouldn't talk that way).

Some examples of Low language are: conversations with children or people perceived to be lower on the social or economic ladder such as waiters and housekeepers, intimate conversations among women, television shows which involve people of other racial groups than white, writings of women and other minorities (the writings of Joel Chandler Harris and Ntozake Shange use dialect and are therefore Low). Those who speak Low as a primary tongue are often discounted by those whose primary tongue is High.

Blacks and Hispanics are told that they not only must speak English but the right kind of English in order to function (get and keep a job) in the "real" world. Women have learned the same thing. High often has more thinking or judgment words while Low has more feeling or relational words. One of the reasons that Low develops is because High does not have adequate vocabulary or meaning to express the lives and experiences of certain groups of people. Even women who have been raised in High-speech homes and schools will use more feeling or relational words when they are with female friends, and return to High speech when in the office. They mainstream their language in their work but not in their private lives.

There seems to be some agreement that important literature is written in H and many people may deny that L even exists, or will ridicule or minimize the validity of L. It will come as no surprise that androcentric language is supposedly deified in scripture through the cultural understanding of direct inspiration by God. "The masculinity of theological and liturgical God-language is . . . not a cultural or linguistic accident but an act of domination in and through proclamation and prayer. While androcentric language . . make(s) patriarchal domination 'commonsense,' masculine God-language in liturgy and theology proclaims it as 'ordained by God.'"[326]

For many people who only speak (or acknowledge) High, anything which is considered Low is heavily discounted, merely background noise until that which is Low is forced upon them by frequency and insistency of use in mainstream media. (The demeaning process we spoke of earlier will not hold sway if a sufficient number of people refuse to abide by it. Persistence and numbers will revive the plasticity of language.)

Thus the movies of such actors as Eddie Murphy, and the talk show of Oprah Winfrey (stars so big that they could not be classified as "blacks' stars") break down some barriers between H and L as they commingle both. Greater frequency of blacks, Hispanics and women as news anchors, television and movie actors and mainstream writers have also assisted in softening the walls which stand between High and Low speech in the United States.

This growing consciousness that men and women have significantly different usage of the same language[327] fosters study of gender and language.[328] The observed variations can be seen as pointers to what we can learn about how sex differences, societal norms and a host of other influences subtly adapt speech choices: vocabulary, tonality, inflection and force. [329]

Women especially have been disconcerted by their heightened sense that language often leaves them out, deliberately or by implication. "Women's words are censured, misrepresented, ridiculed and eliminated in a male-dominated society. . . ."[330] This censorship in matters religious is what I call holy blindness. The churches cannot imagine that women will have anything of merit to contribute and perhaps know that women's speech will tear at the fabric of male domination. "Censorship works to repress new questions in order to prevent the emergence of unwanted insight. . . . Relegating the theological question of God-talk in relation to women's flourishing to the periphery of serious consideration in academy, church and society is an instance of this phenomenon. It is the refusal of insight. . . ."[331]

For a considerable time only a few voices were raised in protest, with many women sensing but not being able to articulate their feelings of discomfiture as the language they spoke expressed a somewhat different reality than that of which they had previously been aware.

All this information on High and Low language leads us to an understanding that when women speak of God in High language (the permissible language of the Bible, and the ambo) we are often strangled by insufficient or impermissible vocabulary to describe our own experience, our own discovery of the presence of God in our lives.

Mary Daly calls this inadequate language taken as adequate. and calls us to take back language, to have new speech while using old words, stripping them of their patriarchal, Biblical meanings and "remeaning" them by using them in new contexts which reflect new experience.[332]

All of these experiences of language need be coupled with one more, women's silence. Forced silence in the secular and in the religious milieu is just as powerful as the language spoken. All of our time of struggle to be self-determining we have been stifled. Our work has often seemed to have no historical context because our sisters who came before have been silenced.[333] As we have seen, men name, men speak High language which is the language of scripture. Paul's *dicta*[334] on women speaking in the assembly have been used as a mute for two thousand years.[335] Elisabeth Schüssler Fiorenza, calling women the "silenced majority," comments that "Women's theological silence in the church is still reinforced today. . . . Although women can study theology, we almost never become professors at influential theological schools and faculties. Women are excluded from preaching and articulating church policy or doctrine. . . . No feminist theologian speaks with official 'teaching authority.'"[336] We have been forced to accept the ways of naming God, in fact, all things sacred, which have been prescribed by men for two thousand years and more.[337]

WHEN NAMES STOP WORKING ✪

Even to articulate the fact that a certain way of naming no longer works is a revolutionary act.

**I just have a terrible time believing in that merciless male God. I am praying toward a more loving and relating God. I really believe that God is involved with us and is not uninterested in our happiness.

**In order to keep being in relationship with God, I really had to find new images which I could picture as I prayed. I feel so much more loved and cared for than the idea of God the Father implies for me.

As names, and the meanings in their symbol sacks, less and less express experienced reality, they fade from speech. Names stop working gradually if they begin to loose contact with human understanding. "If the idea of God does not keep pace with developing reality, the power of experience pulls people on and the god dies, fading into memory."[338]

Societal change and growth in the theology surrounding women and God has led many of us to reexamine familiar God-language and find it perturbing. We began to see ourselves more distinctly as full subjects of salvation history and as imaging of God and we began to reevaluate what we heard in the pew.

Just as in the secular world, males (now ordained ones) responded to women's sense of exclusion from the naming and symbol system with patronization, then explanation (God transcends sexuality) and finally, in many situations, anger. The churches have not only societal pressure on their side but also the long-understood arrangement of sacral reality in which God has been perceived as male and males have been perceived as the ordained spokesmen of God. (See Mary Daly's "If God is male, then male is God.") Elizabeth Johnson points out, "To even the casual observer it is obvious that the Christian community ordinarily speaks about God on the model of the ruling male human being. . . . The difficulty does not lie in the fact that male metaphors are used, for men too are made in the image of God. . . . Rather the problem consists in the fact that these male terms are used exclusively, literally and patriarchally."[339]

The idea of God being like a Father became God being a Father, and thus sanctifying every father as being more god-like than any other person. We spoke before of the power of symbols which underlie our every use of language. Symbols are effective, symbols work.

Nowhere in contemporary literature has the effectiveness of symbol power been so poignantly expressed as in the heartbreaking expression of man's inhumanity to women, *The Color Purple*. Celie has written letters to God for years, until she finally begins to see the connection between whom she is writing to and who is abusing her.

"What God do for me? I ast. . . . He give me a lynched daddy, a crazy mama, a low-down dog of a step pa and a sister I probably won't ever see again. Anyhow, I say, the God I been praying for and writing to is a man. And act just like all the mens I know. Trifling, forgitful and lowdown. . .

"All my life I never care what people thought bout nothing I did, I say. But deep in my heart I care about God. What he going to think. And come to find out, he don't think. Just sit up there glorying in being deef, I reckon.

"He big and old and tall and graybearded and white. He wear white robes and go barefooted.

"Blue eyes? she ast.

"Sort of bluish gray. Cool. Big though. White lashes, I say.

. . . Ain't no way to read the bible and not think God white, she say. Then she sigh. When I found out I thought God was white, and a man, I lost interest. You mad cause he don't seem to listen to your prayers. Humph! Do the mayor listen to anything the colored say? . . . Here's the thing, says Shug. The thing I believe. God is inside you and inside everybody else. You come into the world with God. But only them that search for *it* inside find it. And sometimes it just manifest itself even if you not looking, or don't know what you looking for. Trouble do it for most folks, I think.

". . . (U)s talk and talk about God, but I'm still adrift. Trying to chase that old man out of my head. I been so busy thinking bout him I never truly notice nothing God make. Not a blade of corn (how it do that?) not the color purple (where it come from?) Not the little wildflowers. Nothing.

"Man corrupt everything, says Shug. He on your box of grits, in your head and all over your radio. He try to make you think he everywhere. Soon as you think he every-where, you think he god. But he ain't. Whenever you trying to pray, and man plop himself on the other end of it, tell him to get lost, say Shug. Conjure up flowers, wind, water, a big rock.

"But this is hard work, let me tell you. He been there so long, he don't want to budge. He threaten lightening, floods and earthquakes. Us fight. I hardly pray at all. Everytime I conjure up a rock, I throw it. Amen."[340]

** I Don't want to hear HE anymore. I've had HE shoved down my throat all my life.

**It makes me so sad that all my growing up I got forced to practice naming God as male. Now I am over fifty and I am working to expand my names for God but it is so hard. I have wonderful ones on which I concentrate when I pray but old mad God is still stuck in the back of my head and not leading me toward God but reminding me regularly of fear and sin and negativity.

**God as male is a controlling God, one which wants absolute obedience rather than love. Just like so many men and priests I've known.

**I really need to work on my idea and prayer of how I image God. The old white guy with the long beard and the big stick still lives in my head.

**My prayer life is wounded everytime I have that image of God the Father pop into my head, because I have very few personal positive images of fathers in my life. My father frightened me to death growing up. He was an angry, repressed, abusive person who didn't like women much, and practiced ridiculing my mother and myself. I never heard anyone refer to God as anything but the male God, and as an adult I was very relieved to find that other women and men, too, have a hard time with the Father image because of their own experiences with fathers. I have begun to work on God my mother and it is a very warm image for me, but the practice of it is hard. I sometimes feel like I am doing something wrong.

The respondents, like Celie, are resisting the symbol of God the Father and, in fact, the maleness of God. Exclusive use of this image has limited their understanding of the goodness of God, has hurt women, and in fact, has not led them toward the loving God of Jesus' teaching.

Speaking of God only in patriarchal terms denies the use of any feminine metaphor for the divine while encouraging the domination of men over women and therefore making the terms used diabolic or anti-symbolic, because they point away from liberation and toward female submission.

SO WHY DO WE CARE? ✪

**I know God is there, I know that God loves me. I just have to find God and listen to God's voice in my life without it always being a male God that I hear.

**We in our group have all commented on how wonderful it would be to be able to publicly name the loving God we know, the accepting relating God. Our whole lives and the lives of those around us would be so much healthier if we accepted rather than judged, cared rather than criticized, and if we did it because we believed in a God who we saw as truly that way.

**How will I teach my daughters and particularly my son about a more peaceful God unless we find and practice that naming of God ourselves so that we are able to show that God to our children?

**Boy, you only have to start reading the feminist theologians and pacifists to begin to see the connection between how we name God and what we have done to the world. Read Matthew Fox, read Mary Daly, and then you hear what comes out of your mouth in naming God. The thing I can't get over is that even the institution admits that God is not male, but they sure practice that. I know who benefits from that sort of description getting drummed into us all the time. Makes me sick. I know She's there loving me, and loving our world. I intend to practice She She She every day for the rest of my life. Even if I pray all day it's probably not ever going to make up for the damage that he he he did to me, and to all of us.

The need for God present in life has led many women, and men for whom the male-only image is hurtful or insufficient, to continue to seek new naming even when imagination stumbles and fear overtakes.

Some believe that this move forward is the breath of God as the wind at our backs, pressing us on. The work on God-naming or, to borrow from Mary Daly's much-used and excellent phrase, "naming toward God" (which signifies that in all our human language we cannot corral God with names and symbols, capture God's immensity with words). We have come to know that the male God does not work. In fact, *HE* impedes. The traditional speech has strong symbol value which no longer serves us well, and we go into the desert in order to find new words which speak to our experience. As long ago as 1973, Mary Daly called to us, "To exist humanly is to name the self, the world and God. The 'method' of the evolving spiritual consciousness of women is nothing less than this beginning to speak humanly—a reclaiming of the right to name. The liberation of language is rooted in the liberation of ourselves."[341]

Naming and renaming God does not change God; it changes us. This naming of the unnamable God, this holy mystery, the God who cannot be captured in a bushel basket of nouns, is our attempt to put language to the infinitesimal perceptions we glimmer of God's compassion, creative power, loving relationship to us. Beginning the unsteady, never finished search for—at best—feeble word pictures of God we feel the limits of language. We also glimpse the wonder of that most human of activities, naming what we experience, and giving credence to that naming.

What we know, no matter how dimly, is that the ways of naming that holy mystery speak volumes about what we value in our lives and in our world. Even those who do not believe in God are in many ways shaped by the symbol sack of the word *God* now offered by believers. That host of images tells what is considered perfect and worthy of imitation in our society.

As long as the society worships the war-loving god, it is free to imitate that god, and is encouraged to do so. As long as a society affirms an image of a divisive, conquering, male god, then the society is going to choose that god to emulate. For only women to disassociate by disbelief is insufficient to solve society's firm grasp of this idolatry. It is of great benefit to men to be able to buy into God-power by resemblance. That resemblance continues to be used to justify division among peoples, ecological damage and the selfish use of the world and its peoples, for destruction which may be fatal to us all. To find and name a life-giving, relating God may not only free women but save our world.

"Since the symbol of God is the focal point of the whole religious system, an entire world order and world view are wrapped up with its character. Some views of the divine are perverted, so that devotion to this God leads to inhuman structures and behaviors. For example, God spoken of as a wrathful tyrant can be called upon to justify holy wars and inquisitional torture chambers. Language about God as universal creator, lover, and savior of all, on the other hand, moves believers toward forgiveness, care, and openness to inclusive community. The symbol of God *functions*, and its content is of the highest importance for personal and common weal or woe."[342]

The horrifying possibility of nuclear winter could not come from a population which truly worshipped God as Mother from whom life flows, if we saw the life of this earth and every thing on it as the physical being of God.[343] The rape and murder of women as an act of control, the abortions or infanticides of millions of females because of their gender, the murder of millions of women because men deemed them to be "witches" could not happen large scale in a faith community which genuinely saw women as fully image of the Creator.[344]

We consciously, unconsciously, subconsciously follow, emulate, take our power, our example from the God we worship. The God of masculinity, the male, controlling, distant, uncaring God who gives men power not only to name but also to fill the earth and sub-due it and have dominion (Gen 1:28), to stride with power over the earth has led us to this:

> "Masculinity has made of this world a living hell,
> A furnace burning away at hope, love, faith, and justice,
> A furnace of My Lais, Hiroshimas, Dachaus.
> A furnace which burns the babies
> You tell us we must make.
> Masculinity made "femininity," . . .
> Made our children go hungry,
> Made our mothers whores,
> Made our bombs, our bullets, our "Food for Peace," . . .
> Masculinity broke women and men on its knee,
> Took away our futures,
> Made our hopes, fears, thoughts and good instincts
> 'Irrelevant to the larger struggle,'
> And made human survival beyond the year 2000
> An open question."[345]

We need to "kill" the patriarchal God in order to stop the deeds done in His name, before it is too late for our earth, and for us who are dependent on her.

It will not be enough to search out ways of speaking of our God for our private prayer lives. The Spirit speaks names of healing which we must use publicly, shout from the roof tops, practice in ritual and live, live, live as if we believed these names are true.

WHAT IS RIGHT SPEECH TOWARD GOD? ✪

There is no single answer. Rather there are only the questions we ask ourselves as we move our naming away from the rusty old habits. It is exciting work. In practicing true naming rather than the (at least potentially) false naming of our past which names God male, we are praying new naming into existence. It is recognizing the holy image in each of us, as we incline toward God.

Some wisdom from Elizabeth Johnson: "It is not necessary to restrict speech about God to the exact names that Scripture uses, nor to terms coined by the later tradition. So long as the words signify something that does characterize the living God mediated through Scripture, tradition, and present faith experience, for example, divine liberating action or self-involving love for the world, then new language can be used with confidence. . . .

"It is a matter of the livingness of God. Given the inexhaustible mystery inherent in what the word God points to, historically new attempts at articulation are to be expected and even welcomed."[346]

Is the name sacred on your lips? Is it sacred in your heart? Do you feel yourself in the midst of the holy when you enunciate it?

Does the name name toward, even dimly, the encompassing wholeness of God? Does the naming expand or contract our knowledge of the divine?

Does the name discriminate against, or imply discrimination against one or more groups of people whom God created?

Does the naming call to mind division or (re)union?

Does it aim toward healing women and calling forth wholeness? "One criterion recurs as a touchstone for testing the truth and falsity, the adequacy and inadequacy, the coherence and incoherence of theological statements and religious structures. This criterion . . . is the emancipation of women toward human flourishing." [347]

Does the naming express the experience of women (and men)? "The language and images are saying that the process of maturing that fulfills each one of us personally is also what the world most needs from us at this time. A Native American teacher describes this as 'an unveiling of what is already inside of us. We are trying to form a new world now . . . and what is really new lies in that great womb where all possibilities are. We need to go in and bring it forth.'"[348]

Does the naming flow from being in communion with God, that is, is it a gift of the spirit of our own prayer life? Or do we use names which keep God at arm's length? "As long as we have to call God by general terms like 'The Almighty,' 'The Lord God,' as long as we have to put 'the' before the word to make it anonymous, to make it a generic term, we cannot use it as a personal name."[349]

Does the naming come from our maturity, or from dependency on the male God of our childhoods?

Does the name speak the promise of renewal and healing?

Does the naming bring forth fear or love? Are we even afraid to practice naming toward God, paralyzed by the possibility of getting God wrong? Nancy Hardesty writes, "Calling on God is not a long distance telephone call in which the matter of one wrong digit could connect us with Hong Kong. We do not even have to know the right area code or zip code to contact God! . . . All we need to do is turn to God and open our-selves. . . ."[350]

Probably a dozen other questions also speak to right speech for our loving divine. These are only a few to bend our mind and prayer, like a new green shoot leaning toward the sun.

SO HOW DO THE PARTICIPANTS IN WOMENEUCHARIST NAME TOWARD GOD? ✪

** We avoid male pronouns/nouns for the Deity unless we also include female pronouns/nouns.

**We reduce references to the male when speaking of God, and make other references inclusive, brothers and sisters, Creator God, Spirit, prime force.

**No one is held to any image.

** We use only inclusive Divine and human terms.

** We always adapt language to make it inclusive.

** We don't use material in which language needs adapting.

**We only use people and God descriptions which are gender inclusive.

** If we need to adapt language we try to be open to one another. There are some men who occasionally come to our group and we try to be very careful not to offend.

** The effort to adapt language is part of the effort to break away from patriarchy and help us to focus on what unites us rather than what divides us.

** We avoid all names, pronouns which demean by exclusion. The Church has no idea how many women have felt damaged and angered by not being included, angered that there is so little effort to expand our language to include everyone. It is like standing at the banquet and being only casually tossed a crust of bread, and then treated as if we have no right to expect any more.

**We are in the process of adapting and using non-sexist language. It is great to be free from the regular liturgical routine. I think we internally image God as is good for our individual journeys.

** We always use inclusive language, we do not use Father or Son.

     We use Energy, Circle, Beauty,

** "God, Creator, redeemer and Spirit." We either avoid using gender pronouns or use them inclusively.

**We tend to de-personify the Creator; we do acknowledge and pray in the name of

Jesus the Son, we de-gender, depersonify the Spirit.

** I try to search for the basics in Scripture when I choose the ways I will name God in our liturgies, especially in the Scriptures as newly revisioned by feminist theologians.

The adjectives which are used, and which bear remembering during this chapter are: inclusive, diverse, sensitive, non-sexist, non-judging, non-demeaning, Scriptural and expansive. I find frequently that "non-sexist and inclusive" mean that women are not demeaned or excluded. There seems to be among some of the respondents a naming of God as female, in contravention of their own statements of inclusivity. There were also many responses which did not claim inclusivity and did not practice it, labeling toward God as Mother and Goddess and She. This is not a bad way of naming, but if we are to claim inclusivity then we need practice it.

What we do need to avoid is the trap of idolatry of one image at the expense of all others. The benefit of feminine naming is that we are encouraging the stretch of imagination which greatly enlarges our perceptions of the divine, and as we grow in confidence we can share that gift with others. There are never enough symbols of the divinity's goodness and love, and the usage of female ones directs our gaze toward our worthiness of signing some aspect of the subtlety of God.

Jesus filled his talk about God with rich and varied namings, saying God was like a woman who had lost a coin, like a shepherd, like a sower of seeds, as well as like a father.[351]

**He named from experience, he named healing names, and relational ones.

WomenEucharist respondents also have rich and varied naming. Of all returned questionnaires two reported only two ways the respondents named toward God. The average number of namings was five and there were several that had over ten, with one reported thirteen ways of addressing the divine. This tallies with the findings of Winter, Stokes and Lummis, "Our data show that the great majority of women respondents are inclined to have shifting, changing images of God and not one or two clear, definite images."[352]

IMAGES OF MOTHER/PARENT; DISCOVERING OUR EXPERIENCE ✪

**Our Mother, Mother . . . As a group we see God as Mother and Father . . . In the womb of God our Mother . . . El Shaddai . . . Creator and sustainer of life . . . Mother . . . We use God our Mother . . . We often use God images of Mother Spirit or Mother Creator . . . I like Mother God . . . Mother and Father . . . We call God parent or Mother and Father . . . Mother . . . Birthgiver . . . Nurturer . . . our Mother and Father.

Meinrad Craighead says in the introduction to *The Mother Songs: Images of God the Mother*, "God the Mother came to me when I was a child and, as children will do, I kept her a secret. We hid together inside the structures of institutional Catholicism. . . . This personal vision of God the Mother, incarnated in my mother and her mother, gave me, from childhood, the clearest certainty of woman as the true image of Divine Spirit. . . . believed in her because I experienced her."[353]

Meinrad speaks in the voice of women everywhere when she says, "I experienced. . . ."

God our Mother just will not die, no matter how frequently patriarchy tries to kill her off. Perhaps it is because we all bear the mark of our first connection to life-giving creativity, our navels. And these we get from our mothers, to whom we were tethered by an umbilicus which brought us from a speck to fruition. In the watery world which is our mother's first gift we *experience* all of developmental creation from tiny sea life to fully human.

Meister Eckhart says that God's own gift is to constantly give birth. Every moment God is in labor with her own creation.

Certainly the Old Testament has God often in that maternity bed: "You were unmindful of the Rock that begot you, You forgot the God who gave you birth."[354] This is the picture Isaiah paints: "But now, I cry out as a woman in labor, gasping and panting."[355]

We have always had the knowing of Mother-like God, from the time of the Old Testament to the days of Mechtild of Magdeburg, who saw that "The Trinity is like a mother's cloak wherein the child finds a home and lays its head on the maternal breast," to our contemporary Ed Hays who prays,

"In the beginning, Lord God,
You alone existed: eternally one
yet pregnant in the fullness of unity.
Full to overflowing."[356]

Age after age we call to our Mother. We know she is there, though she has been variously denounced, drowned, and crisped at the stake. We have reached out our hands and touched her breast and drunk her milk and, even though those nursing memories are dim, they call us back because they were life-blooming when we knew ourselves safe and growing. Perhaps knowing still pulses in our spiritual DNA.

"What unites all people of all time is not that we are all mothers but that we have all been born of a mother who was born of a mother who was born of a mother.

"Through reverent feelings for their own mothers, early matristic peoples conceived of the all-inclusive sacred lifeway . . . of the Great Goddess, who was for them merely an extended Model and image of Everywoman and Perfect Mother."[357]

What images do we summon when we name God as like a Mother? Julian of Norwich announces, even of Jesus, "Our savior is our true Mother, in whom we are endlessly born and out of whom we shall never come. . . . The mother can give her child to suck of her milk, but our precious Mother Jesus can feed us with himself, and does most courteously and most tenderly, with the blessed sacrament, which is the precious food of true life. . . ."[358]

This is a mental picture in contradiction. It catches us by surprise. Yet consider the characteristics of mothering: gentleness, nurturance, forgiveness, creativity, protection, full-breasted feeding, comfort, circling of arms around us, acceptance, safety, saving.

Like Julian, many ascribe these very traits to maternal parenting. It should not surprise us that the visible signs of maternity, bulging bellies, full breasts, remind us of the creative urge of God, through which we all have come to be.

Miriam Therese Winter has a beautiful song which calls forth this memory in us.

"Mother and God, to You we sing:
wide is Your womb, warm is Your wing.
In You we live, move, and are fed,
sweet, flowing milk, life-giving bread.
Mother and God, to you we bring
all broken hearts, all broken wings."[359]

Isaiah speaks "For thus says the LORD: . . . As a mother comforts her son, so will I comfort you."[360]

So, what became of the comforting nurturance of paternal love? There is much study being conducted in anthropology about our earliest ancestors and the kinds of lives they led. Here is one construct:

"Our earliest ancestors who revered the Great Goddess as Mother Nature —as Mistress of the Animals and Mistress of the Plants—were transient gatherers and foragers who lived intimately with . . . animals, birds, trees, . . . They roamed from one camp to another according to the availability of food. Since there was no one particular place where they resided, . . . *home was wherever the mothers of a group were situated at a particular time,* caring for children and old people. . . . The mothers did not rule over others or dominate them as fathers have dominated and ruled over others in patriarchy, often acquiring and maintaining their prestige and authority through physical force, intimidation and raw power. Mothers were accorded prestige and authority by their very existence, . . . by their automatic centrality to everyone's life.

"Saying that mothers were *central to society* in matristic cultures means that the values intrinsic to women's roles as life-givers, life-enhancers, and life-sustainers set the PATTERNS and standards of cooperation, nurturance, and mutual support that determined all other values and priorities in peoples' lives. . . . And with the sharing, nurturing. . . . model as the prevailing PATTERN of both male and female lives, our kind survived and thrived in cooperation with each other and our environment—with plants, other creatures and the earth—*until the advent of patriarchy.*

" As archetypal reversal occurred beginning about nine thousand years ago with the advent of pastoralism—with the first controlling of animals, the first conception of other creatures as beneath-Self—but the proliferation of hierarchical thinking and warring began with most effect only about five thousand years ago. The big cultural and philosophical change at that time consisted basically in going from viewing the world as whole, as non-hierarchical and interrelated—as if Self were always Other in some real way—to viewing the world as divided into dyads of opposition, pitting *dominators* (a few powerful men) versus the *dominated* (all Others, including weaker men).

"With dominator behaviors came a hierarchical, dualistic value system—including the warrior sky-father gods that model, and thereby justify and sanctify, dominator behaviors. This philosophical system—with its religious icons—supports struggle and opposition-to-others-and-Nature as the Ideal to strive for, as the prevailing PATTERN and Model for human lives."[361]

To turn the question of Professor Higgins around, "Why can't a man be more like a woman?" Or to phrase it differently, will men, if they are able to image God as mother, be able then to find in themselves the traits of nurturance, care, peacefulness, at-oneness with others, deep relationship, which can save the Body of God which is our biosphere from another crucifixion?

When we call God Mother/Father or Parent we enter into the mystery of how both can be one and like God.

Just as for thousands of years the ascendancy of the Old Testament God was the model for paternal parenting, now (only 2000 years late) we are called to image the maternal parenting of Jesus-God, so that we have a shifted symbol towards which we can worship.

"Behind every new spirituality and any creative re-visioning of the world—at the root of any real theology—is an experience of God. Yet every religious experience comes from a meeting with a new and challenging face of God in one's own time and social situation. I suspect that although it is imperative . . . for feminist theologians to develop new interpretive paradigms that function to liberate people, only women's *experience* of God can alter or renew our God images and perhaps our doctrine of God." [362]

What is it that we bring to consciousness when we see the parenting of God? God-in-relationship is exactly what parenting implies. We have practiced far too long the non-relational model of fathering, which is distant, disinterested, uninvolved. Many of us have very limited experience of being fathered. Our fathers, many of them, went outside the home to work, and spent little time with their children, and we did not understand fathering in the tender way that Jesus meant when he spoke of God as his Father. The idea of God as a remote and punishing Father emerged as European society began to shift from an agricultural life-style in which the father was present, a visible and often equal care-taker.[363]

As we in American society inch away from dirty diapers and feeding as women's work, as we see more women in the work place and more men wearing babies in back-packs, we can begin to see again fathering as nurturance, *fathering-in-relationship*, and embrace again the cradling, playing, teaching father of Jesus' growing.

Numerous theologians speak to the need to reunderstand God in friendly relationship with us, quietly shelving the concept of the totally unrelated, distant Father, as being less authentic in our burgeoning understanding of the God whose very nature is love.

"Classical theism emphasizes in a one-sided way the absolute transcendence of

God over the world, God's untouchability by human history and suffering, and the all-pervasiveness of God's dominating power to which human beings owe submission and awe. Is this idea of God not the reflection of patriarchal imagination, which prizes nothing more than unopposed power-over and unquestioning loyalty? Is not the transcendent, omnipresent, impassable symbol of God the quintessential embodiment of solitary ruling male ego, above the fray, perfectly happy in himself, filled with power in the face of the obstreperousness of others? Is this not 'man' according to the patriarchal ideal? "[364]

It is the wholly lonely God whom we now begin to reach out to, only to find that God has ever and always longed for us. We tricked ourselves because by our own unfortunate imaging we have held back or turned away, temporally certain that we were only conditionally loved and in union.

**Creator . . . loving Maker . . . Creator . . . Source of All Being . . . I like Creator God best . . . Divine Creating Energy . . . Creator . . . Maker of all . . . Creator.

Carter Heywood, in a wonderful homily, has this marvelous picture:

"Various 'process' theologians suggest that God created us because God needed us to help God continue to become. It may be that God created us simply because it is the nature of God to create, or that God created us because God, having begun to 'come to life' Godself, realized that the only way to experience life would be to share it.

Long before Jesus, God made Godself known as One immersed in the affairs of being human. Human history was, in fact, sacred history, the story of God's own being moving in creation itself. . . .

"God will hang on the gallows . . .
God will be battered as a wife, a child, a nigger, a faggot.
God will judge with righteousness, justice, mercy those who batter, burn, sneer . . .
God will have a mastectomy.
God will experience the wonder of giving birth.
God will be handicapped.
God will run the marathon.
God will win.
God will lose. . .
God will be bursting free, coming to life, for
God will be who God will be." [365]

To understand our God as deeply intertwined, sublimely caring of our every experience, yet letting us freely respond to Godself and to our sisters and brothers is to begin to comprehend the heart of relationship between ourselves and God. We do not know a God who is care-less.

"Being related is at the very heart of divine being," Elizabeth Johnson writes, "God's being is not an enclosed, egocentric self-regard but is identical with an act of free communion, . . . At the deepest core of reality is a mystery of personal connectedness that constitutes the very livingness of God . . . the very nature of the holy mystery of God herself."[366]

In this loving communion WE uses

**Sister . . . friend . . . lover . . . caregiver . . . Eternally caring God . . . Calling Forth . . . Sister God . . . The one who connects all . . . Good Friend God . . . Brother Jesus . . . One with us . . . Blessed caregiver . . . Eternal lover . . . living healer . . . blessed peacemaker.

These namings reflect the loving relationship of God with us, the passionate friendship of the Creator, and also the best that exists in our human condition. They lift up to be mirrored those roles of women which have previously been seen as lowly service, and dignifies them publicly as God-like. They are sweet, non-threatening terms which can remind us all to reach out, image friendship, practice healing, be a lover. All this and also trust that God is present in our own experience.

Rosemary Radford Ruether reminds us that every theological statement, every verb and adjective we use can be judged as to whether or not it promotes the full humanity of women. If it does not it is not redemptive. [367]

When women begin in the liturgical circle to use words which sing of our own experience, our relationing, our sistering with and befriending of God we begin to blessedly be healed. It is not that God's arms have not been open, it is that we have not known that they were open to us.

One man writes, "I changed when my image of God changed.

"Unfortunately, the God I grew up adoring was German. My God was a self-righteous German who sat on his . . . judgment throne. . . my God could see all the mistakes and errors in everyone else. If my self-righteous God did not like what he saw in others, he could even separate himself from them by sending them to hell. And if my God could be a self-righteous German, then no matter how many healing prayers I prayed, I would probably never change. I became like the God I adored.

"But if my God doesn't treat people that way, I can't either. We find that a key to personal and social healing is healing our image of God."[368]

We remember again that symbols work because they "give rise to thought," they direct the eye, and beg the heart to follow. And follow we will the God whom we symbolize.

**Goddess . . . Goddess . . . goddess . . . god/ess . . . Goddess . . . the Goddess . . . Goddess . . . We name her Goddess, and I don't believe her to be a different God, she is still the Goddess who sent Jesus, the one of the Trinity, only more fully, better realized, in our lives. She is such a relief to me.

It seems wise to address the image of Goddess separately from image of our Mothering God. The feminine, nurturing qualities of the divine have been visible, though most often not stressed, in scripture. However, the concept of Goddess in a Christian world has often been linked to paganism, to falsehood, to sensuality and bodiliness from which a male god must rescue us. Naming the feminine Goddess must be heretical; She has been driven out. The demonization of the ancient Goddess seems to have paralleled the rise of the patriarch, in which a masculinized society required a God made in the likeness of human male, and that the feminine be driven out or taught as myth, beyond which we, thinking rational people, have progressed.

Androcentric education and religious training have led scholars to debase the Goddess. "Religious norms affect . . . consideration and interpretation of given data. This is subtly evidenced in the use of language as well. The Goddess tradition has been referred to as a 'cult' instead of a 'religion,' implying to the modern ear something less than acceptability . . . The female deity stories are considered 'myth,' . . . Given our linguistic bias, it is difficult for contemporary people . . . to take seriously the beliefs, symbols, and creation stories of ancient peoples . . . even when ancient writings on clay tablets or papyruses bear witness as the oldest religious stories of our species."[369]

We continue to ask ourselves, who benefits by a patriarchal God?

It is wise here perhaps to remember P.J. Fitzpatrick's suggestion quoted earlier: "to *look* rather than to say how things *must be."*

The amount of literature which has appeared in the last twenty years on Goddess is sufficient to tell us that She has never been expunged and is reemerging as a significant image of the divine, not just for women, but for all who seek speech and symbol of a divine who unites and heals.[370]

This experience of the divine is of the Source and Ground of all being. It is liberating, it is hopefilling, it is, above all, healing division and rejoining the body and the spirit as part of our whole gift. The expression of the divine does not dichotomize. Rosemary Radford Ruether says, "The God/ess who is the foundation . . . of our being and our new being embraces both the roots of the material substratum of our existence (matter) and also the endlessly new creative potential (spirit) . . . it leads us to the . . . harmonization of self and body, self and other, self and world. It is the *Shalom* of our being."[371]

Goddess points us toward and leads us to the original harmony of creation, and away from the alienating, divisive struggle of spirit vs. body, of human vs. earth, of male vs. female and masculine vs. feminine, of black vs. white vs. brown vs. yellow. Goddess liberates us toward rejoining ourselves to the body of God which is the earth and toward our sisters and brothers without judgment or domination.

What effect does the identification of the divine Goddess have in the lives of women?

**I never could see myself as the image of God until I began to image God as like me. When I came upon the term "Goddess" it made sense. This is the feminine present in creation, and the more I thought about it, and prayed it the more I felt comfort in the image.

**The symbol of the Goddess works in my prayer life. I am empowered to see my own place in the universe, instead of one that is merely derived from men related to a male God.

**I experience Goddess as the wonderful, healing power in the universe. This is the greatness of God lived out. I believe that Goddess signs the need to be brought together, rather than pushed apart, separated and angry. While I have known the war-like God I believe that Goddess calls us to heal and make peace.

** The male God with whom I was raised always held out violence as a way to peace. Odd to think about. For Goddess this way is unthinkable. If I pray to Goddess I am always being called to find peaceful solutions in which power-over plays no part. She leads me along right paths.

Women in great numbers are growing toward a personal experience of creative power and recognizing that this power is good, and therefore must reflect the Primary Creative Power. This inspiration goes best under the title of Goddess. In this way many women name how it is that the divine is directly available to us. Carol Christ comments, "The simplest and most basic meaning of the symbol of the Goddess is the acknowledgment of the legitimacy of female power as a beneficent and independent power . . . (a woman who names Goddess) is saying that the divine principle, the saving and sustaining power, is in herself, that she will no longer looks to men or male figures as saviors."[372]

Feminists understand the need for women to rediscover power in our own lives. This experience of personal free-agency is required not only for societal adulthood, but also for spiritual maturity. The power which we seek is power-with, not power-over and that is the potency of Goddess. Rae and Marie-Daly say, "A major ideological distinction between the tradition of the warrior god and the Goddess tradition is that the invaders defined power as 'power over,'—the power to take, the power to control—while the Goddess tradition honored power that gave life, 'power with,' power that acknowledged the natural rhythm of nature . . . . And so it is to this day."[373]

Some women believe that Goddess is the most powerful symbol of change for women, and one that is important to practice into comfortable speech. There is a need here for language planning which lets us practice safely new/old ways of naming. [374] This deliberate practice does direct our symbol sack away from the transcendent patriarch and toward an indwelling loving life-giver. It does not erase previous naming, but heals and builds on previous imaging. However we need to be aware that this language experience is not of a male-identified Godhead who has been softened up for our time by the addition of a few feminine characteristics. Such re-imaging would be dangerous, putting a benign mask on the God of patriarchy. [375] On the other hand, it is valuable to note Elisabeth Schüssler Fiorenza's comment, "The Goddess of radical feminist spirituality is not so very different from the God whom Jesus preached and whom he called 'Father.' In ever new images of life, love, light, compassion, mercy, care, peace, service, and community, the writings of the New Testament attempt to speak of the God of Jesus Christ, and of this God's life-giving power, the Holy Spirit. . . . in various ways (the NT authors) spell out that Jesus rejected all hierarchical forms of power."[376]

No, Goddess awareness focuses "on the power of experience, of connecting with the Goddess Within who gives birth to an awakened, empowered personal and communal response. The Goddess is immanent . . . in nature, in relationships in communities. She is *here*, an unconditional presence and power."[377]

As such, Goddess is salvational to a world where human life is often mean and short-lived, where materialism and pollution are rampant, where women, children, people of color are often valued only for their labor-potential and are objectified throw-aways. "Today our spirituality is rooted in experience and in story: the story of women, . . . the experience of the poor and oppressed of the world; the experience of the aging; the experience of the fear of nuclear holocaust and the far-reaching evils of nuclear buildup for the sake of national security, power, and domination; the experience of the woundedness of the earth and the environment."[378]

We live in a world where we have lost the feel of our basic connection to the ground of our being, to the seasons of our lives, to the cyclical nature of the earth and to the very passionate relationship of Creatrix to all that is. The Goddess calls us to remember, repair, and reconnect.

"Now She is reborn in our age, as the central focused energy, the 'from everlasting,' pleading, exhorting, demanding. To choose Her is to choose interdependence, nurturance, vulnerability, balance, integrity, compassion. To choose Her is to choose mystery and deep silent wisdom. To deny, delay, marginalize, or hold Her in quiet contempt is to choose death."[379]

We need to constantly recall that we emulate the divine whom we symbolize.

**Spirit, Ruah. . . Spirit of Love. . . Sophia . . . I use wind images . . . Great Spirit . . . Holy spirit of wisdom . . . We use Spirit a lot . . . The Spirit of God is the way our group most often names God . . . Divine Wisdom. . . Breath . . . Breath of God or ruah . . . Holy Spirit . . . Spirit of Jesus . . . Sophia Wisdom.

Wisdom and Spirit images are frequent in the praying experience of many respondents, continuing a tradition which finds its roots in Old Testament writing. The first appearance of the spirit is before our time began. When the earth was a void and chaos reigned " a mighty wind swept over the waters. Then God said, 'Let there be light' . . ."[380] This same breath of God mixes with the dirt of the planet to bring *ish*, first human, to being, providing us with the remarkable image of how much each of us is a miraculous mix of soil and spirit.

Is it the spirit who comes in the guise of angelic visitors to the tent of Sarah and Abraham who makes Sarah laugh, or is it the one who flames up before Moses as a bush which burns and is yet not consumed?

She also lives as guide and leader of the Israelites in the book of Exodus. There it is the wisdom of Shekinah who, enrobed as cloud and fire, led the people toward the land of milk and honey. It was her wisdom which sat in the tent with the people of God, it was out of her that the Lord spoke, it was her insight which led them through the desert.

Research indicates this most lovely and gracious Spirit has a long life among the peoples of the world. The Goddess religion and feminine deities of the Near East informed ancient Judaism. "Goddesses were worshipped as the givers of life, as creators and redeemers. They represented both social justice and harmony with nature. And they were an independent women's tradition, even if they were integrated into the Jewish tradition. From the third century BC onwards the figure of wisdom was revered in Jewish wisdom theology."[381]

She has a whole book dedicated to her qualities. The sages call her a tree of life, more precious than corals. She is named intelligent, holy, unique and subtle. They see her as clear and unpolluted, powerful and penetrating. The very breath of the power of God who orders all things well.

Isn't she a treat?

This tender picture of spirited goodness flows directly into the books of the New Testament. Is it the Spirit of God whom we find in angelic form in the house of Mary at Nazareth, inviting her to set foot on a challenging journey? Is it the Spirit who fills up Elizabeth and the child within her, leaping for joy? We find the spirit speaking to Joseph in dreams, calling the family into Egypt, for the safety of the child. It is the spirit, in the story of Jesus' baptism, which announces the pleasure of God. When Jesus' earthly work is complete he sends that Spirit to his friends and, with this inspiration in which fear died and liberation happened, the community which we call church was born.

The Gnostics believed that every one who joined them had been directly called by the Spirit, and as a result they had no hierarchy, since all were equal before God. In claiming the authority of the Spirit, one of the longest standing conflicts of the church was born, as the tradition became uneasy with and attempted to control the flow of the Spirit among the people of God.[382]

"But this initial clash between the authority of Church officials who mediate the message of God from the past with the free spirit of new ongoing, and uncontrolled 'revelations' was an instance of a fundamental type of conflict. . . . The hierarchically controlled church is faced with the accusation that it has maintained order and continuity at the price of suppressing or at least restraining the spontaneity and effervescence of the Spirit."[383]

Many women who called out to the spirit are people who had a sense of religious presence but were denied a role in the Church. For the generations preceding our own, Gerda Lerner points out, "It was precisely because they were weak, uneducated and simple, and because they were excluded from the great privilege of the priesthood, that God had chosen them as His instrument. . . ."[384] The Lord speaks to the mystic Hadewijch (c .1200),

> "it greatly honors Me.
> that unlearned lips should teach
> The learned tongues of My Holy Spirit."[385]

This kind of perception continues to be heard through the centuries. In the twentieth century we are still getting the same kind of statement.

In 1911, Hatty Baker was moved to comment sharply, "'The logical basis for male ascendancy is the resolute denial of the existence of a soul in women', Miss C. Hamilton recently wrote. It may be, it often is, sub-conscious, but male ascendancy is a striking feature of the ever man-filled pulpit, and although one hardly goes as far as to declare its logical basis to be the denial of the existence of a soul in women, yet it does seem as if it led to the denial of the out-pouring of the Holy Spirit—with all his accompanying gift of prayer, and prophesying to women."[386]

Elizabeth Johnson explains, "Divine Spirit is . . . the creative and freeing power of God let loose in the world. More than most terms for God's dynamism it evokes a universal perspective and signifies divine activity in its widest reaches."[387] Those widest reaches extend even into the lives of women. It is often the whisper that calls us forward and is also the wind at our backs pushing us on. This is the spirit which many have sensed when it seemed that other faces of God were turned away from them.

**I have truly begun to trust the spirit of God speaking in my heart and in the voices of other wise people. I am sometimes ashamed that I have turned away from this voice of goodness in the past because I worried about what other people might think, or because it didn't come from the Church.

**Without question it is the Spirit who gathers us together, and we name her as the one who leads us together to hear the meaning of Jesus' teachings in the scripture, and points us to the Creator.

**The experience of Spirit is so life-affirming to our group.

**We name her wisdom, and I believe that we are becoming wise women as we gather together and pray and celebrate. I have a new interior life, braver and humbler than ever before, but not afraid any longer, not afraid. This is Wisdom and she is wonderful.

**Not too much after my WomenChurch group began, while I was still not really sure I should be doing this, I quit smoking, and I began to breath better than I had in years. Every month I would go to WomenChurch and I found that I was "breathing spiritually" better than ever. I choose to celebrate both my kinds of better breathing on the Sunday evening each month that we pray together. I can not remember a time when I have felt healthier, in body or soul. This is the breath of God in my life.

**She is unrestricted, calling us away from our fear and toward greater freedom to do the work that needs doing.

**The experience of the Spirit is one of joy for us.

**I experience the spirit as very democratic. She/it doesn't just come to be present in cathedrals and synagogues, certainly not in Congress, though I believe she is there but often not listened to. I have found her in the Second Harvest where I work, and I have found her in my women's group—certainly!—and she comes and sits in my single mothers' support group, and I have heard her in the voices of other people in the simplest places.

**We believe the spirit helps us to be concerned about all life of this earth, not just about human beings. When I began to hear the spirit inside of me saying I am valuable, then I began to see the life of animals and plants as a deeply important part of creation. This insight (which I *know* is from the spirit!) has really helped me to treat life preciously.

**I feel the spirit in the call we all have to rediscover the preciousness of our planet, before it is too late. Our group is very aware of the flow of the seasons, the growth of plants and children and our own lives.

**I live near a polluted city where the air is sometimes bad. How we all are happy on the clear days when the wind has blown the pollution away and the skies are clear! We have used this in our group. It is something we all understand because we live with it and even sometimes cause it. The Spirit as wind in our own lives, it blows away the pollution of our spiritual lives, and lets us see and breath more easily. This was an image that really took hold!

These women speak of a vital breath, one which animates their spiritual lives. Such a model of the deep relationship between the God of our every breath and ourselves, the one in which we live and move and have our being, is wonderful because it is not only unmediated, it is also life-giving, not controlling. It undergirds the possibility that our every move and thought are held deeply in the breath of the Spirit blowing through us.

We already know this at a linguistic level. We have an idea and name ourselves inspired. We breathe and call it respiration. We plan together and in doing so we conspire or breathe with. Our very prayer lives we call spiritual, full of the spirit of God. Special people who call us forth are often described as high-spirited and when we have breathed our last we have expired. Our very spirits, and the Spirit of God within us has slipped away.

It is no wonder that WE participants find the Spirit so thoroughly present. The tradition of friendly spiritual presence in the difficult journeys of human kind, encouraging and guiding, is an experience with which WE can identify.

Women also name the Spirit as appealing to our need to heal the world physically, beginning by seeing our intimate connection to every living creature of God. The concept that we are all enspirited by the breath of God touches the growing sense of nonviolence and repair to which we are drawn.

The encounter is with the breath of God in living rooms and barrooms, in shelters and deserts and around the tables of sinners and it is a miracle. When women feel as outcasts and yet know that they are invited to do the work of God it can be because the breath of God breathes where it will, blowing down walls of false restriction and graceless division which separate the people of God.

This wind, forever old, is being felt as a breath of fresh air in WomenEucharist gatherings across the country. We are inspired.

Brother Jesus . . . Redeemer . . . Savior . . . Jesus Christ . . . Sanctifier . . . Christed One . . . Friend Jesus . . . Word . . . Jesus . . . Jesus the Christ . . . Child of God . . . life-giving Jesus . . . liberator from all oppression . . . .suffering Jesus . . . Jesus, like us in all but sin . . . Jesus of justice. . . .

Why Jesus at all?

It is, after all, Jesus himself who, through his choice of twelve males has been used to justify the exclusion of females from ordained ministry, and de facto, from much of the ministry and decision-making in the Church. *Inter Insigniores* declares immutable the position that Jesus, born as male, did not entrust the priesthood to women. The encyclical asserts that if the Church will not change it is because Christ wished it to be a certain way.[388]

This position, frequently restated, and the "male is God, therefore God is male" theology which is twisted through it, has driven many women from a relationship with Jesus, who has been presented as divine-male rather than divine-human and here to save females only indirectly.

Is Christian community a discipleship of equals, we ask, or is the "God of Judaeo-Christian revelation a male being who sent a divine male to save us, thus revealing the normativity of maleness and establishing the superiority of males in relation to females in the order of salvation"?[389]

There are many women who no longer claim Jesus because they find their experience of oppression in his church so powerful. The maleness of Jesus has been used to explain why women were witches and men were not.[390] Wars have been waged and millions destroyed under the banner of a male Christ.

This sexual idolatry is being challenged by women world-wide.[391] We might hark back for a moment to the "God Is Dead" controversy of the late 1960's. It is the Male Only God who is dying in the symbol sacks of women, being overlaid in part by the charismatic human JesusGod who must agonize over the destruction done in God's name.

In the midst of all this, the major study on women's spiritual experience (which draws information from women of many different Christian sects), *Defecting in Place,* says that the dominant image of a gendered experience of God is still Jesus.[392]

How is it possible to keep on choosing Jesus? "For most women . . . Jesus is associated with the gentlest images of God and is humanly helpful and accessible . . . it is the supportive qualities that prevail."[393]

In the list of names at the beginning of this section, the adjectives used are ones which move toward wholeness and healing rather than towards judgment and desolation.

**It is through Scripture study which liberated the stories of Jesus from repressiveness that I can still claim Jesus in my life. I, as an active feminist, am delighted to be able to say that.
**Our group names Jesus, and so do I. For a long time we were into only using feminine images, and Jesus was reserved only to the consecration. We are now seeking the feminine, healing ways in Jesus and finding it a comforting place to be.
**Our group works with the homeless in a soup kitchen, and it is Jesus who had no where to lay his head whom we name often, as we see him so visibly in the food line. The wood cut of Jesus silhouette which the Catholic Worker uses is the one we worship.

Jean Vanier speaks of Jesus the Healer in a way which many women may understand, "Jesus manifests himself as He walks through Judea, when He comes to give sight to the blind, to enable the lame . . . to walk and the deaf to hear. . . . All these are essentially symbols of something much deeper. He opens the eyes of the heart. . . .

"The message is for the wounded and the little ones, the poor ones, those who are awaiting the liberator and the good news."[394]

As long as women continue to see themselves as embattled and demeaned in culture and religion, Jesus can be prayed to as an equalizer, defender, protector, as a person who contravened unjust law and came to bring a new covenant in which women can be liberated.

In the words and stories of Jesus, a love of the land and the water can be found. Jesus prepares food, converses with women, cares about children. He consistently enters into the daily order of people's lives, their hunger, their illnesses, their sadness, and while feeding, healing, comforting (all seen as the work of women), Jesus identifies the connection between the life of the world and the love of the Creator. Jesus does not stand outside the pain of the world.

Joyce Anderson-Reed writes:

"Jesus was
manipulated,
stepped on,
violated,
abused,
annihilated so as to be forgotten and replaced.

And why did this happen to him?
After all, he's not a woman.
After all, he's the Son of God.

Imagine.
My vulnerability
and Jesus' vulnerability
intersect
at the point of womanhood. . . .

Now,
if I have validity as a woman before Christ,
Then
my gifts have validity for ministry,
For
Christ affirms me:

My daughter, your faith has set you free."[395]

**I almost never pray to Christ. I pray to Jesus. The difference for me is that I have learned most from the way Jesus *lived*, and I am most interested in the life and teaching of Jesus. This doesn't mean that I don't think he is God. But his death and resurrection are of less import to my daily life.

**We name savior and sanctifier, but really see this in terms of our lived experiences. By teaching a way of living, forgiving and healing his life moves into our own. I don't think we need to be "saved" at the time of our deaths, we need it every day.

**I reject the way that "Christ" has been taken over by a male world, but I can deeply identify with the spirit of Jesus, a carpenter who came to teach and model a life which reflects the love of the Creator.

**The spirit of Jesus lives in our lives. It is this spirit who joins with us as we gather for Eucharist, it is this spirit whom I know is with me, and with all of us every day.

This liberating model is named Jesus-Sophia by Elizabeth Johnson, "God who is Spirit . . . is present yet again through the very particular history of one human being, Jesus of Nazareth. The one who is divine love, gift, and friend becomes manifest in time in a concrete gestalt, the living, gifting, and befriending first-century Jewish carpenter turned prophet. According to the witness of Scripture, Jesus is a genuine Spirit-phenomenon, conceived, inspired, sent, hovered over, guided, and risen from the dead by her power. . . . Through his human history the Spirit who pervades the universe becomes concretely present in a small bit of it . . . Jesus is Emmanuel, God with us."[396]

The women of this study seem to be facing toward the Spirit of Jesus whose presenting characteristics are forgiveness, teaching, making holy, and freeing. This is the divine human encounter, which stresses liberation into love. This Jesus chose an unorthodox path, centering himself in the love of the Spirit instead of the social convention of his time. The radical life which flowed from this choice is the model from which women, often bowed by convention, can find our own holy patterns.

So what can we conclude? The subtle and constant implant of male *imago Dei* has been deeply harmful to women, who have few symbols which lead them toward witnessing to their own worthiness as a channel for thought about the mystery of the divine. Waiting no longer, numerous women are practicing their own language-planning, accustoming their ears and their prayer and that of their sisters to symbols, words and phrases which evoke the deity present in nature, in creation and in the feminine self.

✪✪✪✪✪✪

HOW DOES IT FEEL?

FORETHOUGHT ✪

This chapter addresses several issues posed in the questionnaire. All of them revolve around the personal responses, the feelings, which are evoked as we join others to celebrate Eucharist. I first inquire about the ways in which WE circles meet the spiritual needs of women seeking alternative ritual. Then I ask about uncertainties or misgivings which women may harbor as they attempt to step out of the habit of previous worship styles, and whether these actions are seen as radical or revolutionary. Finally I ask about fear and rejoicing, and other emotions which this new path may bring forth.

✪✪✪✪✪

*Blessed are You
who call us out
from the cocoon of comfort and contentment
to embark upon that unique path
which You have set forth
for each of Your sons and daughters.[397]

*Strong sisters who have walked with me,
and wept and laughed and soared with me,
Can we not yet on this life's plane
reach out, and up and up again
until by reaching, soaring, searching
at last we find the prize of living life
through women's eyes?

And then by Love and Faith and Grace
we'll share with other waiting hearts
the treasure of this Women's Place.[398]

*When we do not know what to do, confronted with challenges that baffle and frighten us, we have to rehearse in the dark . . .We have then to improvise on the basis of gut feelings, following primal motivations . . .We need to shift our magic circles and redefine the sacred.[399]

How do we recover, discover and imagine what our spiritual needs are? The catalogues of contemporary publishers are full to overflowing with titles addressing women's spirituality. And yet, and yet—the quest continues among ordinary women to follow the thread of our own spiritual lives, which may or may not be like those described in the press.

In a lovely word picture, Andrea Cook Cockrell says:

"God wants to hold you up and
Listen to the sound the wind makes
Blowing through you,
Will teach that sound to you as your own
The only thing that makes you different." [400]

It will take us a generation at least, probably considerably more, to shed the cloak of male spirituality, the one-size-fits-all approach, in which many of us were muffled, to teach us the things which make us different in the life of God. The freedom to scrutinize others' prescribed ways of human-divine relationship comes first. WE seeks the light-hearted autonomy in which to imagine ourselves questing toward God. It's like having the liberty to examine piece by piece, a wardrobe picked out for us, yes, and worn by us all our lives. But do we really like these outfits? Does each article fit? Do they chafe, or itch? Am I willing to chance nudity or rags until I find my own spiritual wardrobe? Must I gather my own fibers, weave my own fabric, in order to get a spiritual garment? Will I do it alone or are there others who will help me? Will one simple outfit of my own choosing be a happier fit than a whole closetful of someone else's?

We are entering the age in which we may select our spiritual wardrobes. We know what the patterns are; many of them we have used. Now we come to examining with the eye of our souls what is really our own. It is uncertain time. Throwing out the old may lead to feeling spiritually naked. It takes courage. A delightful model might be Francis of Assisi, who, called by the Spirit to heal the church which was in ruins, stripped off all his garments, including his breeches, and trusted that all and anything which might be required would be provided through the love of God.

What we can do is listen to the pattern stories of other women. Free of statements which demand our own sense of obligation, we are called to define what our spiritual needs are and how they are to be (ad)dressed. A personally chosen spiritual life comes from the willingness to try on and select or discard many spiritual outfits, listening for spirit-sent affirmation, hoping for the courage to discover what fits us best.

Carol Christ says, "The current interest in feminine perception of the ultimate stems from a widespread sensing that women's stories have not been adequately told. Women have lived in the interstices between inchoate experiences and the shapings given to experience by the stories of men. In a very real sense, women have not experienced their own experiences."[401]

We work on practicing ourselves into a spiritual reality which we recognize as our own and God's together, because it fits like a second skin. Many women share this un/dressing room with us. They support us as we experiment. We support them. Their choices will not be exactly like ours; after all, there are as many "spirit-shapes" as there are body types. Yet no doubt there will be similarities.

Be willing to try on a lot of outfits. Look in your soul mirror often. Remember that this process takes time. Keep mindful that the quest should not be speedy. The journey itself is at least half of what we are about. Be patient with yourself, as the spirit is being patient with each of us. Look for the divine in the far-away and the near-at-hand. God is present in the previously unknown and also the right-here, right-now. Gertrud Mueller Nelson says what so many have said before, "The religious experience, the 'epiphany' we all long for, may be so utterly a part of our daily lives that we may be looking elsewhere, traveling great distances only to discover what was truly close at hand." [402] Trust, trust, trust the spirit of God available in our own experience and be willing to ask and honestly answer the questions this chapter addresses, "What is my spiritual response?" and "Does this better fit my spiritual needs?"

These may be the two most polite and important questions which can be placed before anyone in the community, particularly women. Women have often been metaphorically gagged by the institution of the church. Synods, conferences, all manner of councils have met without us. Our input (and the input of the Spirit speaking through us) is not sought. Decisions are promulgated which bear tremendous weight in the lives, physical and spiritual, of women without any effort to engage us in the process. This is an insult to the human family. This book and others which touch on like areas would not be necessary if women had been asked all along within the assembly, "What is your personal response (to any matter of concern)?" and, "Does this fit your spiritual needs?" And then the assembly needs to listen attentively and respectfully as someone who is *imago dei* expresses her experience.

Even if the assembled community demonstrates no interest whatsoever in the way we incline toward God and God toward us we need to learn *to ask ourselves* the questions again and listen respectfully to spirit and self and the dialogue within.

What is spirituality? Ann Carr gives us a good launching spot, "Spirituality is expressed in everything we do. It is a style, unique to the self, that catches up all our attitudes: in communal and personal prayer, in behavior, bodily expressions, life choices, in what we support and affirm and what we protest and deny. As our deepest self in relation to God, to the whole, and so literally to everything, spirituality changes, grows, or diminishes in the whole context of life . . . it bears the character of grace as lifted beyond previous levels of integration by a power greater than our own."[403]

This is a splendid definition. It is non-sexist. It can drape safely around women and men alike. The deepest self in relation to God—not mediated, not separated and regulated. Unique to self, it has personality at its core, one's own and God commingled. As so many women already know, spirituality is not a separate event, enclosed in the religion box, and brought out a few minutes every day, or week. Mary Jo Weaver says, "Spirituality is rooted in desire. We long for something we can neither name nor describe, but which is no less real because of our inability to capture it with words."[404] One of our responders speaks of the "mystery and magic of God." Our spirituality is enfleshed in each thought and action, belief and response. God is present and entwined in every connection and relationship, and our spirituality reflects that.

Beyond this, what additional phrases would we use to understand the concept of *feminist* spirituality? And is it even fair to ask that question?

If it is as humans that we relate to God, then being male or female should not be definitive in that relationship. Women have wished for centuries that the churches genuinely honored Paul's observation that "in Christ there is neither male nor female." However, human comes in two different packages, and it is through our individual experiences within these packages that we tread the path toward the Holy Mystery. It is this casting of genetic lot which shapes the experience of our spirits in relation to God, and therefore shapes our expression.

There are numerous definitions. The work of Sandra Schneiders yields this: "First, feminine spirituality is both rooted in and oriented toward *women's experience,* especially their experiences of disempowerment and of empowerment. . . . Second, feminist spirituality is deeply concerned with the reintegration of all that has been dichotomized by patriarchal religion . . . the fundamental reintegration is that of body with spirit. . . .

"Very closely related to the emphasis on the goodness and holiness of the body is a third characteristic, a profound concern with non-human nature. . . .

"A fourth characteristic . . . is its rejection of cerebral, rationalistic, and abstract approaches to religious participation.

"A final, but perhaps most important, characteristic . . . is that from the very beginning it has involved commitment to the intimate and intrinsic *relationship between personal growth and transformation and a politics of social justice.*"[405] As we explore the spiritual responses of women to the celebration of the sacrament of thanksgiving, let us note whether and how the threads of feminist spirituality unwind through them.

So, what are our personal spiritual responses in all those WomenEucharist celebrations which occur in apartments and meeting areas and family rooms across the United States?

THE PRESENCE OF THE DIVINE ✪

This is what respondents write about the encounter with God:

**I find my group and our celebration connect me in a very real way to the mystery of God.

**I take a lot of time to reflect before choosing a theme. My reflections lead to faith in God's presence among us being very powerful.

**This keeps me in touch with the feminine face of God.

** This is foundation and celebration of what I have come to believe God wants. Just one more step in my claiming my baptism freely and believing I am part of God's family.

**This group helps me feel united with Christ and others. I feel grateful and indebted because I feel He gives me the right words, I feel we are all partners with Christ in this endeavor.

**I am so grateful and so appreciate the feeling of the closeness of God my Mother in the presence of all those women who are mothers. There is a sense of Mother God in the place.

**I feel the presence of Jesus.

**Jesus is more present here for me than in the traditional church because He becomes weaker in those settings when I experience discrimination there.

**We are reverent, prayerful, in union with my God.

**I am deepened in my connection to the Divine within me and in others and in all the universe.

**On the days of celebration, when the group is gathered, the feeling of presence of the Spirit is truly overwhelming.

**We are truly following the idea that we are a priestly people and we are a sacrament, sacramental in the coming together and sharing. We need no mediation or stand-in to find God, to be in the presence of God, to be healed or empowered or challenged or forgiven.

These questions (especially the one eliciting personal spiritual response) garner animated responses. Not one responder skipped this question and some of the most emotion-filled answers came here.

Women seem to be performing badly needed interior work, and as they have begun they have found a God-sent wellspring of good feeling in their efforts. "I see emerging today, in groups of people and groups of women, a quest for spirituality, a hunger for God and for meaning. . . . Women in particular, in my experience, are on a quest for God. They may name it by different names, but ultimately, it is a seeking for nurturance for their souls and for some, for the finding of their own souls."[406]

The ways of expression point us into the community of God: women say they are "united with Christ," "in union with God," God is a "presence among us." We find that within the circle of celebration Jesus is here. Where we gather, when we ask. This finding is reflected in the multi-religious study of women and spirituality, *Defecting in Place.* "They are discovering that the very lives they live are the locus of God-with-us, and are beginning to shape a spirituality on the strength of an inner spirit which they associate with God's own indwelling Spirit as guardian and guide."[407]

The women of this survey are in the process of taking personal authority over their own spiritual lives, recognizing themselves as fully baptized. Clement of Alexandria said that God dwells in those who are baptized. "This mystery is indeed revealed in the Word: God in people and in people, God."[408]

We are being rewarded by the inner confirmation of God present and willing and loving in the circle.

THE IMPORTANCE OF THE CIRCLE OF WOMEN ✪

Numerous replies stress how important the group itself is to us, almost indispensable to spiritual life. Many are grateful indeed for the community aspects of Eucharistic prayer:

**It is the best thing for me right now in terms of communal prayer. My pain would be more severe without it.

**Definitely I have a need for a real community.

**The past three years this group has been my primary worshipping community. One of the most creative, intimate, trusting communities I have been a part of. I am more wholly myself, more lovingly woman, respectful of myself and others as creations of God, much more aware of the pains and struggles of my sisters.

** The trust of each other shown in our group is awesome, even in the presence of total strangers (though there are no such really). Such a delicate precious gift. It enhances my fulfillment of my spiritual needs. It is quite a different dimension. This is akin to the very early church, people meeting in homes in small groups for spiritual uplift, healing, walking together in the way of Jesus that we may *hear His word and do it.*

** (I'm) not sure what "spiritual needs" are. I enjoy the women who gather, I push for action in the group, the discussions are good. I reject the dichotomy of the spiritual from other aspects of life. It is all one.

**My community of WomenChurch is a very special part of my church life. There is a special feeling that comes over me when we're gathered. I am totally loved, safe and secure.

**I feel more of a oneness, a joining.

**I am uplifted by sharing Eucharist with other women, not just talking. This is a very deeply spiritual thing we are doing. It is not better, it is more.

**This (celebration) stirs my spirit but usually heightens my awareness of community with these friends I've been meeting with for over 10 years.

**I am a more intimate part of the participants' lives. Very often I am edified by the struggle each is enduring.

**I find we are hope-filled because as women we share the Scriptures from our points of view and give each other spiritual support.

**I look forward to celebrating. I like the openness and sharing in a prayerful context.

**Our prayer, reflections and sharing are very meaningful to me. The group celebrations satisfy my need for liturgy.

**This feels like my spiritual home.

**I love the members of our group, the simplicity, honesty, ability to be silent together and the ability to share on a deep level. It is very grace-filled.

** Usually they touch my spirit.

**I feel privileged to know the women in my group. They have given me so much.

**It is always good being with other women who are spiritually alive.

**I find it very real, rewarding and am grateful that I am part of the group.

** I feel that this is a more personal celebration for me. Our group is the community that keeps me going.

A host of respondents spoke of the delights of the communal nature of celebrations.

Our churches have taught us both the best and the worst in community life. On one hand we were expected to be like stuffed dolls propped up in pews who swelled the ranks and were mandated to keep silent in the assembly, appreciated for our numbers and our ability to labor. On the other hand, we have had our times of mystery and glory and joy shared with and recognized by our sister and brother church-goers. These snip-pets informed us about the wonders which lie in community around us, if only we can brush off the cobwebs and bring them into the light. After all, the first community is the Trinity—all Goodness as lover, beloved and love.

Early in the responses we hear the term, *real community*. What is real community? The adjectives used in the next several answers give us an idea: intimate, trusting, respectful, open, creative, and aware of the lives of the people around us. And when prayer enters in, the spirit of God here and in each other leads us to call this home.

PUTTING ON OUR SPIRIT ✪

A number of participants named the spiritual growth which is a part of this articula-tion of the Eucharist.

**I have a really peaceful feeling, as we celebrate New Life. I have the sense that I am doing "soul work."

**I'm with people who are also searching for God and all that comes from that source.

**I've found that being involved in creating rituals makes them more meaningful for me. This feels like the way it was before the institutional Church stifled growing, self-awareness and love of all people.

**Your whole way of viewing life changes when you take responsibility for your religious growth and worship.

**I am affirmed, encouraged, revitalized, given hope, energized and deeply moved.

**Our celebrations keep (me) in touch with others' change of view and I am challenged to grow spiritually.

**The celebrations force me to stop and think and meditate upon the spiritual.

**This is my base, and the way I learn who I am and who I want to become.

**My spiritual response is one of renewal, rejuvenation and affirmation.

**These celebrations fill a real need in my spiritual life. I feel empowered. This is something whose time has come for me and for other women. I am comfortable with our celebrations and find them very meaningful.

**I find the rituals often transformative. They touch deeply into my life and enable me to connect to more universal rhythms. They are often quite powerful. The group is essential to me because no other group helps me to integrate body and spirit.

Being part of the group, being able to share stories, we know that all of life is spiritual. In worship groups we learn and are challenged to grow. We meditate upon the sacred. We respect the growth of others, and honor their willingness to share.

Janet Walton has this observation, "The stories of women's ritual experiences are expressions of visions born of necessity. . . . Each story recounts what is emerging from within ourselves. . . . They represent our quest to know what is true . . . the women involved in these stories have committed themselves to name and let go of what is damaging, to empower one another to speak and act in light of the truths we learn and share, and to call forth the beauty and potential in each person."[409]

Women are claiming that the very things which ritual, good ritual, should do are being done by and for and around them as they pray together.

Tom Driver says, "ritual is best understood from a vantage point created by a 'preferential option for the poor.' That is to say, we cannot well appreciate the power of ritual unless we see its usefulness to those in need, especially those who, having little social power and, being victims of injustice, have a need for the social structure to be transformed." [410]

Traditional church ritual has both awakened in us our connection to Divinity and participated in our distancing from Her. The deepest longing focused through ritual can also be quashed by the manner of its performance. With WomenEucharist comes a freeing from the second part of the drama, and a chance for learning. We encounter our selves as *imago Dei*, and also see others in the same Light. Ritual which is reattached to the realities of our experience becomes alive again. "Ritual brings the far-away, the long-ago and the not-yet into the here-and-now . . . ritual becomes part of the work through which a people throws off its chains."[411]

As women do the "soul-work" mentioned above, as we name the challenges and connect with others and with our God, we grow spiritually and see the possibilities of the not-yet being birthed into the here-and-now.

HUNGER AND FOOD ✪

Several women used the metaphor of being led by hunger, and being fed spiritually. These very feminine images are ones which women understand deeply as, often, the primary feeders of families and communities.

**The group and our celebrations comfort, nourish and sustain me.

**The liturgy nourishes me and nurtures me for the next month.

**Our worship is a form of nourishment, usually enriching. It is amazing how often I feel full spiritually and full physically because of the wonderful bread and wine that we eat. Jesus is so much more real and "juicy" when the bread and wine are not puny and bad tasting.

**They are my source of spiritual nourishment.

**I feel spiritually nourished.

**I receive nourishment for my life of social justice.

**I feel very nourished because our sharings are very freeing.

**I'm hungry for the nourishment this group provides.

**I am nourished by our celebrations, both in body and soul.

**I feel less spiritual hunger in the days following our celebrations.

In this context, at these holy meals, the women can be recognized as genuinely ladies, or loaf-givers, to each other.

Jesus spent a whole lot of time feeding people, and we know that, being human, he was also often fed. Martha was busy getting the meal together at which Jesus undoubtedly ate his fill. When he fed thousands he must have had some bread and fish himself. In that interesting little story, Jesus is so hungry that when he comes upon a fig tree with no fruit, he curses it. (Would he have kicked the vending machine which was out of fig newtons?) He and his friends were perhaps part of the reason the wine ran out at Cana. It is bread and wine transformed that he offers even in this generation. What is the promise recorded in John 6:51? The bread of life is so nourishing that we who eat it will live forever. We will never be hungry again. Then why at church do we so rarely feel satisfied?

It may well be rare indeed that women feel nourished around the official table. "Many women are beginning . . . to admit . . . that the rites of institutional religion do not touch that innate hunger for God crying out from deep within them, nor do these nurture their spiritual lives."[412] It is rare enough, indicated by the number of responders referring to spiritual hunger and satisfaction.

The symbolism of the meal is highly visible in many WE liturgies. Almost every group has one or more bakers and thin little wafers are not allowed to meagerly suffice in an attempt to feed our spirits and our bodies. Diann Neu makes this point, "Women-church purposefully reclaims th(e) meal character of Eucharist. . . . (In) all feminist Eucharists we redeem and reclaim the gospel message of table sharing: women bless and eat food, bless and break bread, bless and drink the fruit of the vine, tell stories, give thanks, claim power and actualize promises in memory of her."[413]

It is as if when we ask for bread we are not given a stone by Bakerwoman God.

CELEBRATIONS OF JUSTICE ✪

Respondents discover through WE the focus for spiritual growth in social justice issues, as related to the gospels. Rosemary Radford Ruether has written that one of the main responsibilities of intentional liturgical community is to find its place in the arena of justice, " A community needs to engage in some social praxis that makes it a community witnessing to a new option for human life beyond the circle of its own membership." [414]

Many women are either employed in service professions or volunteer in such arenas and there is much information, much heart ache, much struggle which we bring to our worship. We do not lack sources of material. Many of us have known in the past that our rituals are a part of the tradition which has kept things as they are, rather than assisting in transformation. We need to consciously participate with the Divine in the in-breaking of goodness, justice and love into daily life. To carry justice/mercy issues onto our altars is to recognize the holy in every moment of creation.

•

**I have spent so long working in a shelter. People come to us and are the victims of the faceless "system." Sometimes I grind my teeth while trying to get someone in the county offices to do something for homeless families, pregnant women, retarded men, vets. It is crazy. My group of women not only help me to pray the injustice of the situation, but also donate toilet paper and soap and tooth brushes. So some justice, some help comes just in and through our group.

**I am so touched that our group has helped to bury the dead. We have a couple of times had the chance to take care of winos who have died and who have no one to bury them. One of the guys had no legs. He lost them in Vietnam. I cry every time I think about his pain. But he had a wonderful funeral. We feel helpless in our group but we do pray together, and some good for the world comes of it.

**I like to be challenged to be more than I have been; to be called to deep gospel values, and a chance to examine what my life means.

**I love learning new ways to look at God, justice, women.

**I go to worship and to be in solidarity with other feminists with progressive politics who are concerned about the poor. We share similar values.

**We see our prayer together, not as withdrawing from the pain of the world, but as an entering into it. Our praxis is prayer, discernment, action. If we cannot take it to God and seek wisdom then our response is not necessarily wise. It is in the heart of Eucharist that we are able to pray our own struggles and the struggle of the world.

**We are looking for a ministry which we can work in together. Even though we all have chosen individual ways in which we serve, we think that a joint ministry which comes from group discernment will enhance our celebration of Eucharist. I am anxious to begin.

**We have protested together on hunger issues. Fortunately we are in a city which has frequent opportunities for this kind of event. We are all very politically aware, and doing this kind of thing because of the Gospels is important. I am spiritually deeply touched in our eucharists, as I see us together in prayer, and know we have marched before for justice and we will march again.

**Originally a number of us came because of our discomforts with the church, but we have grown to see that discrimination against us is quite the same as discrimination of others in other circumstances. I am a kind of white-haired lady who wears good suits, but I am really beginning to see how my pain is somewhat like the pain of many other people. This is a great gift to me. I am considering going as part of the peace watch to Haiti.

Feminist theologians write voluminously about the connection between justice issues and prayer. When prayer is not removed to the hermitage, when prayer is about life on the street and on the 6 pm news which brings us Sarajevo and Beirut live, when prayer is about gays beaten on the sidewalks of major cities, then women who have had to pray our daily lives hear the voice of Joan Chittister, "The call of the spiritual life, then, the call to ministry, is the call to take all the insights into the life of Christ that we have ever been able to gather back down the mountain to the world of our own time. The call to ministry in this century is the call to be aware of the root causes of suffering in this world and to work a few miracles of our own."[415]

In WomenEucharist there is little separation between the worship in which we join and the work which we do. While some participants struggle for the freedom of our sisters, gradually we see that the membrane of suffering connects us all. "A Christian feminist spirituality is universal in its vision and relates the struggle of the individual woman—black, brown, yellow or white, rich or poor, educated or illiterate—to the massive global problems of our day. For in recognizing the problem (the sin) of human exploitation, violence, and domination of male over female, rich over poor, white over color, in-group over out-group, strong over weak, force over freedom, man over nature, it sees the whole through the part. . . . Christian feminist spirituality resorts to prayer as the only hope for its vision even as it struggles to act, here and now, to bring it to reality."[416]

For many women it is relationship that counts most. This thread has woven itself through the previous chapters. Sometimes we have spoken about theories of women's development from a perspective of research; sometimes we have simply listened to the voices of our respondents describe the need they feel to be as one with others. To speak now of justice issues is to carry the thread further. If we are genuinely to wish relationship, goodness for self and others (not power-over), then we must wish and work toward the well-being of all to whom we relate. When this is hoped for, prayed for and worked for it leads to at-one-ment with all. It is relationship fulfilled, it is the divine present, it is justice done.

MORE CELEBRATIONS OF JUSTICE ✪

A great number of women see their celebrations also as necessary and/or related to the inequities of treatment that we, and many others, have received from the patriarchy.

**I could not stand the distance and lack of respect in the traditional Church.

**I'm supported and gain power to face the unhappiness of our world and Church.

**I like some of it (gathering) as it provides a meeting place for me to meet others who feel angry like I do about women's status in the Church.

**Were it not for this community I am not sure I could celebrate worship as a Catholic.

**This is a support group for my struggle with the Church as well as an opportunity to act out my priesthood.

**The celebrations have been real eye-openers for me. At no time in our institutional Church gatherings has there been opportunity for people to vent their personal pain, suffered at the hands of the clergy or others. In our group there is room for this, and the stories cry out for compassion; the true face of Jesus responds from these women. This is one purpose of His sacrament fulfilled.

**It is much closer to home than Mass. Mass is a whole different experience for me, the formal obligated worship of God.

**It feels so good to have a forum to discuss the sexual inequities of the Church, and to worship God in a whole way. I am touched by other women's journeys, pain and joy.

**My parish environment was more sinful than the gathering I am now a part of.

**It supplies a need for me because I am alienated from large group celebrations, preached over by males.

**This is very valuable to me. It is the only place that I can *honestly worship.*

**It helps me stay in the Church, maintain sanity, and sustain belief. I need this sharing to survive.

Women pronounce the pain of injustice. For many of us, it is the experience of WomenEucharist which gives us perspective on the religious institutions into which we were baptized, but which have, at various levels, discriminated against us ever since. Yet many of us feel called to remain. We recognize the other good and searching souls among us in the parish and feel bonded with them also.

Many women can be said to be *defecting in place,* " a metaphor that tries to capture the paradox of the Christian feminist position in relationship to the church."[417] These women remain active in their parishes in recognition of the community there, in hope of changing or inflecting discriminatory ideas and actions. They can also be viewed as not unlike the members of the early church who remained a long while within the Temple precinct, sharing the good news.

** There are people (in my parish) whom I love and who do not join me (or not yet) in celebrating Eucharist as the group does.

**I find I need both this group and the larger community of my parish to meet my spiritual needs. I'm sure it helps that many members of my group are involved in the parish also. There is a fairly large number of people in the parish who are supportive though they do not participate in the group.

**This group meets my spiritual needs, but I also need my daily community and my Sunday community. I find the face of Christ in many places.

**I belong to a "people" parish which has many ministries of which I approve and in which I am active. I worship there regularly but find that the group is important for deep prayer and support.

**I need my liturgy in the parish. It is a black and white group of people. It is life-giving, especially the music and singing.

**I feel called to be a part of my local parish. I have been there for many years. There are people whom I love, with whom I have worked on committees, and done liturgy planning. I keep on lectoring there, I still do liturgy. I am one voice calling for inclusive language in the reading. My presence is a part of my struggle to call the men of the parish to keep on including women. That needs to be said over and over again. The parish feels like work. My women's group feels like home.

Recall that a tremendous number of the respondents are still parish members not only in name, but also in commitment and activity. We are mostly still deeply invested in our parish faith communities. As women who don't "go it alone," holding relationship as an important spiritual value in our lives, we ache that our parish churches are not necessarily our spiritual homes. We often live a parody of Robert Frost's line, "home is the place where, when you have to go there, they have to take you in." The institution takes us in but makes sure that we know Sunday after Sunday that we are not completely welcome.

Rosemary Radford Ruether says it this way, "Women-Church means neither leaving the church as a sectarian group, nor continuing to fit into it on its terms. It means establishing bases for a feminist critical culture and celebrational community that have some autonomy. . . . It means some women might worship only in alternative feminist liturgies; others might do so on a regular basis, while continuing to attend liturgies in traditional parishes into which they seek to inject something of this alternative. . ." [418]

Our writers echo a woman quoted in *Defecting in Place,* "I am pulled between the idea that the parish should be the center of my worshipping life and the fact that the most spiritually enriching experiences that I have had have not occurred in the parish." [419]

WHERE ARE THE PROBLEMS? ✪

Even though all respondents are celebrating members of WomenEucharist gatherings, not all find the experience free of difficulties. The spiritual garments don't always fit just right.

** Too unstructured, too often just a group therapy session or social session.
**I feel myself getting impatient when discussion/homily rambles, then I get upset with myself at feeling this way. I must confess disappointment that we can't get scripturally/theologically deeper.

**It doesn't go deep enough for me.

**I am not deeply moved by them. I come away sometimes feeling empty, sometimes feeling that it was "nice," but I feel I'm at a different level than the group. It also bothers me that the group seems afraid to include Christ and traditional Christian messages of redemption.

**While the institutional Church has oppressed, misled, denied women as such, I do not have as much a WOMAN issue with the Church, which may be why a woman's group does not (has not yet?) fulfilled my need.

The spiritual journey can feel uncertain and messy at times, especially one in which we are not only somewhat unsure of the directions, but also the map has gotten smeared and rained on, and we're fuzzy on the exact location of our destination. Leaving the synchronized march of some Catholic liturgy, with a director who blows the whistle and tells us where to step next, can result in feeling adrift, uncertain, unsatisfied. As we work with the faithful form of Eucharist, we ritualize from month to month, seeking what works for the human in each of us so that we can know ourselves engaged with God and our spiritual needs embraced and satisfied.

There were responses complaining about too much ritual and not enough ritual, and also the recognition that in this setting we possess the power to change whatever needs adjustment.

**I have been moved by (the liturgies) a couple of times, especially when the ritual is in response to some event in the participants' lives, e.g., birth, death. I'm not too excited about rituals.

**Some rituals are adequate, others are not.

**Sometimes we seem more experimental than worshipful, as we attempt to find our spiritual stance, a way of worshipping which is most meaningful to us as a group.

**The group does not meet my need for music in ritual. I love music and it is a very important part of my prayer life.

** We do need to work more on developing our own rituals.

**I find it lacking, not because of the intent but because the format lacks beauty and inspiration. Rituals are important to me.

**This is a more personal experience for me, and requires more of my input and participation than formal church does.

**I have come to have a gift. The spirit speaks through me (and through each of us). When one of the liturgies or a series of them leaves me feeling lacking I know that this feeling needs to be verbalized within the group. I am amazed at how often when I speak up (or when someone else does) there is much agreement, as if the spirit is speaking in each of us and it only takes someone being willing to speak so that we can address the problem. There is such respectful listening here. The spirit of God is as much present in the planning as in the actual Eucharist. I feel that the God-in-me and in each of us is honored here. As a result, we have the most splendid liturgies.

Others experience maturing change as the women have met for a period of time.

**I see growth in the depth of celebration. The group is becoming more intimate, and our ability to share is much more.

**When we first began we were so greedy for "our own space," and our own prayer that we were all over the place ritually. We did most of Radford Ruether's stuff. We had shells, and presents and bulbs and sand and water, sometimes all in the same event. It was confusing and exhilarating at the same time. We wore ourselves out celebrating. It was wonderful, too. We felt so alive. I was like a kid in a free candy store. I wanted to taste everything. Now we have calmed down quite a bit, we choose one theme, one symbol, one set of readings. More focus. This is good, too. I am learning, and we all are, to see this as a phase of celebrating the freedom of Jesus to be present with us in many ways. I am comfortable with the certainty that we will have more ritual phases after this as we continue to explore what we need. I have faith that this is the spirit speaking to us.

The need to be patient with ourselves, the need to honestly express our feelings about this new worship, is evident in some groups once the novelty of freedom has worn a bit. It should surprise no one that insufficient or unfocused ritual, and some dissatisfactions about worship components and style should be a temporary outcome of this experience. With all the other social biases we have inherited, we have developed the belief in instant gratification. Patience is not our strong suit as a culture, and we will still be pushing toward the heavenly Jerusalem generations from now. The blessing is that we shall be listening to each other with respect as we go.

Some are struggling with what it is we are doing after all. We need to be continually aware of the gifts, the sensitivities which every one brings to the table. Uncertainties keep us in awe, awake to what we are about, treading cautiously. This may also be akin to putting on red after years garbed in black. It seems so unlike us, just a bit scandalous.

**A secret fear . . . what if I'm being blasphemous? The socialization of the 50's comes up to haunt me occasionally. I don't let it stop me from living out my faith. I rejoice at all opportunities to be priest.

**It has been just over a year that we have celebrated and it has taken me all that time to have it almost fully settle down in my mind and soul. My remaining hurdle is the "mode" or "acting" of consecration. I believe that I understand what it means to the others but I cannot see it as true consecration. That act in Mass is so absolutely sacred to me and my belief, that anything that remotely "mimics" it bothers me, or has bothered me, very much. I have read and prayed over this, and I am very close now to settling in my mind that I deeply respect whatever meaning it has for the others, but for me it is but a reminder of what Jesus gave us — Himself.

Old habits are hard to break, and in fact, not all of them will be broken. A part of the gift of the new is to help us to see in a fresh way all that has come before; to reevaluate and reconsider and try on again those spiritual garments which we have worn so long.

The most frequent complaint is also a back-handed compliment to these WE circles:

**We don't meet often enough, just once a month, and I need more.

**It's not frequent enough.

**We don't celebrate often enough. It should be once a week.

**I need more frequency.

**I am hoping we move toward weekly gatherings, and that they become deeper.

**We don't meet often enough at once a month.

**The liturgy is so well prepared and such a good experience that I'd like it more often

**The celebrations of my women's group are best, but because of infrequency, my parish gives me community more constantly.

Another area of comment pertains to the need for a wider community. This is most often voiced by women who have husbands and children. Finding a wonderful path of celebration, they wish to share with those they love.

**I value this and my parish.

**The only problem I see now is if we become too small to continue our worshipping together and our outreach activities.

**I long for this to become a bigger, more stable and comprehensive community of closeness, sharing, prayer and social justice encouragement.

**I need both this and the larger community of the parish.

**I need a larger community and to be involved in deepening of community life and use my ministerial talents on a broader scale.

**I would like to have men join us but some of the women aren't ready.

**This is great but it does not meet my family's needs.

**My husband would really like to be here with us.

**Our group was not able to address the need for me to worship with my husband and children. There were three of us who all felt the same way. We spun off a different group which now has seven families who meet for Eucharist and potluck twice a month. Four families had not been part of womenChurch, and the three of us who were still see the women's group as a basic part of our spirituality.

Small intentional worship communities have their own special gifts: women beginning to experience themselves as fully equal, personal responsibility in contribution and planning, subtle values shifts as justice issues are mulled by the light of the Gospel, increased sense of dignity in worship, and best of all, a growth in unmediated embrace of Jesus. It is only natural not to wish to keep this all a secret, but to share this enthusiasm (being filled up with God) with others we love. On the other hand, larger communities hold those whom we care for who are not ready to join us; they offer a sense of stability which numbers and a building imply, and often the gift of a choir or an organ or a sense of the largeness of the congregation which small communities cannot duplicate.

Each form of community has its blessings. Women feel intensely the need for a reunderstanding of power, a reclaiming of it within the whole community, while grieving the loss of the larger group, or the anger of participating in it. Those of us who are over fifty know ourselves to be the bridge generation. We remember and sometimes treasure the smells and bells of our early years, while rejoicing in the freedom of our new experience. No wonder we have mixed sentiments!

James and Evelyn Whitehead identify these emotions: "All the church is groaning as we let go of old styles of leadership and accustomed forms of worship and ministry. The groaning is painful but it is a sign of life. The body of Christians is not dying but stirring. It is moving in new and unfamiliar ways."[420]

Three respondents indicate that their spiritual requirements were not being met at all, or poorly, in their groups.

**I am not deeply moved by (the celebrations).

**This helped for a while. I need more.

**The group met my spiritual needs for awhile, but then it began to "ooze" too much.

Several found that of the variety of spiritual needs they have, some are satisfied and some are not. This should not surprise us since, with the explosion of interest in spiritual matters, we have a panoply of choices spread out before us. (Refer to the previous sections on need for larger community and on ritual and the lack of it.)

**I have my group prayer needs met here but am personally
committed to a contemplative style of prayer.

 **Women's spirituality isn't evident. Some of our people are more political than spiritual.
The group doesn't yet meet my spiritual needs, but this has to do with group dynamics.
We don't have a very feminist style of leadership.

**I need more contemplation at times and a larger group.

**Sometimes yes, but it depends on the mood I carry into it. The intimacy of the group
can cause me to think of my own present sad circumstances.

**Sometimes truly uplifting, sometimes indifferent, sometimes just comfortable.

**My spiritual needs are met by many sources and in so many ways. I bring who I am to this group without expectations.

Just as we have discovered that there is more than one way to celebrate Eucharist, we have also found many outlets for our spirituality as our understanding of that word has broadened. We find our spiritual selves addressed in art, in meditation, in massage, in spiritual direction, in gardening, in sex, in poetry and *lectio divina*. Expansion of our vision to see the spirit present in every nuance of our existence is one of the real gifts of this age.

WHERE THE JOY IS ✪

Overall, there is a very high level of satisfaction with WomenEucharist as a place where many spiritual needs can be engaged. For the majority of respondents the reality is that their WomenEucharist groups are enthusiastically the center of their current soul-work.

**This group is essential to my spiritual life.

**Definitely better for me.

**I rejoice because I have found a supporting and challenging community with which I can worship.

**Not all, but many of my needs are met here.

**I experience tremendous spiritual joy and a certain connectedness with the other women in the group as well as with all women everywhere.

**This is definitely better.

**I make sure that my life schedule does not interfere with the twice monthly worship. It is too important to me to miss even one.

**There is no contest.

**It meets my group spiritual needs

**My group is essential to me.

**Absolutely better.

**In many ways this is better.

**Yes!

**It certainly does.

**My main source of community worship.

**Definitely a better place for me to worship!

**I have been in the desert for so long. This group and our Eucharist is like a long cold drink of spiritual water. I was dying of thirst.

With such a significant number of accolades, do members of WomenEucharists have misgivings or uncertainties about what we actually do? Many have mixed responses to surrounding areas of life, anger at the circumstances which bring such an event to be necessary.

**I have no misgivings because very fine people gather for prayer and it is *good*. Rome, thankfully, cannot control private groups from gathering for prayer.

**I don't have uncertainties or misgivings, though I did at first. I am not afraid, but I do not rejoice either. Right now I am struggling with conflicts and anger surfaces regularly. Very often I think nothing will happen in the official Church in my lifetime. What I have been doing is what many of the others have been doing at this time in history—questioning the tradition. This is a watershed time, a time of chaos, when we are changing directions, not unlike the time of Exodus, or the Babylonian exile, or even the time of Christ.

**No uncertainties. I am in *grief for a clerical church that continues to deny* its addiction to power and that is deeply unhealthy in regard to sexuality.

**As a married priest I'm about the cause of empowerment of the base. But I'm male and am frustrated by the sisters' propensity to sit in criticism instead of banging at the door of tomorrow with female conviction. I'd like the Pope and his friends to die so we can get on with today for which we are already late.

**I feel sad, frustrated, disappointed in my church.

**Some anger is connected with the power-dominated Church. Many church leaders are inhumane. The official Church is not a church of God's people. Many of us who have expressed a deep faith in public have been emotionally "burned at the stake."

**I am angry at the oppressive stance of the hierarchical church.

**Since I go to Sunday liturgy in a parish I don't have misgivings. I believe that if we were told to disband I'd be very supportive of the group. I think women's liturgies are a natural outgrowth of what would/should happen when the Church rejects women.

**The totalitarian behavior of Rome is a bit scary. When I don't think of Rome I'm happy.

**I do not have misgivings about legality vs. illegality of what we do, nor do I think God will punish us. I've moved away from the institutional Church, not from my belief in God. By doing this, my image of God has broadened and softened. I have a great deal of commitment to feminist issues in the Church and I believe the image of God must be changed if other changes are to occur in the world. Male divinity is at the root of oppression. Women who dissent are trying to transform the structure of the Church not merely to seek equality. We need to change our theology, and from that change the structure.

**I am deeply saddened by the pain and destruction the Church institution continues to cause in women and men because of its oppressive, misogynist, clerical, dysfunctional structure of patriarchy.

**I used to be uncertain but after seven years, not anymore. I'm concerned about other women—if they don't find a group and feel alienated from Church where do they go? Just drop out? I'm concerned about the future of the Church. I've tried in the past year or so to go to Mass at several places just to attempt to "refind" meaning but the *homilies*, the use of sexist language, the lack of clarification of Scripture, leaves me no other way.

**I felt uncertain at first. The only reason I've remained in the Church the past twenty years is because of a conviction re transubstantiation brought about through the hands of a duly ordained RC priest—now I've read new age, feminist, other religions and spiritual literature. Maybe it is all one.

**No misgivings. I am saddened that we have such a male-oriented Church with no allowance for women. I am sad that so many women still do not realize their oppression. I have a need to do this and I keep searching for people to celebrate with.

**The church can't punish me. I've evolved beyond that adolescent concept of God and Church.

**I'm only uncertain in the sense that I do not think that most people would understand, or respect the significance of this group to be as "important" or as "authentic' as a parish community. In my dark days, I do hear the voice of the traditionalists getting to me with their "It's not Eucharist you are sharing" comments. Most often those comments don't match the power and significance of the experience in my life!

**I'm not afraid, but I know I can never go back to Catholicism.

**Uncertainties? Of course. Many of the women in my group are extremely knowledgeable about scripture, church history, etc. I am fairly ignorant concerning these matters and sometimes feel as I have little to contribute. I am, however, quite confident of my own spiritual experiences and hope to eventually share them.

**(I have) some worry about my growing alienation from the institutional Church. Can I be a part of a loosely-knit WomenChurch and feel connected to a viable group of post-patriarchal but not post-Christian people?

**I'm afraid to let go, yet celebrating the sense of spirit of community.

There is a real sadness embodied in many of the responses about misgivings and uncertainty. Though the question, "Do you have uncertainties, misgivings about your participation?" did not focus on the institution as a possible source of any misgivings, it was, with occasional exceptions, seen as the prime cause of such negative emotions. The distress seems to flow from a sense of being almost driven out by hierarchy.

Some deny any emotions of negativity and instead, spell out their reasons for happiness.

**I feel quite lucky to have been a part of this group over so long a period. It feels easy and at home to me. It is a safe space.

**Not afraid, I'm rejoicing. Comfortable. I am concerned about what I would do if the group dissolved.

RADICAL SPIRITUAL REVOLUTION ✪

Given a chance to discuss whether WomenEucharist is radical or revolutionary, the women have a high level of response. A number chose to define the terms. Women find many ways to suggest their understanding of radical or revolutionary, and several areas where the terms could be applied.

A number of celebrators saw a return to the roots of early Christianity.

**(We're) radical in the sense that we are recreating the *root* of human community, revolutionary only in the sense and to the extent that we refuse to participate in the hierarchical church and its trappings.

**Radical is "rooted" in my terms and I think we are really rooted in the earliest Christian traditions. I also think it's revolutionary, for women/people taking charge of their own lives is what brings change and the feminist movement is carving major changes in the hierarchical Church. One way I judge that is by the control which the Vatican and others try to exert over our lives.

**Radical, yes, back to basics.

**If following Jesus' break with Jewish customs and rituals is radical then perhaps we are. The fact that Jesus took action against a domineering Church leadership makes our actions credible.

**I've often felt nervous about "doing it wrong" but since deciding on seminary I feel empowered to follow my own leanings even if it breaks with tradition. The group is how I believe the first Christians did it. I think it is good to return to this simplicity.

**It is somewhat radical, yet I feel it is what Jesus would espouse.

**In a quiet way we are radical. We are returning to the roots of our heritage; meeting in each others' homes; establishing new models of leadership and worship; rediscovering the gospel message and rejecting the status quo.

**It is revolutionary. We are daring to *claim* our birthright as Church. We are re-imaging and re-fashioning our Church so that it once again would be recognizable to Jesus. We are bringing down the institution.

One woman saw the situation as somewhat turned around.

**I think *we* are on the path that Jesus gave us in celebrating the Eucharist. It doesn't have to be in total conflict with established Church, rather an augmentation of spiritual growth. I feel Rome and many of the established Church practices are revolutionary in that they take away (from) or actually go against what Jesus said to do and to be, i.e., loving toward oneself and one another.

A number of responders saw the shift as happening within themselves, a shift which is accompanied by a growing sense of personal spiritual authority.

**When women take their lives seriously and share them, when we do so consciously and deliberately in a faith context, reality is transformed at its root. That is radical.

**I believe my Baptism is foundation and I am responsible for what I do.

**I feel radical. We are creating new images of God out of *our experiences.*

**Yes, it's radical, but also very natural. After fourteen years we have taken the Church and made it our own. We have no need of the institution. We are really free.

**Yes, in the view of only ordained priests "from the line of Melchizidek" consecrating, our claiming our own membership in God's priesthood and consecrating is quite a step. I have heard it said that change in the Church always happens with the people first and the Vatican following. This is definitely an example of that, laity and women consecrating.

**What has happened inside of me is revolutionary. I'm 58 years old. At about the age 45 I started questioning then questing. Before that I was the traditional "good Catholic," living on the surface of spirituality, having all the answers. I like the way I'm growing up.

**It is radical for me to find guidance in the wisdom of many and in my own experience and being.

**We re revolutionary in that we deny the hierarchy any right to control our lives. We consider all community members priestly people.

**We're radical. This is the root of my spirituality, the sacramental act. We take the power into our hands.

**For me personally this is revolutionary.

**We're revolutionary in that we are all trying individually to create change and coming together and naming worship and Church for ourselves.

**I feel it is radical by stepping outside the bounds of the institution and doing what "they" say we can't do. It may be revolutionary in that it provides people with alternatives and new experiences.

**We are revolutionary because women and men have equal roles in participation and it is not controlled by the bishops.

Is it possible that what we are doing is just now coming to light, but has silently co-existed for a long time?

**Maybe this is revolutionary or maybe WomenChurch has always been with us in some way. After all, men publish history, which (they) determine is essential. Her story may have been quite interesting had it been recorded.

An assortment of responders view the revolution specifically as related to the future.

**My fear is that the Church will not survive if it doesn't change, so we're revolutionary, yet this is the way of the future. Women will be equal in the Church or the Church will not survive. Women will revolve, bringing much-needed change, oneness, not duality, compassion rather than legalism.

**We're radical according to Church tradition and the present Vatican. I think it's still new to walk as though you really are Church. I wish it wasn't. Perhaps it is revolutionary to believe in the Gospel Christ rather than Church law.

**This is revolutionary because this issue of *Feminism* is crucial for our Church and society today to survive!

**We seek a peaceful, loving revolution. I guess we're cautious, willing to exercise some patience, but we're no longer waiting for permission!!!

**We are recreating a wayward church in the Spirit of Christ.

**I didn't feel radical at first, but now I feel like I'm really in the front line of change. I believe it's coming, before my group began I had very little hope I'd ever see change. Now I'm positive it's coming, a major part of it is already here.

**We are a part of a radical expression of 21st century paradigm shift in religious understanding.

These women vocalize a prophetic faith that growth and healing are coming to be within the community which we name church. The ability to dream of the new paradigms is a gift of the Spirit. She is whispering to us the good news that all can be well. Matthew Fox says "It is no small matter in the history of civilization to learn that ordinary people are all called to prophetic vocation. This could truly be the energy that brings about a New Creation, were it believed in . . . *trusted*. . . . It is a trust not based on human apprehension or human power but on the grace of the Holy Spirit, which is truly poured out on all humankind.

"The prophet knows something about trusting anger, trusting one's moral outrage, trusting what is intolerable. And molding that anger and outrage into creative possibilities."[421]

This whole study has touched repeatedly on anger, on outrage, on the recognition of the intolerable in our lives. The Spirit gives us the wondrous gift of imagination, linked to blessed fury which spills out into the dream of the future. It fascinates that not one respondent speaks of "getting back" at the inflictors. Consistently we dream of repair, of rediscovery of God in community, of building up. No revenge, only making all things new. A touchstone scripture for this moment is the prophetic fulfillment which Jesus quoted in the synagogue at Nazareth,

> "The spirit of the Lord GOD is upon me,
> because the LORD has anointed me;
> He has sent me to bring glad tidings to the lowly,
> to heal the brokenhearted,
> To proclaim liberty to the captives
> and release to the prisoners; . . .
> to comfort all who mourn ;
> To place on those who mourn in Zion
> a diadem instead of ashes." [422]

It is a voice reminding us that, yes, evil is present, but we may take its pain and reshape it so that good may come, that healing may take the place of wounding and that communities may reassemble with a new paradigm of wholeness rather than division, with dichotomies put aside. This sophia dream of the future, and the possibility of its coming to birth, allows us to put bitterness aside and work for the inbreaking of the new creation.

Responders also saw our actions in WomenEucharist as evolutionary, a "becoming" which is a natural outgrowth of the move of the Spirit within us.

**Not revolutionary, instead a natural evolution of people seeking something better.

**I'm sure others are doing things much more radical. I just hope we continue to grow in the Spirit and not think our way is "the" way.

**What we do is natural except I want all to come along and because our cause is so confrontational we wind up fighting with our friends who are afraid.

**I don't feel radical. Others have done this over the centuries.

**This isn't radical or revolutionary. It is what needs to be done to birth something new and valid.

**Other countries are way ahead of us.

**I suppose it would be considered radical/revolutionary by those outside the group. I simply consider it normal—the most meaningful way to celebrate and live according to the Gospel. It is honoring my roots as a Christian and a Catholic. As far as I am concerned, the institutional Church is not honoring the message of the Gospel in its entirety.

**Five or ten years ago this all would have really disturbed me. Now I am delighted and excited about this emerging church.

**Only seems revolutionary when I think of what others would think, e.g. my elderly mother, but for me, no.

** I'm not radical or revolutionary, but a follower of Jesus and men and women who were with Him.

**This isn't radical, it's a matter of enlightened survival.

**I don't think it's revolutionary and that in itself is odd. I think it seems natural because it comes from the simple mandate of scripture, "Do this in memory of Me."

**I long for the day when I wouldn't experience discrimination in the parish church. So, until that is a reality, our Eucharistic group is a God-send. It doesn't feel radical or revolutionary. It's only a way of holding onto Jesus and all he means in my life. I feel it is a creative way of keeping Jesus alive and well in our lives.

**I felt radical ten years ago, but no more.

**If we are together becoming a huge undercurrent, then maybe we're not so radical anymore.

Here is a litany of the ways in which women described their responses in celebrating together.

** It sustains me, always enlightens and enriches me so much.

**My response is mostly elation, community, renewal and hope.

**Joy, wholeness, justice.

**Indescribably moving and enriching.

**Healing and affirming.

**Joy!

**Mostly I rejoice that I have such a powerful group of women to share my journey with.

**Intensely, profoundly moving.

**We're overdue to let the Spirit move us and shake us!! I rejoice to be with other women who are thinking critically about their lives, society and the Church and I am tired of resisting the results of patriarchy.

**I feel satisfaction, energy, creativity, excitement, solidarity, bonding. We're radical!

**I am not afraid in my soul; I do rejoice over what our group has as a gift from God; had

I not participated with them I would be much further from God. I want so much to be close to Him/Her. There is a deep peace here as well as ferment over how to be effective in changing the institutional Church which is sorely damaged. I rejoice in women gathering for liturgy. I'm excited by the spirituality and wisdom I see in these women.

**I am not afraid. I feel great joy and a deep sense of community during our celebrations.

**I feel rejoicing, awed, warm, challenged.

**I put all my trust in God who gives me the heart and words for this ministry. I am at peace in that.

**I am hopeful and rejoicing in the struggle.

**I'm rejoicing and celebrating myself and my connection to all women and then all people.

**What we are doing satisfies me. I don't label it.

 **What we do is holy and wholesome.

**I'm quite at peace with my involvement. This is more like what Jesus did, gathering His friends and celebrating.

**(I'm) excited about the emergence—rapidly continuing—of WomenChurch, base communities. It is revolutionary! We are daring to *claim* our birthright as Church.

**I'm grateful. It's simply meeting the needs of the time.

**I'm not afraid and rejoice sometimes. I'm relaxed and at peace and satisfied.

**I'm at peace, energized and glad—quietly.

**I'm rejoicing and sad that others cannot move out to such a group.

**I wish more men and women could experience this real spiritual opportunity.

**I feel liberated, free to love the Creator of *all that is* more freely.

**I love my participation.

**Rejoicing, thankful, excited, confident, anticipating, free, curious, bewildered: how does anyone stay locked into the patriarchal threats of loss of soul?

**The celebrations are prayerful, meaningful experiences for me.

**My response is joyous and melancholic. Joyous because it is so wonderful. Melancholic because there are so many who will not join us. Who don't know they can break free.

**I feel joyful and uplifted.

**Connectedness, joy, Presence, service.

**Liberating.

**Peace, quiet joy.

**Is grateful an emotion? My group is one of the best things I've ever participated in. The meetings seem so perfect now, it's exciting to envision what this will evolve into. This sounds like rejoicing to me. I'm sure this seems radical to many people. I don't think historically it is. Certainly the agents of change usually come from outside the main Church.

They are experiencing sacramental effervescence, the bubbling up of delight which comes with practicing the liberation ritual of thanksgiving. They are dancing before the Lord, they are singing their own Magnificat. Having found this joy which is the truest sign of the presence of all that is Perfect Joy, it is hard to willingly go back into Egypt.

How do all these pages of responses square with the definition of spirituality and, in particular, the feminist variety? Go back and consult those definitions. Do you find echoes? Are the celebrants growing toward a mature personal and communal spirituality? Is it a whole new spiritual wardrobe which we have assembled, or are we searching spirits, sorting through what had been assigned in the past to find the divine pattern for our lives?

Remember Francis . . .

✪✪✪✪✪

WHO CARES?

How might authorities in the patriarchy respond to WomenEucharist? The question evokes fears but also the growth beyond fear. What about members of our families, and what about our friends? This chapter addresses our concerns about the impact WE might have on these relationships. The result of the struggle is an inner resilience of both individuals and WE groups growing into a new understanding of church. In relationship with the institution we struggle with our own feelings about alienation, rebellion and emerging.

✪✪✪✪✪

✳*What would happen if one woman told the truth about her life?*
The world would split open. [423]

✳*"NUNS' 'MASS?"*
QUESTION: Recently on a national radio show, a lady mentioned that there are women 'celebrating' Mass. She said that the bishops are looking the other way. What do you know about this?
—Name withheld, Henderson, Ky.

ANSWER: I have read articles about these attempted eucharistic liturgies and have seen several on television reports. Usually, a group of nuns, although occasionally there are lay-women, are gathered around a temporary altar or seated around a table. Usually they recite a text of their own making but in keeping with consecration formulas.
Most bishops are aware of these aberrations, but the matter is more complex than you suggest. Many of these women belong to a religious order, which does not fall under the jurisdiction of a bishop, but rather answers directly to Rome.
Canon 1378 provides that 'one who has not been promoted to the priestly order and who attempts to enact the liturgical action of the Eucharistic Sacrifice' shall be punished by an automatic penalty of interdict and be subject to excommunication.
However, for this to take place, a legal process is involved, which would require that these women be identified along with their communities, charges filed with the Holy See, and the women involved given the right to respond to the charges. In the case of a layperson, the bishop of a diocese in which the woman resides could take direct action. [424]

✳*I tried to live small.*
I took a narrow bed.
I held my elbows to my sides.

I tried to step carefully
And to think softly
And to breathe shallowly
In my portion of air
And to disturb no one.

Excuse me for living.
But, since I am living,
Given inches, I take yards,
Taking yards, dream of miles,
And a landscape, unbounded
And vast in abandon. [425]

✳*There is no fear in love, but perfect love drives out fear because fear has to do with punishment, and so one who fears is not yet perfect in love.* [426]

While looking inward toward the center of the circle, we continue to look outward at the contemporary landscape of our lives, reacting to what others may think and do. It is a great sadness that questions about fear have relevance in our survey. The questions were generated because of the frequency with which women speak of fear when they speak of the Church. We are shaped in a faith which had, during the years of formation for many of us, a teaching of everlasting damnation as a central component. Regardless of what official theology might say, the daily encounter with God often included the invocation of His power to imprison in eternal fire. A lot of us discovered a loving God in spite of the threat. Yet many still bear a cautionary concern about how authorities, who have taken on the mantle of the Almighty, may see fit to wield power over our work lives, our parish commitments, our ministerial charisms, our religious communities. Fear of retribution is reinforced by the landscape of daily life and shaped by the regular reminders of the power which men have over the lives of women. It is for many of us a significant factor in how we make decisions about disclosure.

Gordon and Riger, in a study of the fears specific to women observe that many of them learn fear early and keep it long. Fear is specific to each woman's experience as it cuts across the micro and macrocosm of her society. Their study indicates that fear for most women is a real, palpable and fairly frequent emotion. [427]

It is the awareness of this fear in my personal life and in the lives of others which first led to making the survey anonymous. While there are not more than twelve to fifteen responses which indicate a strong sense of fear of retribution, many affirm by various caution statements that they are aware of the chance of trouble and about half of the respondents, given the opportunity, returned questionnaires unsigned and not back addressed. Several which do include such personal information ask that it not be revealed. Well over half indicated some level of circumspection

It is worth remarking upon that not all participants in a given group expressed the same reservations or level of fear. There are participants who verbalize considerable concern for their safety while others in the same group indicate a lower level of fear or none at all. This may well have to do with individual employment, ministry and previous disciplinary encounters.

FEAR ✪

**The group by and large feels it is emerging Church, but is careful about too much of the wrong publicity. Those still in the institution in official capacities are careful about discovery.

**We are secret. I feel that we might be forbidden to do this, which would put us in an us vs. them position. We don't want that. If someone comes to us seeking we welcome them. You can't separate our pain from our reason for being. It feels very right and blessed, so fear is not a major focus. We just have an unspoken agreement to be careful whom we talk about it with. I have grappled with the fear, and have chosen to take part in spite of it.

**The group loves the time of prayer. A few may have questions but the only fear surfaced when an article was written (about us) in a local newspaper; some were not willing to have their names used.

**We don't go out of our way to be discovered. This is a very conservative diocese.

**I could easily lose my job if it were discovered that I participate.

**There is a priest I know, fortunately not in my parish, *but he is in some people's parish,* who publicly refuses people communion if they have remarried outside the church. I am pretty sure there are priests who would refuse me and others communion if they knew what we were doing. Yet, I don't know what else to do or where to go. I don't want to leave my parish. I love many people here and they love me. But the oppression of feeling the spirit call on one hand and the forbiddance on the other is terrible. I know God is with us, but my fear has been justified over and over by what happens to women when they upset the priest or the hierarchy.

**I was a campus minister of a local Catholic college and felt once or twice a bit nervous if word got out that I was inviting students to these gatherings.

**I do feel the necessity to conceal my active part in the group from some in my parish lest I get less of a hearing from good but conservative people.

**I wouldn't want the local bishop to know, or some of the local clergy.

**A priest in whom I confided said that there is a canon law against what we are doing. Would he tell the bishop? Would the bishop forbid a pastor to give me the Eucharist? My job, my ministry could easily be on the line.

**I feel some trepidation in having my pastor know that I participate since I see him as very traditional.

**Some have fear of discovery because we are largely a homosexual group and they fear discovery and persecution.

**Fears: it's mixed. Some are very open about participating. I am fearful at times, fearful of losing my place in my parish and I feel vulnerable because I am a lesbian.

**My community at daily Mass is very important to me. My parish is almost good enough . . . a wonderful place. My pastor is nearing retirement and becoming more conservative and afraid about how the chancery will respond to different things in our parish. If he can back down on various activities because he doesn't want to rock the boat so near his retirement, then he may feel he is placed in the position of telling me (and some others) that we are forbidden to pray together as women.

** I don't know whether our clergy know we do this. One parish staff woman knows, she has been invited but hasn't come. I'm on the fence about whether I would be willing to tell our clergy, they may well be very understanding but I don't know.

The trepidation women feel can be justified through personal experience, or per-haps through observation of the encounters of acquaintances; still others have vague quivers about possible disapproval. We need to ruminate on the power structures which lead supposedly mature women to suspect it is necessary to conceal their prayer lives from those around them. We need to study and pray about the misuse of power which would lead prayerful women to live in caution of the church men around them.

Not one reply indicated sensations of guilt. Sandra Schneiders points out, "They are not controlled by guilt, in relation to the institution. . . . They are busy *being* church rather than trying to reform the male establishment which is usually regarded as church." [428]

Fear, yes. Fear of condemnation. Catholic women, women of many strongly patriarchal denominations fight a life-long battle to claim their own spiritual authority.

Fear is forgetting that Jesus has promised constant companionship. Fear is forgetting that Jesus often challenged the power of entrenched religious authority to cure on the Sabbath, to feed the hungry on the Sabbath, to love above all else, to be in service to others. Fear is also forgetting the joy which many women find when they gather. Does fear subside as confidence in the Spirit grows?

The circumstances surrounding these gatherings are reminiscent of the early days of the Pentecost community in which women and men who shared belief in the risen Christ first were filled with fear and then with growing confidence as the Spirit of God pushed out the dread of discovery. As Peter said then, so women are saying now, "Indeed, upon my servants and my handmaids/ I will pour out a portion of my spirit in those days,/ and they shall prophesy." [429]

NOT IN FEAR ✪

**The qualms we have are the growing pains of claiming our own faith. We are not in fear of discovery, we are not in hiding. We are an open group and welcome newcomers. We are simply faith-filled women doing our thing.

**We used to be a bigger group and that bothered the organized church. Now we are small and I don't think they care about us anymore. We are doing what we *must* do to worship in an authentic way for us. We would like to share our celebrations with others. All are invited but we will not change our way of celebrating just to get more people to attend.

**We have no fear of discovery.

**When I was teaching scripture classes I let those know who seemed like they could handle it. The priest at the parish could.

**Our circle of women has few qualms or fear of discovery because we continue to be *truly* nurtured, fed and healed and challenged by the celebrations.

**No fear, no qualms.

 **We are not afraid because we have no secrets.

**My group is largely drawn from my parish and it's ironic because we belong to the most progressive, most social justice-minded, most open parish in the diocese. The pastor knows what we do and has no problem.

**We have not advertised our existence to the institution nor have we hidden from them. Basically it is not terribly important to us as a group. Who cares if we are discovered.

**We are quiet about what we are doing, but we don't hide. Some would disapprove, and we are discreet.

** No fear at all. I find the celebrations a source of great joy and peace. The institution has no power over me.

**I stopped giving them the power to frighten me. This was a long slow process. Now, what we do is beautiful, we are discovering how to pray better, be more loving, and we are doing it without having to look over our shoulders to see who is watching.

**When women are new in our group some seem concerned about who knows that we celebrated the Eucharist. Gradually relief, faith maybe, takes over and they worry less. There are a couple of women who come occasionally who do worry about their jobs. I have sympathy for them, but for myself, I am past the point (mostly!) where this is a worry for me.

**Some individuals usually attend traditional liturgy. I personally experienced not being able to attend traditional liturgy because I WOULD BE DENYING THE EXPERIENCE OF OUR RITUAL. I am finding there are many groups which have come together as our group has. Our faith in what we are doing is too strong for qualms. It is well known that we do this, though not necessarily accepted. I love explaining my experience to some who question what we do. The response has been quite positive.

**I am not afraid but I have exiled myself, or maybe the Church has exiled herself from me. I am much calmer and more at peace now.

**I have stopped letting people of patriarchy (not just in church, but in job and in society) have so much power in my life. My qualms settle as I realized that my prayer life is for me and for the community with whom I worship. There is not one place in scripture that I can find that Jesus wanted women to be afraid of him, and most certainly not when he sat down to eat with them.

**We stopped worrying about the response of the institution gradually as we became more confident and prayerful and deeper in community.

**In the beginning I was afraid of receiving condemning edicts from the hierarchy. This has not happened. I was afraid of discovery because of this fact, however I believe that if other women knew of our findings, they would be relieved to find a way to stay in the church rather than leave because of what they experienced at traditional Mass.

NO FEAR AT ALL ○

Such a group of pilgrims! Such a sense of journey!

Some women indicate that discretion is an aspect of their worship circumstances. The implications of this reply may be a sensitivity to the possibility of conflict or condemnation, else why the need for caution? While not exactly shouting our good news from the housetops, some of us are increasingly able to whisper it around, as we inch along in the "growing pains of discovering our own faith." One responder says she has "few fears of discovery." While not specifying what those few are, she indicates that nurturing celebration carries greater weight than anxiety.

Another names a significant pull of WE when she says, "We are doing what we must do to worship in an authentic way."

A wonderful fact is that an increasing sense of authenticity can grow from reflection on our actions and others' reactions. There seems to be for some responders an increase in faith and confidence as simultaneously their level of anxiety decreases. When Spirit-filled hope and love blot out fear (even if it is very gradually) whole new vistas are revealed. There is a joyous quality afloat in some of the above responses, which comes from the delight of being personally and in communion, nurtured and challenged.

All this is indicative of what the consequences are of the spiritual freedom spelled out in *Dignitatis Humanae*, the Second Vatican Council's Declaration on Religious Liberty. The document (with my profound apologies for exclusive language) says, "It is through his conscience that man sees and recognizes the demands of the divine law. He is bound to follow this conscience faithfully in all his activity so that he may come to God, who is his end. Therefore he must not be forced to act contrary to his conscience. Nor must he be prevented from acting according to his conscience, especially in religious matters. The reason is because the practice of religion of its very nature consists primarily of those voluntary and free internal acts by which a man directs himself to God. Acts of this kind cannot be commanded or forbidden by any merely human authority. But his own social nature requires that man give external expression to these internal acts of religion, that he communicate with others on religious matters, and profess his religion in community. Consequently to deny man the free exercise of religion in society . . . is to do an injustice to the human person and to the very order established by God for men." [430]

Imbedded in the document is a theological understanding shared by its authors and the participants of WE. The ground of the document is the belief that divine activity in human life supersedes all human understanding, and that God's presence is mysteriously and wonderfully available to everyone.

Women attempt to pray out and work out the demands *of the divine law* and the *free exercise of religion* in the circle of WE.

WE represents for participants *voluntary and free* internal response to God's invitation signified by the practice in community of the sacrament of thanksgiving. "We are doing what we must do to worship in an authentic manner," one woman says. "Nurtured, fed, healed and challenged," says another. "Celebrations are sources of great joy and peace." "Too strong for qualms."

The very responses dovetail with the words of *Dignitatis Humanae.* It seems that the promise, the intent, of the document is well fulfilled in the answers which women write. "Calm, joy, peace."

This set of responses is quite distinct in tone from the previous group. Here are women admitting to having had qualms, but they are now related to personal growth rather than to authority; and women who knew fear in the past but now find relief. These are women whose experiences minimize or erase misgivings. Some suggest a willingness to accept ambivalence on the part of others, an ambivalence which is recognized but does not deter.

One observation: fear and religious freedom do not comfortably coexist. For too many generations women have been controlled by the very church which is also home. Until we are able to extricate ourselves from the destructive fears on which patriarchy is based (whether it is in this house we call church or elsewhere) we will not be able to freely worship. Many theologians praise diversity in facing the fearsome many-headed monster of religious patriarchy. One lesson to which we need to attend is that if women can find God present in these heterodox celebrations, then perhaps there are many other ways which are equally valid for being truly in the presence of God.

Each woman has her own share of inspiration, her own fears to confront, and therefore her own stories to bind into prayer and action. "The fundamental commitment that feminists in religion share to end male ascendancy in society and religion is more important than their differences. What is clear is that, if feminists succeed, religion will never be the same again." [431]

IN RELATIONSHIP ✪

It is not only reverberations from the institution which we are called to address. In what ways do we view the reactions of those around us: our families, friends and work companions?

**I am happily married for 33 years. My spouse supports me but I am careful not to let right-wing friends know about the group.

**My significant other is in the group also.

**I am a widow. My husband was an active member.

**My husband strongly dislikes all organized religion but our group is so disorganized that it's okay with him.

**My spouse sees the group as a healthy place to be born or to share with like-minded Catholics the purpose of Jesus.

**I have a significant other of ten years and counting. She is part of the group and a major musical contributor.

**I am a part of a religious community. WomenChurch is known in the community and supported by a significant minority there.

**I'm quite open about the group in all my circles. I am a member of a religious community and several of my sisters are part of WomenChurch.

**My husband has good feelings about the group but is not included.

**Our group includes the director of religious education and the spiritual director of the parish as well as most of the women who are the movers and shakers around here. I think it is the very openness of the parish which has encouraged us to move forward in many areas, including women exploring ways of worshipping that are perhaps not normative.

**I met my partner at WomenChurch. She and I really love the group. It is not subversive to pray.

**I have spoken at our parish on behalf of WomenChurch. I have left behind those relationships where there would be criticism, or am polite as in the case of my in-laws.

**My significant other is also in the group. We met there.

**I'm not afraid to tell. Who could quarrel with a monthly gathering for prayer, faith-sharing and supper?

**My husband supports our efforts.

**I am married and he wishes he could better appreciate my needs. He goes to a parish even while believing little of the traditional creed.

**We are in a neighborhood parish and I am quite open. (I have) a supportive interested husband.

**I am unafraid to share my activities with other Franciscans.

**I don't worry anymore. I agreed to go public via a newspaper story when a woman reporter urged me in this direction. I'm a member of a religious congregation. Some members understand and accept, others seem condemning. Since I went public everyone knows. Otherwise, I would have been afraid of the bishops.

**My husband is not religious. He sees it as something that fulfills me, so he is happy about it.

**I am married and he sees it as a natural outgrowth of my feminism.

**I have no need to conceal. We are a very poor parish and people are important. Activities center on bringing blacks, Hispanics and other colors and types together. Celebrating is important.

**I'm always inviting new people. I usually talk to people after Sunday Mass. Inevitably, people express disenchantment with the institution or that particular Mass not meeting their spiritual needs. I use those opportunities to invite them to my house Church. My husband is supportive. though I don't think he completely understands.

**I get bolder in talking about our group all the time. I used to be cautious, but after sharing with one person and then another, I find growing confidence. This is a wonderful thing we do. Why have we been afraid in the past to tell?

**I am married. He does his thing spiritually and I do mine. We honor each other's spiritual paths.

**We don't advertise, and don't feel that our Eucharist takes the place of the community gathering. We are unusual in that we have the best of the new living circle church with equality and inclusion in our parish.

**Telling one person and getting a good response ("I'd love to be doing something like you do") has given me greater confidence. My worship has been like coming out of the closet. It is amazing that so many people, when you talk to them, envy us and want to join us in the freer, more personal worship which we share. I am always asking people to be with us.

**I don't hide the existence of the group. My pastor knows I'm involved and he's open to it.

**I feel comfortable telling specific individuals in my parish. I am partnered with a woman who is also a part of the group. We are the parish's token lesbian couple and the group's as well.

For some of us there is still an uncertainty, a thin gauze of secrecy which we drape between our celebrations and those whose opinions cause us apprehension. The uncertainties seem to have a broad spectrum, from mild to severe discomfort levels. We continue to respond to conditioned perceptions, many of which are tied to concerns of censure. "We allow ourselves to feel low self-esteem and our fear is magnified. We tried to fit ourselves into rigid little boxes of how to live our lives. . . . We limit ourselves to old options because we're afraid of loss. We're afraid to differ too much from one another. . . . We don't want to be criticized or condemned or thought of as difficult. We're frightened of losing our image or maybe of having an image that stands out." [432]

The dark side of the gift of relationships is an over-concern with the criticism of others. It is possible to value another's opinion so highly that we let it deflect our own best interests. Emotional sensitivity to others is not only an anchor but can serve as a ball and chain.

Responses certify that the freedom to worship, and to talk about it, sharing with non-members, inviting interested individuals, is increasing. "I'm always inviting new people. . . ." A number of responses certify a growth or progression in public comfort. "I get bolder in talking about our group." There is a swell in confidence as information is received with enthusiasm. Some seem sufficiently inspirited that they have no reluctance to spread the word wherever they will be heard. One woman, using the language of contemporary life, says it is like "coming out of the closet." Her sense is that something which was previously secret can now be shared with personal confidence. As one participant puts the question, "Why have we been afraid to tell in the past?"

Yet a number of participants still have pockets of problem people:

**My family of origin might have some trouble with it.

**My bigoted aunt . . .

**I never tell my family about my women's liturgies. They are conservative.

**There are friends who, if they joined us for worship would be uneasy.

**I hold my group close to my heart and cherish it. It's not something I'd care to share or attempt to explain to individuals who might become hostile.

**Some friends might see this as dangerous.

** Within the IHM community, how to celebrate Eucharist with the congregation has become a significant question and painful for those on both sides and down the middle.

** My parents know about the group but do not really approve. We make a point not to discuss the group with them but we don't conceal our participation from them. Some of my friends would not understand.

** I don't share with many that we consecrate. My partner is a part of the group also and we are the only lesbians. We are accepted but there is some unrecognized homophobia. I doubt if my pastor or some conservative fellow parishioners would appreciate what we do.

**I am married. I've been reluctant to tell my husband of all that happens there because I think he is more traditional than I, though he does have his differences with the Church. He has never questioned me or made any snide remarks. One of my sisters is a mostly lapsed Catholic following 17 years in the convent. I generally don't bring up anything Catholic with her. (Our family is notorious for not bringing up anything difficult directly. Religion is very delicate.)

**Can't tell those conservative Catholic relatives.

**My grandmother is old world Catholic. She would have nightmares!

**My family might question the validity of such a celebration.

**With some of my more traditional Catholic acquaintances I am careful. I work as a chaplain and have no wish to shock anyone.

**My significant other is not spiritual and prefers not to discuss the group though she attends once in a while to support me. Even within our Dignity chapter our separate women's group causes hurt and angry feelings for some.

**Many friends and the Catholic faculty in the school where I teach don't know.

**I wouldn't tell my parents and aunts and some members of my (religious) congregation and perhaps some of my patients. (I am a psychotherapist.)

**My work supervisor is a Roman Catholic. I wouldn't care for him to know even though he would never say anything.

**I do not share this with the groups I give retreats to. If an individual seems to lean in this direction or otherwise has a problem with structured Mass I might invite her to the group. I am a Catholic sister. I have several priest friends and it could bother them because they do not understand. My brothers do not understand either but there is no tension.

**I probably would choose to conceal the existence of my group, not because I'm uncomfortable with our activities, but because people can be such pious jerks. Not a very Christian statement, but. . . .

**I have a Very Significant Other. She is happy for me, but skeptical about anything that is spiritual or religious. She is searching for her own spirituality. and has not had much success. With limited exceptions, most gay people haven't found a lot of open arms in religious communities/churches. I've made a personal decision not to let the ignorance of others get in my way. Some of my family members have questioned the need for such a group. My response usually is that it is another way to celebrate and serve God. That answer is far too simplistic. Everything we do in life (cleaning, planting, working) should fit that explanation. It seems to satisfy them. As of late, I've begun discussing my group and my spirituality among my friends who pretty much exist in a spiritual void or who have such conventional beliefs that they don't question or really understand what they believe.

** My husband is pretty passive about what I do. He sometimes says that I'm going to lose my faith, especially when I talk about Goddess worship. He doesn't like what I'm doing, but we've always tried to respect each other's independence so he lets me alone. One of my friends was worried and disapproving but on the whole I'm at an age (62) where there aren't too many people around who can give me grief about anything I do.

A most interesting part is that the fears felt by these women do not keep them from celebrating; these fears are balanced by an interior call which is also compelling. Do these women feel that they are painting fishes on the walls as the members of the early Church did? The catacombs of today are the living rooms and family rooms of our homes.

**I often reassure myself by remembering that Jesus felt that he could heal, that he could share food even when it was forbidden by the law of his time. They obviously were not "forever" rules because they do not apply to us today. I still have times of insecurity about discovery but they are less now than in the past.

**When I remember Jesus' behavior to authority figures I feel strong. We believe he is here among us, calling us to put aside that which enslaves, such as fear and thoughtless obedience, and asking us to pray with him for the return to a theology of love and not forbiddance.

The hope and trust in the call of the Spirit run parallel to some uncertainties. There are those quoted who have many positive emotions braided together with the negative ones. "Trepidation" is parallel with "great joy and peace," "fear' with "right and blessed," "nervous" with "faith-filled," "secret" with "open," "forbiddance" with "celebrating," "conceal" with "confidence."

Mary Collins OSB, in a talk on women and the institutional Church has this wonderful observation, "In my judgment present disillusionment is grace offered to women and through women to the whole church. . . . A whole company of women who gather for eucharist is beginning to question Jesus again in search for the living and life-giving God. Some men are among their number. Dare we believe there is power here not yet evident on the surface of things?" [433]

Perhaps it would be wise to look upon any fear in the same way. Is it, like disillusionment, a gift offered to our community? Does it lead to a chance to question yet again what it is that we profess by our eucharists, a grace which will lead us to bring into the light a power which is not yet revealed?

**Sometimes I am afraid of discovery, yet I realized that when I am I have put my thoughts in the wrong place. The fear drives out love. It is a negative emotion. I try to place myself in the company of Jesus and I pray for Pope John Paul, for our bishops and for all of us that we may keep learning to make loving, non-fearful community. Eucharist, especially when we find ways and reasons to rejoice, should be shouted from the housetops.

**The fear and the joy go hand in hand. Sometimes one is uppermost, sometimes the other. I know Jesus is present in the joy and not in the fear. A lot of my growth in courage is in the discovery of my heart that Eucharist is worth praying for!

While some women have friends and family who disapprove, or who they fear will disapprove, other women have found that they have spouses who not only approve, but wish very much to be included.

**I am a bi-sexual married woman (BMW). My husband is fully supportive and would attend if he were invited.

**I am married 29 years. He doesn't like the name WomenChurch, feels excluded, is disillusioned with the Church but still goes.

**I'm married. He feels a bit left out, but wants me to go forward. We are searching *together* and I don't necessarily want to find an answer that excludes him.

**My husband feels left out. He would like to share the experience with me. I'm not quite ready to share it with him though. I know for myself it would change my sharing during our period of reflection.

An issue which women will need to address is how all people of good will are to be incorporated into WE communities. The comments above admit ambivalence, one which has often been voiced, "yes, but not quite yet." Frequently conceded by feminist theologians, and voiced by respondents, is "the need for a period of withdrawal from men and communication with each other is essential for the formation of feminist community." [434] Numerous Catholic writers suggest the need to build spiritual knowledge and strength as Women-Church, uncovering for each other the gifts that we, specifically as women, have to share.

**In our group I have heard women's actual voices which I have almost never heard before because their husbands speak for them. And some of the ideas and opinions! Wow!

**I like to worship with both sexes, but the additional impact of being just with women is healing because we've really come a long way from Rome's grasp.

**In our praying and speaking together we have said anti-patriarchal, not anti-men, things which I am pretty sure we would not feel able to say if men were with us. There really has to be a time to pray this stuff out of our systems. Probably younger women won't need a lot of this praying-out time because they have been less dominated.

**My husband feels like he is a real feminist, which I think is great because it is something he obviously thinks is important, but he still reverts occasionally to putting down my emotions and the emotions of others. It will take awhile to have me feel strong enough in prayer to want him to be with me in our WomenChurch group.

**My husband of 30 years is just great. I would love to have him in our group. There is nothing I can't say in front of him, but I'm not sure others will be so comfortable. I hope the time will come.

"We are not talking here about separatism as total ideology, but as a stage in a process, a stage that is absolutely necessary but not an end in itself, a stage toward a further end in the formation of a critical culture and community of women and men in exodus from patriarchy. We should be clear that when we talk about women withdrawing to collectivize their own experience . . . for most women this means, at best, a few hours a week taken out of lives lived in the presence of males."[435]

Lesbians with whom I spoke did not hold for a totally sex-segregated group.

**I work with men all day and have many male friends. I would just like to worship freely with my partner, together with many other men and women. Free to pray as we wish, free from fear of condemnation.

**My sisters in our group are very special to me. I would love to have a time when we can worship freely with men, without being afraid they're going to put us down. THEY will have to change though, to make that possible. Even gays in Dignity feel like they have some sort of special handle on the truth, that they know better "What the church is about" when they go through persecution just like we do.

Some groups already work toward a time of more inclusive worship. There are numerous groups which are family-inclusive, mapping how men and women and children can pray coequally.[436] They are fruit for another study.

ALIENATED? REBELLING? EMERGING? OR ALL THREE? ✪

Given the opportunity to characterize their worship groups as rebellious (openly opposing the patriarchal church) or alienated (being estranged or indifferent or hostile) or emerging (rising from previous circumstances or coming forth or manifesting out of a previous inferior position), respondents offered a plethora of descriptions. Very few responders found that only one word was sufficient.

A number found that none of my suggestions fit.

**We are Church, not rebelling or alienated, but a place we can *honestly* come to worship without having to leap over hurdles of unacceptable traditions.

**I always say we are "unaffiliated." We were asked to disband by the chancellor of the diocese but we didn't.

**The group has no relationship to the institution other than as critics. We write letters of protest about various issues and have demonstrations. We feel that we are part of the creative Church.

**We are Catholic-rooted. We participate in an Ash Wednesday vigil and are delighted with the publicity. The event includes doing a ritual in front of the cathedral while Mass is going on inside.

**Many of us consider ourselves to be Catholics despite (and perhaps to spite) the institution.

**As a group I'm sure we would be viewed as lunatic fringe by the institution. From our point of view we are both substitute for and supplement to it, depending on who of the group is talking.

**We go to our local parish and are very active in parish concerns. I feel that we are part of a rediscovered aspect of Church. We don't feel that one has to be a man in order to celebrate. Probably our gathering would be criticized by old time Catholics but that really doesn't bother me.

**We're antagonistic.

**We do not experience ourselves outside the Church.

**We are all individually members of different religious communities, but as a group we have no relation to the institution.

**We have an adversarial relationship with the institution. We come together to protest.

**I consider myself a retired Catholic. My group is my contact with the people of God.
**We are, most of us, practicing Catholics, active in our parishes. No one seems to want to set up in opposition to the Church. Rather, we are opening ourselves to the birthing of a new church which is growing out of the old dead church. This new church will not have a hierarchy, it will have a communion of persons seeking to help each other on the spiritual journey.

Several women saw their circles as still caught in the negative emotions of estrangement, a necessary stage through which all pass at some level of intensity.

**Many of our members belong to religious congregations. Some have been very alienated, and have left for other religions, others are in rebellion.
**We seem mostly a rebelling and alienated Church and a place of refuge.
**Our relationship is peripheral. Some of us belong to the institutional Church, some do not. We are alienated.

Some felt that it took at least all three modifiers to express the shape of prayer and practice.

** We are a part of Dignity which claims that we are gay/lesbian Catholics who dissent from the teachings of the Church on sexuality but are still Catholics. The institutional Church shuns Dignity in general, and this small group of women who gather to celebrate together has no official tie or recognition from the institutional Church. We sometimes feel rebelling, often alienated and occasionally emerging.
**We write the Archbishop once a year and invite him to join us on Ash Wednesday and pray for repentance for the sin of sexism. Rebelling, alienated and emerging!
**I see an "institutional" shift towards new realities such as WOC and other intentional eucharistic communities. Ours is emerging, alienated, rebelling.
**We are an underground group, not formally connected to any parish, but many of us worship at the same parish and serve on committees together. The Catholics among us are committed to justice for women in the institutional Church. I think Catholics feel it is a rebelling Church. The searchers feel alienated and yet all of us refer to our group as

church, as in *emerging*.

**We're definitely emerging. There is an upbeat feeling, but also alienated and rebelling.

**The group's relationship with the institution is one of anger, frustration, some hope. Most don't go to a regular parish, not one person is totally comfortable with the Church. Rome doesn't approve of women celebrating, so we are rebelling. We're definitely alienated, and yet we have to be part of the new, emerging Church.

**We see ourselves as baptized into the community of faith but not institutional Catholics. We're all three, rebelling, alienated and emerging.

**We are rebelling and emerging. We have alienated ourselves because we refuse to go back. We are trying to go public.

The most frequently chosen descriptive word employed is *emerging*, even though it is often couched in modifications. Not only do those above see emergence as part of the character of their group, some see it as the primary focus.

**We are all historical Catholics, some are vowed religious. We are emerging Church.

**We are all in *pain*. Some of us still cling to an institutionally sanctioned eucharist on at least some Sundays. The number who do so is getting smaller and the occasions less frequent. We are emerging out of the ashes. God will still bring forth life, in Her way.

**We are emerging, though for a long time we were rebelling and still feel alienated when we attend regular institutional parishes.

**A majority (of our 17 members) still attend Sunday liturgies at a parish but a couple don't go at all or they connect with another church. We're emerging.

**Individuals sometimes participate in their local parishes but we are emerging as part of the WomenChurch movement.

**Most are practicing Catholics, some are dropouts, all are angry and wanting change. We are emerging.

**I am one with the living Catholic Church, not with Rome. We're emerging. We are not rebelling, we are claiming what is rightfully ours.

**We hope we are part of an emerging church born out of alienation. Our bishop says as long as we celebrate privately he can do nothing about us.

**Some are alienated but we are witnessing the emerging Church.

**Mostly we are practicing Catholics, though on the fringe. We're emerging, challenging the patriarchy. We welcome newcomers and invite others openly.

**Our relationship to the institutional CC is very close because we are its members. We do what we're doing presently because the clerical element does not understand the pain we experience when they exclude us on the basis of our womanhood. When we can be accepted as are they, we'll join them. But until then we'll need to do what black people did and that is gather about Jesus ourselves and leave our doors open for them to join us if they wish. We were alienated, trying to cope with the plight that was ours and yet find a way to stay within the church. Now we see ourselves as emerging. I don't have any qualms because I believe that God has led us in this direction.

**We are emerging, the church of the future. Public notice is given, the public is invited. We're very peaceful.

**We sometimes as individuals feel rebellious and alienated but we do not seek or encourage these feelings. We want to help the emerging church.

This is such encouraging news, news that the spirit of hope is abroad in the land! In the midst of negative vibrations, many of us want to continue to be connected to and a part of our faith family. We see dimly through the faith communities which are small and supportive that there is hope. We are practicing a paradigm of partnership in which there are no winners or losers. WE is a circle of equals emerging in community. "Not power *over,* which would simply be a rearrangement of the old paradigm, but partnership with, a new paradigm, a paradigm of partnership, a communion of co-equals, trusting one another and celebrating one another's gifts in a common service of the faith."[437]

These feelings oppose both despair and indifference. Despair would lead us to assert that any involvement or alliance with the institution is hopeless. There are many good women who have come to this conclusion.

Indifference is a sign that we have no feelings of relationship with the institution and don't care what thoughts the institution has about us. Indifference is the opposite of love. While some of us have lost interest, others of us still see ourselves deeply in relationship with the Church. So many responses are couched in relationship terms, even if those answers indicate outright hostility. If we are alienated *from* the Church we are not indifferent to it but estranged from it. If we are in rebellion *against* it, we are not indifferent to it but in mutiny against it. These are still deep relationships. Certainly they are currently negatively defined relationships, but they are relationships none the less. For all the pain that alienation and rebellion foment it is probably preferable to despair or indifference. Continuation of the relationship also bears an often hidden seed of hope. We cannot "discount the current gathering of the forces of reaction and the closing of ranks in Rome. But conversion often occurs 'in extremis,' and that may well be the state of the institution in the months and years ahead. . . . In the meantime, hope endures in the people of God who see, even through darkness, that something profound is indeed happening—that a new age in the history of the Catholic Church lies ahead, that the authentic and beloved tradition will be recovered in a renewed community of faith."[438]

It is of deep value to realize that alienation and rebellion (or similar emotions) are necessary older sisters to the struggle of emerging. Without them we would not know the need for transformation. Without them we could remain safe and unchallenged in the cocoons of earlier spiritualities. Without them we would not hear the bells of spiritual liberation ring. These feelings, coupled with faith, bring us to the flickering but active hope. We practice that hope in Eucharist. We do not passively wait to be rescued, to have everything made right by some power figure. WE accepts that this is a God-given time of discovery, reflection and action. As we accept the invitation of the Spirit, we are emerging, being brought to new levels of faith and celebration.

For a significant number of participants the parallel between psychic and spiritual emergence and physical birthing is no doubt obvious. The labor, the sweating, panting, painful bringing forth is work equal to and worthy of the wondrous results. For women to struggle is "sweat equity" in the building of the house of the people of God. It is bringing to light, through struggle, the new possibilities of life in the spirit of Jesus.

PERSONAL EMERGENCE ✪

Groups emerge because the people within them emerge. The individual impact of this worship on the women braids together to make possible the growing strength and affirmation which is felt by all. Some women find the primary sense of emergence or impact in their personal lives.

**It has centered who I am.

**(My group) has provided mutual and continuous growth.

**Everything is different because of my group. I believe I am a better person and I hope I am kinder and more helpful to others. Once you believe in and take responsibility for your own religious activities, then you can do almost anything.

**I now know that if I can create my own spiritual experience I am able to do the same with all other areas of my life.

**Very freeing, less fear, peace, joy.

**It strengthens my belief in resurrection.

**Enriching.

**It changed my life. I began to believe in myself and my own thoughts, feelings, intuitions. I am responsible for how I spend my time. I feel I have given my three children (now in their twenties) a boost by "following my bliss," trusting myself, seeking a loving, kind, forgiving God, not a "god of power and might."

**Empowers me. Improved self-esteem. Brings me closer to the Mystery.

**It has opened my eyes and set me on a course that is so soul-satisfying that it maddens me that it took me so long to find it. I see God in a totally new way and it has helped me settle some old psychological fights deep in my soul.

**It's keeping me sane.

**More freedom, more open, happy, expectant, hopeful, than I was ten years ago.

**My spiritual life is much richer and more meaningful.

**Empowerment—spiritually and politically.

**Exciting, enlivening, challenging. fruitful.

**It's the backbone of my purpose for living.

**This experience seems to have stretched and refined me. It's made me enter more deeply into prayer and to trust God. I trusted a gracious and loving God would lead me and this God has.

Such responses certainly sing of the presence of the Spirit of God, a spirit of empowerment to be fully human, a spirit of hope and trust, growth toward freedom. One comment, "It's the backbone of my purpose for living," reminds of what is the true center, where our purpose always was and where we need to consciously return. Her statement is a guidepost as we search for our truest ways of celebration.

A variety of responders set the impact on their lives within the context of the groups themselves.

**I grow to know myself and God in new ways. I have a community of Faith where I can "come Home" and experience acceptance, belonging and refreshment.

**I have enhanced spirituality and a sense of belonging to a small group. A feeling that God loves me, that I am accepted, worthy.

**Gives form to my inner desire for priesthood and lets me see that it is possible. Unites spirits and this is so healing for me, to be in deep communion with others.

**It has helped me to become more aware of how God works in our lives. The sharing that is done has given me precious knowledge. I no longer look for God in one way only. It is helping me to learn the many, many ways God is all around me and in me. God no longer has one face.

**The impact is the realization that prayer is infinitely explorable. The varieties of prayer are endless and women and men should be encouraged to diversify the rigid standard that Rome has given us.

**This has afforded me a measure of community living which I miss, because of living alone. It keeps me honest; keeps me up-to-date; keeps me engaged in eccelesiological awareness.

**Adds another dimension of prayer and spirituality, non-traditional ways, new friendships.

**It keeps me from total spiritual aloneness and gives me community.

**I have a sisterhood who share my search for a meaningful expression of God, my frustration with the Church proper. I am not alone.

**Deep sense of support; group validates some of the countercultural values I espouse and we as a family try to live. Neither mine nor my husband's families are in town so it's like home: aunts, uncles, cousins who share lives and significant events and rites of passage.

**It helps to build spiritual community.

**My group is only about eight months old, yet it has become a very important part of my life. The experience is transforming for me. It has provided a missing link. Perhaps it can simply be explained by it being the difference between being a sports spud and an athlete. It's much more rewarding to participate than to just watch.

**The integration of God's Spirit into my life is wonderful. I hear others share their faith and their pain and their progress, always with their eyes on God. It is wonderful, hopeful that others can survive pain and heartache, there is such promise there for each of us, the promise that through Jesus, with Jesus, in Jesus all things are indeed possible.

THE CIRCLE ⊙

In reality, women live a constant circular flow. Growing personal awareness and transformation enrich the group. The subsequent strengthening of the group in the life of Jesus flows back into the personal lives of women. The process is continuous and spirited. New members who join are impressed and amazed by the capability of women as they ask Jesus to join in ritual. Friend supports friend when misery overtakes. The grace is returned on another occasion when roles are reversed. To do this in the conscious presence of sacrament empowers and emboldens women to work together to see goodness in this work, transform their lives and the lives of others in the reflection of God. Mary Jo Weaver reflects, "Roman Catholic feminist theologians have begun to make it possible for Catholic women to reimagine the church on their own terms, and the WomenChurch movement . . . has begun to provide a setting in which Catholic women along with their Protestant sisters can experience the power of the Gospel in a new, self-created space." [439] She makes an important point. It is not by theology alone, not by intellectual pursuit, that we *know* the goodness of celebration, with all its attendant blessings. Having read, heard, been told, we must *do*. This praxis combines reflection, prayer and study brought to action, then reflected upon and prayed so that we discover, in community, how we are to emerge and renew our world.

These women see an impact in their own lives and are called to reflect on how their changed persons/selves encounter the world around them. We use the insights emerging from growth to observe with new eyes.

*I feel it has been a very positive experience in my life and has changed my view of the institutional church forever. It has made me much more of a radical. It is a source of challenge, hope and support.

**I want to stand up and be counted, be willing to risk. This is my Church; I won't let anyone put me out. We are the Church, Jesus' Church.

**I have now an almost constant awareness of the nuances of sexism and racism.

**I find it difficult to hear what the hierarchical Church has to say on many issues.

**Feminist values are an internal part of my life. Most significantly for me, this impacts on my relationship with my religious congregation. In conscience, I cannot take on canonical status because this aligns me with the patriarchy while also putting me under its direct control. I therefore choose to be a non-canonical associate and am actively involved with other associates and also canonical sisters working to create alternative non-canonical full membership as an option for feminist women.

**Freedom. Knowing the Spirit is not limited to Catholic Church structures.

As one reflective woman insists:

**I know I can't go back!

Out of the birth canal, into the light, we emerge. Emergence implies both *from* somewhere and *into* somewhere else. Emergence has the texture of newness and renewal. It speaks of a past and of a present, as well as aiming toward a future. It is an action word, full of expectancy and promise. Butterflies emerge, transformed. Babies emerge. We emerge because we must. Our time has come, is coming, will come. One by one, apart and together, it dawns on us that we are already a part of birthing a new understanding of what our church is about, and the Spirit of wisdom is midwifing this delivery. As Leonardo Boff puts it, base communities "may still be in embryonic form, but we can already see in them the shape of the church to come. Today's basic communities hold a prophecy, a promise that is slowly becoming historical reality. We shall have a new church, a church born of the faith that nourishes God's people." [440]

**This has been a part of the evolution of my faith journey. I'm on the way—to where I'm not sure. It's great to have companions who are with me.

**This experience is so Spirit-led for me and for my sisters. I experience the Spirit of Jesus inviting us forward, calling our names, wanting us to creep, leap forward. This has led me to ask myself over and over, how are we a part of the present Church, leading inevitably to the future Church? We know for certain that we will continue to become the church that we celebrate. If enough of us practice the loving and forgiving and compelling spirit of Jesus we will emerge as a part of the fresh and powerful people of God. It gives me hope.

✪✪✪✪✪

JUDGING OUR IMPACT, IMAGINING OUR FUTURE

FORETHOUGHT ✪

This last chapter hears women assess the ways in which we believe we influence the institution, and shares our hopes for the future.

✪✪✪✪✪

✳*For freedom Christ set us free; so stand firm and do not submit again to the yoke of slavery.* [441]

✳*We are cultivators of*
the unsayable, weavers
of singulars, migrant
workers in search of
floating gardens as yet
unsown, as yet unharvested. [442]

✳*Nothing is fixed or perpetual*
not rain
or seed
or you
or I
or our grief in this world that is bleeding
because we're forever cutting paths
opening our way along unfamiliar roads
conquering the fury of oblivion verse by verse. [443]

For those of you who have labored with WE through this whole book there will be no surprises here. After all, WomenEucharist is in itself an attempt at the future-in-present. What you have read so far is part of our practicing ourselves into tomorrow. WE rehearses the what-will-be right now, and you have heard our voices.

You may come away from this chapter disappointed. WomenEucharist does not have all the answers. To expect that would be to be seeking answers outside oneself. WE marks some guideposts for some people for the present-into-future, but not all guideposts, and not for all people. WomenEucharist grows from the conviction that the Spirit of God has made a dwelling place in the heart, the soul and the experience of each of us. She does not establish herself in only a few of us to give final answers to the rest of us.

Give yourself a few minutes before you continue here. Ask yourself: what dreams do you have for the future of the people of God? What is *your* part in the story? How are you beckoned to be part of the continuation of salvation history? Does your Eucharistic ritual speak more of liberation and transformation or of status quo and bondage to the past? How are you the face of Jesus to other women, men, children? How do you build up the Body of Christ? What is there that you cannot do alone, but together with believing sisters and brothers can make real? Is Eucharist important enough to you to make it worth saving?

The journey described in these chapters is an attempt, often faintly understood, to live what we celebrate. Women who speak in these pages are trying to hear more clearly the Spirit's invitation to the promises of the liberation ritual of Eucharist and to the stories told within it. No one would claim a complete comprehension of the process. No one knows exactly what is needed for complete transformation of ourselves by and through the Eucharist. That exists in the eye of God, and only gradually, through praxis, do we stumble toward it. However, in these pages we have, in a sense, had no choice. We have already set our feet on the path of the future. We only can choose how we will walk it.

We exist in a certain historic moment, with its own cultural, linguistic, ecclesiastic and ritual models. As much as we might wish to be a part of other times, this moment is our gift. Our challenge is to address the ways in which God is walking with us now.

A large part of the WomenEucharist experiment is a conversation with Eucharistic tradition. What, we keep asking, is normative to the celebration of the sacred meal? In the past the eucharistic prayer has emphasized at one time one element of celebration, at other times another. Different traditions have given us images, prayers, expressions with which we praise and thank. What is wonderful and worthy of preservation? What is an unfortunate accommodation to past culture which we now know hobbles the people of God? Our ritual life is important because, if we live what we celebrate, then the celebration defines the boundaries of our world and how we believe God sees us. Do we wish to continue for ourselves and our children a ritual which enacts the ethics of submission of half the human race? In WomenEucharist we encounter the challenge of reflecting, praying and hearing the Spirit's invitation. We are led toward the mystery of Christ embodied in our gatherings.

IMPACT ⊙

David Power points out, "In the need for women's liberation from patriarchy, within society and within church, the remembrance of the pasch has to be recast in order to ground a renewed communion in thanksgiving and at the table of Christ's body and blood. What feminist theology and liturgy are now exploring has to be incorporated into the common Eucharist. . . . When women play a larger role in the church, they do not simply fit into the structures but they change them. . . . The initiative, however, is at present with women who are exploring their own modes of expression. Their rites, their forms of remembrance, their prayer, as these are shaped in a variety of circumstances, have to become integral to eucharistic development."[444]

Generations held, almost as an article of faith, that the Church and its ritual celebration were unchangeable. Of course, for a long time we have known otherwise. Many of us, though, had no concept of what initiatives for alteration we should take. What was necessary? How should it be accomplished? Only at a snail's pace are we learning that women are now central in transformation. We are central in naming the changes needed to become more genuinely the community of Christ, and to serve more genuinely the liberating meal. We are among those whose call it is to make heaven on earth begin (again) now, to arrive at the place that we started and know it for the first time.

Women are historically less likely to be prime movers in transformation at Church and table. For so long we have had no access to the halls of religious power, nearly voiceless at any official level. Alternately, women are perhaps more likely to be at the forefront of movements for change. It is women (third world, vowed, Hispanic, white, middle-class, divorced, handicapped, lesbian, black, wealthy) who have the most to gain from expanded roles at Jesus' banquet table.

How do we approximate the impact which WomenEucharist has on the institution? Quite a few responders felt that the existence of WomenEucharist will not be much of a battering ram against what seems to be the double-barred doors of the institution. The Vatican administration which can offer such a document as "Ordinatio Sacerdotalis" in May 1994 is unlikely to be viewed as genuinely open to the kind of dialogue which women now require.

When we ask questions about what impact WE has, we are actually seeking to discover whether women as image of God can be accepted by ordained men. Is the feminine in divinity a gift which the institution is willing to receive? Is the Vatican willing to set equal places for half the human race at the sacred table?

NOT MUCH, NOT NOW ✪

**I doubt if we'll have much of an impact but I really don't care.

**As long as we have a conservative pope sending his conservative message, promoting conservative (frightened/intimidated/ threatened) bishops and priests and seminaries accepting any warm male body, things will only get worse before they get better.

**The institutional RC structure is impervious to lay people, especially women, their ideas and needs. Nothing has an impact on it.

**I don't know if I care much if our group and our prayer together has any impact. We are all older and have had some pretty bad times in parishes. It all saddens me when I think about it but I try not to very often because it all upsets me again. It is easier to just not hope anymore that the church will change.

**I feel so small and know that my opinions just don't count in the Church. It is easier to not worry about the institution and try to build up our little community of women.

**Who cares?

**Whether we make a difference or not has stopped being the question.

**Our group and the institutional Church have such different viewpoints that I can't honestly see them being reconciled in my lifetime.

**Over and over our hopes for some response have been dashed.

**I am too tired to try any longer. Now my position is that since I do not honestly believe the institutional Church will within my lifetime care to listen to me, my sisters and brothers, I must spend my energy in building up the community of the Spirit in my own milieu. This is far more satisfying and rejoicing work.

**I'm a skeptic. I think the only thing that impacts the institution is money or the lack of it, so I doubt they even notice.

There are those of us whose experience just does not lend itself to any hope that the ordained community and its supporters will flex sufficiently in the near future to welcome the gifts which women bear. Some responses reflect cynicism or indifference. These can be seen as protective stances against the pain which the Church has caused them in the past. But there is pain here and exhaustion. Women are wounded and worn out. Though they participate in WomenEucharist groups, some are a part of the population which has ceased to worship in a parish because they do not believe they count there.

For the women who voice these feelings WomenEucharist is a home, a resting place.

New understandings are being developed, discussed and prayed which help us to uncover the reality of church which exists when we gather to celebrate in hope and in faith. No longer expending energy on attempting to get new wine into old wineskins, these women have staked their claim to Eucharist as the heritage still worthy of claiming. The issue of impact on the institution has, as one respondent remarks, "stopped being the issue."

Finding the grace to be church while not needing to be of the Church, these women may bring a sense of unbowed equality before God to our future.

HOW AND WHEN ○

**Certainly we will have an impact, although it may take time.

**I hope we have an impact but feel very cautious and skeptical about changing the institution.

**I think WomenChurch will have an impact although I'm not clear about the length of time involved in the process.

**Yes, we'll impact if we remain inclusive, positive, remembering Jesus, Mary and their group who never forgot to praise, work for justice and celebrate their love for all.

**Sure, in a century or so.

**If the "boys" started realizing that we are going about on our own, I think it could have a positive impact.

**If we could get even a few bishops to listen to us, and they could listen to each other and to the Spirit, instead of getting cautious. Yes, we could have an impact.

**I sit in my parish, which I love, and imagine what it will be like in the day that justice is done. That may be a long way down the road but I believe that the day will come.

**The core group of 10 has been together a long time and will continue. In the future perhaps we will have an impact. Right now our contact with Church is too limited. Perhaps as Church is forced to change due to lack of clergy, etc., we can be an effective force.

**I don't think we'll have an impact, but we have to try. We know there are many groups like this in many places all over the world and some day "The Hundredth Monkey" will win over all churches.

**Being able to believe that somehow the revolution toward love and acceptance for all which Jesus promised is possible and is possible in the institution, that is what keeps me in the church, trying to have an impact for inclusion of all, but meanwhile I have found my group to be essential for the prayer and courage to keep on being in the institution.

**I am one of those who bought the idea that I can have more of an impact within the walls than shouting from the outside. I believe that all institutions change, though very slowly, to more greatly reflect the society around them. The Catholic Church will also. It is still in the dark ages though. Our way will have an impact, but I tend to take the long view, just because the church has taken so long on everything historically.

**I stay in the Church because I think we some day will have an impact. I grasp small moments. It took us ages and lots of energy but we finally got the lectionary for daily Mass to be inclusive. Victory! We had to go through the same battle to get inclusive scriptures for Sunday. We had them for awhile, then someone said the pastor would be reported to the bishop, so we are back to non-inclusive on Sundays, so a few of us have taken the tack of approaching individual readers if they don't personally make the language inclusive. It is so slow but maybe someday we'll be able to see progress. After all, Vatican II was only 30 years ago and a lot of those changes which are wonderful are now "institutionalized."

**I am actively committed to reform. WomenChurch and the gospels give me courage and stamina. The only place of positive impact is at our parish level. If (actually when) we get a new pastor we may have to begin again. I look at the priests available in our diocese for pastorates. It honestly scares me. They are getting so old, they are so protective of their positions and they have so much power to determine the way we worship. I just hope that I (and a couple of good sister friends) will have the energy to start again if (when) we need to. Having an impact takes *so* much energy. I see so many younger women who just don't worry about it. The church has had so much less impact on their lives and they feel free to not come or just walk away. I kind of feel like an old war horse, pretty battle scarred, but I don't know any other life, so I keep on going into this battle.

These are the women whom Sandra Schneiders names feminist Catholics. She compares us to "the earliest Jewish Christians who, while continuing to participate in temple and synagogue, also met together in their homes to share and celebrate their Christian identity and faith which could not find expression in the Jewish assembly."[445]

The women who have stated a "maybe" position couch hope in conditional terms, "cautious," "skeptical," "if." Nonetheless, hope is what we demonstrate, even if some of the responses have a "hope against hope" flavor to them.

Those of us in this group will probably continue to have an impact, merely because we have stamina. We probably judge it correctly to be small and slow. We draw strength from the experience of the Spirit and carry that strength back to the parish. Strength is drawn from "the gospels," "praise," "work for justice," and "celebration." Women who inhabit this camp tend to see the future yoked to the institution and therefore look for food for this journey, seeking virtues and exercises which provide the spiritual calories for constant work for change. We tend to look hard for small gains, and draw small satisfactions from them. Through protest, refusal to tolerate exclusive language, challenge to the patriarchy within the walls, we chip away at unjust and unequal foundations. "The work of feminist Catholic theologians, ministers, and parents toward this end (the full and final repudiation of patriarchy) is carried on in the firm hope that one can use the master's tools to dismantle the master's house and that from the debris of the house of ecclesiastical patriarchy we will be able to construct the home of equal discipleship within which the reign of God can be realized."[446]

These women are long-distance runners for change. The goals are distant but achievable. We carry the hope that the institution can change and that we would like to help it to happen. However, WE has impact in lives. There is a safe place to pray and rejoice. One of the women quoted in *Defecting in Place*, says, "I think the power of women's spirituality lies in the opportunities it creates for helping us make meaning in our lives. This world has a long way to go before all that happens in women's spirituality groups can be incorporated into the traditional life of the church. Every woman should have the opportunity to be a part of a women-only group for at least ten years."[447] Without WE many of the responders in this group might place themselves in the first group of responders. WomenEucharist has an impact because such groups of alternative worship make it possible now and into the future to remain in the parish and continue to call ourselves Catholics.

IMPACT NOW ☼

**We are already having an impact.

**I think we will have a positive impact on many individuals. I would hope it would have an institutional positive impact but I'm discouraged.

**The first impact must be on the individuals in our group, and groups such as ours. As we begin to, or continue to, experience the power of the Spirit in ourselves, we cannot help but have a greater sense of respect for God-in-us, and God-in-each-other. This cannot help but flow out not only on the Church but on every aspect of our lives: work, relationships, government. It may take a long time, but this whole movement isn't happening in a vacuum.

**I think the impact is indirect. There is currently no formal feed back to the institution with our group.

**In our parish we have an impact just because the pastor knows that we do meet for Eucharist. He knows we don't feel quite so dependent on him.

**The existence of women's liturgy groups has already had an impact on the institution and will continue to do so.

**Every encounter with the Lord strengthens us. Whether we know it or not, it "infects" us. If we are truly in love with our small communities, and how they make Jesus present, we will keep on being there. When we go back to the parish (those of us who can!) we, by the very differences in us, bring a "new self" with less disappointment, more faith in God, more willingness to challenge. These all have impact. Multiply our growth in faith and courage by ten, we can change a parish. Multiply by a hundred, we can change a diocese, and that is a lot of parishes. Before we began this I would never have had the courage to invite the bishop to breakfast, or to protest an unjust firing to my employer, or to stand up and write letters about the rights of women in the Church. Yes, we are having an impact right now.

**Of course, we impact the Church. This experience is making us stronger Christians.

**This will continue and all shall be well. It has a positive impact because it changes us. I expect more of the Church and am not silent about it.

**Definitely definitely. We impact because we keep the Spirit alive as it withers in the dark corners of many parishes.

**Yes, we will break open patriarchal structure, at least in the Roman Catholic USA communities.

**The impact is that the group empowers people to take charge of their spiritual lives.

**The impact for me and for other women in our group is discovery of the scriptures as liberating. The gospels tell us that we are equal in God. Paul tells us that there is neither female or male. I take my strength from the words of God, and feel that it is my responsibility to live accordingly. I see the world and the church with different eyes and that can't help but make a change.

**We're having an impact. My brothers and their wives yearn for connection with a loving community to worship with.

**An impact on the Church? Well, who thought the Iron Curtain would disappear when it did?

Relevant to these responses is this idea Joan Chittister gives about us: "I think a great new sense of grace is coming into women. I know people want to attach a secular language to it—that it is aggressive, or at least assertive, or it is uppity or out of line. But I think it's what happens to a person who comes face-to-face with the grace of God in life.

"I think you become capable of anything. And no system, no matter how sincere, can ever again convince you that your relationship to God must be mediated by a man, or that God doesn't want to deal directly with you. . . . Somehow you begin to know that what is going on inside you is of God." [448]

This group seems to be the happiest. So many responses contain present-tense verbs! Their responses are not focused on the pain of the institutional encounter. The answers are far more directed toward the growth which is already taking place. "Already having an impact," "continue to experience the power of the Spirit in ourselves," "The experience is making us stronger Christians." *The first important consequence they see is personal.* Reflected in these comments is that sense which Joan Chittister spotlights, "what is going on inside of you is of God."

This kind of joyous discovery can not help but have a secondary impact on the structure. Growing spirit-affirmation within ourselves cannot be hidden. Our every encounter is informed by the God-gift of power within.

Some women already write of the effect this delightful awareness has brought, "brings a 'new self' with less disappointment, more faith in God, more willingness to challenge," "before we began this I would never have had the courage to invite the bishop to breakfast," ". . . take charge of their spiritual lives," "this cannot help but flow out not only on the Church but on every aspect of our lives."

Change has already taken root because we have first heard the Spirit's invitation with our own ears. Every institution is made up of individuals first. Individuals change slowly and they change one by one. But change they do, and not in a vacuum. Our lives take nourishment from many sources, and results are visible. Women who are fed a diet of equality in school, at home and on the factory floor will expect the same in their place to worship. We are reminded that the Church and the world are woven of the same fiber. We who are the church are the world.

We as Christian women really present with Jesus in Eucharist might wish to view our actions and reflections as part of the ongoing conversation with those around us. Those include our friends, our American society, the institution which we call church. It is through the *practicing* of our faith lives that we are led to fresh insights, new understandings of what it is to be a believing woman at the end of the second millennium.

Our impact, short-term and long, individually and as a worshipping circle, will be exactly as much as we live what we celebrate.

HOPE FOR THE FUTURE ✪

The way we get to the future is practicing one day at a time. The journey motif of Exodus reasserts itself in any discussion of what will come. We have heard words and phrases such as "forefront of any movement," "prime movers," "get to," even "snail's pace." They all speak of movement, of not being tonight where we began this morning.

So it is with the people of God. Of course, we are as ragtag as that motley crew of Miriam's and Moses' people. We all have our baggage and our flocks of injuries, issues, individual stories and worries. We all have our own sense of God and how we need to make God more visible to ourselves and to others around us, how we can be more loving and lovable, how we can be Jesus-available to each other, how the signs of Jesus in bread and wine can be less veiled and more transforming.

Next is some of what we have experienced that is good, consoling, food for our ongoing journey.

We're talking future. Renewal, transformation, alternatives, envisioning. The virtue of hope, faith in the future. Dreaming, imagining a new church.

WE HOPE FOR SMALL COMMUNITIES ✪

**It is my hope that there are (or will be) enough of these little groups that at some point the powers that be have to stand back and notice and respond affirmatively. Although even if the c/Church was perfect (now that's a radical thought), I would not want to give up my group. Worshipping in a small community has far greater appeal for me than traditional worship.

**I hope we will grow in all ways. Yet I would not like to have the group become larger in members. Its impact is strong largely because of the small size of the group. So we may perhaps have to divide into more small groups in time.

**I am more and more convinced that for the Church to be meaningful, celebration of the Eucharist must move outside of Church buildings and into the familiarity of the home; small supportive communities are necessary.

**Maybe we need a place, and many places which are safe, beautiful and appropriate to meet and worship. At the moment I can't see how the traditional churches will provide (this), so we have to have smaller groups in smaller places.

**We'll stay small and grow in community.

**I see us as the way of the future. I hope it stays small and intimate.

Small is a gift for the future. The virtues of smallness are becoming more appreciated in many venues as the population and problems of the world enlarge. What are its treasures? A small group offers greater opportunity for personal acceptance. This is a principal gift for (and from) women. Jesus welcomed all sorts of individuals at table, tax collectors, the ritually unclean, those uninvited to the tables of the righteous. Yes, it bothered the religious authorities: "While he was at table in his house, many tax collectors and sinners came and sat with Jesus and his disciples. The Pharisees saw this and said to his disciples, 'Why does your teacher eat with tax collectors and sinners?'" [449] Jesus made sure that we would know that around this table we all have a seat. Jesus wanted to be certain that his friends could see God "up close and personal." He provided a safe house and so does WE. Smallness encourages communion, being at one with. You can't be at home with each other, you can't be at home with God if you are sitting too far away to hear the voices or see the faces.

With the gift of small communion is the possibility of love. We can be loved and we can love, not in theory, but in fact. The love found in small groups cannot be achieved in the abstract. Love moves out of the ivory tower, out of the pages of a book, to be given and received specifically. "Love one another, as I have loved you." This is being able to recognize the face of Jesus without judgment in the story, the smell, the quirks of the person next to us. This loving as we have been loved is easiest in theory, rather more difficult face to face. Mary Hunt describes this as "voluntary human relationships that are entered into by people who intend one another's well-being and who intend that their love relationship is part of a justice-seeking community." [450] When we love another we will wish no harm, we will not judge, and we will work for and with the goodness of the beloved. They will do the same. The risk-to-reward ratio favors taking a chance.

Small Church in the living room encourages sharing on the issues of empowerment and the identification of charisms, and the need for forgiveness and the call to justice. Intimate Church in the kitchen encourages mutuality and participation.

It is far easier to share our faith around a breakfast room table than in a church which holds five hundred. Our lived experience in many places in North America is one of loss of community, of increasing rootlessness and facelessness. Transience for jobs, the corrosion of neighborhoods, the internationalization of even small towns through television and newspapers, all break down the sense of safety and being known. Huge parishes with cattle-car Sunday liturgies do the same; teeming Masses, indeed. Rules are made for a great faceless horde of humans; circumstances cannot be individually considered. How can we share our faith and tell our stories unless we know those on our right and left? Some respondents know they can encourage personal interchange by staying out-side the institutional church buildings and praying in living rooms and kitchens.

Smallness is counter-cultural and a variety of individuals have begun to sing its prais-es. Arthur Baranowski who has studied diverse faith communities remarks, "The way we come together as church is primary. . . . Faith and love are experiences. The more these experiences are shared—*and this can happen best in a small group*— the more people notice God and God's call to be church for one another."[451] (my italics)

Smallness in worship does not guarantee com-union, but we notice each other. We notice each other in the context of God. We believe that when we meet in such manner we are church. Not some offshoot, but the very body of Christ which is a kind of sacra-ment, even if there are only two of us. Leonardo Boff says, "(Small church communities) represent . . . a renaissance of very church, and hence an action of the Spirit. Seen in this way,. . .(they) deserve to be contemplated, welcomed, and respected as salvific events."[452]

When we can see our small communities of sacrament as salvific events, we have shift-ed the axis of power from outside the circle to Christ who is the power of goodness, the power of transformation, the power of death and resurrection at the center of our gathering.

Some will worry about how small groups can be served when there are already too few (ordained) to serve them. WE shifts the center to the faith life of the community, where charisms will, as they always have, become evident, and ministries-in-service will be raised up. Imagine four or five or ten assorted humans marooned on an island. Passively waiting for rescue is a mistake; the focus for survival is centered in ourselves and in the other castaways. Small groups allow individuals to recognize their own calls to min-ister, and to identify such calls in the others sitting around the table. When we must do for ourselves, instead of passively being ministered to, we gradually become empowered resources of service for our own groups and the world at large. Smallness encourages hospitality to Spirit-driven talents and therefore should be fostered.

Small gatherings do not preclude the occasional larger get-together (the "cathe-dral" moments) in which we can be gratefully amazed at the throng of sisters and broth-ers. The cathedral moments should be exactly that, moments. The seduction of size (See how successful we are!!) reflects concern about how others view us. This is not a contest! The Catholic Church, and most other churches, have played the numbers game long enough to recognize its flaws.

The WE groups indicate that smallness is a gift indeed which in the present/future must be preserved.

WE WANT OPENNESS AND ACCEPTANCE ✪

**My group is a way of coping at this time of history in our institutional church. I still look for the day when the official men of my church will enter into dialogue with us women and not speak for us but with us.

**The stronger women become, the more they will pressure the Church to humanize itself.

**I am led to seek people with whom to share my longings for a greater role for women in the Church.

**The group will go on because God is with us. We are hopeful that our church will become increasingly open to us rather than defining us and putting us in boxes in which we're not comfortable. They don't know us because they don't have our hearts and minds. We're not who they want us to be, but we are their friends, not enemies. They need not fear us. We need to love and respect one another, to truly commune with each other. This movement will provide an outlet for those in suffering from oppression and suppression that now exists for its women.

**We will continue to wean ourselves from the patriarchy, women will grow in ministry with, not over others.

**We will as individuals and as a group of prayerful women continue to become more whole/holy as we work to find out how God is here in us and with us and working through us.

**If the patriarchal Church refuses to give up unjust power over adult women, we will go on without them. We will pray for them, but no longer allow them the power to oppress us. I and my sisters already gather to pray and more and more women in the future will join us, all probably in small circles. The spirit of God is present in these gatherings. God doesn't wish for the lack of inclusion, and for the demeaning and the disrespect that the institutional Church dishes out to women and to all people who are less powerful. This has been a perversion of the Gospels in many ways, the institution should be embarrassed.

Given a chance to dream the future, women hope for "dialogue," "greater roles for women," "an outlet for those in suffering from oppression," "inclusion."

Women of WE have faith that there will be in the future a recognition of our full baptized humanity in the circle of church. This is the cry which goes up from women across the world. We believe that WomenEucharist and similar women's spirituality groups provide some genuine practical clues for the future worship of the people of God. Moving past the constraints of Church which has deemed baptized women as less equal, small prayer communities seek new ways of seeing each other as the image of Christ, and practicing that vision into being.

These liberation structures are thus described by Letty Russell, "Feminist and liberation communities seek to live out a vision of new creation in which there is a possibility of wholeness in relationship among women and men of all races, classes, sexual orientations and abilities, as well a the whole of creation.

"Clues to this unknown reality may be discovered in the new formations of women's spiritual support groups who gather in the round, searching for new connections: to themselves and to the world; to God and to their communities of faith."[453]

Though there are multitudes of women who have moved to spiritual- life states where they would label themselves post-Christian, those of us who remain as members of Christian community continue to see ourselves as defecting in place. Imbedded in the very idea of feminist WomenEucharist community is the belief that within the patriarchal Christian tradition there are aspects which are salvageable for women. We can pick apart tradition and find that which can be rewoven into useful goods. "For some, the vision of transcendence within tradition is seen as an authentic core of revelation pointing toward freedom from oppression, a freedom (we) believe is articulated more clearly and consistently within tradition than without."[454]

For that authentic core of revelation to be revealed for feminist Christians the future must hold the certainty that women, and all peoples, will be *genuinely* recognized as Spirit-bearers, will be treated with dignity, will have their experience honored as part of the message of Christ-made-flesh in our time.

And, as respondents said, "We want love and respect, true communion" . . . "We are their friends, not enemies." These phrases are of hope, possibilities of growth and forgiveness. They honestly sound like Jesus' words. They are from the victims of discrimination and oppression, who know the pain of patriarchy, and yet look for communion. These statements alone are signs of hope for our tradition.

We practice in our Eucharistic rituals a world of inclusion, a rebirthed tradition of dialogue, greater roles for women and an outlet for those suffering from oppression. We are rehearsing in liturgy a world of inclusion.

There are those of us who believe sufficiently that we become what we celebrate to spend our futures in the work.

WHAT ABOUT MEN AT WOMENEUCHARIST? ✪

**Recently we discussed the possibility of allowing men to join at some point in the future. I have mixed reactions. The liberal in me dislikes excluding groups of people based on gender. The radical says, "too bad." This doesn't have a lot to do with life style preference. Men change a group and as well intentioned as they may be, very few are really able to overcome a lifetime of conditioning in terms of behavior and attitude. If this sounds like stereotyping, it probably is.

**Sometimes we struggle about adding men to the group. So far, we have had times when some of our male friends and family members have attended. However we feel that the woman-centered experience is important to us.

**I am deeply in love with a man, but I cannot pray the deepest prayers of my heart, of my own experience, if he is present. I have to be careful "how I sound." My sisters in prayer in my group understand. This is the first time in my whole life that I have experienced freedom of religion. It is wonderful. I do not want to exclude men at all, but we need time . . . I want this to be an opportunity that many women have, and for a long time in the future. This has been an unveiling of God for me. What a great gift we could give if this were something we could offer others.

The people of God exiled in Babylon asked, "But how could we sing a song of the LORD in a foreign land?" [455] Many many women look upon organized Christianity as a man's world, a place where women are captive but not welcome. The songs of the Spirit, the songs of liberation are heard faintly, if at all. WE is an attempt to gather freely and hear clearly the voice of God in our own time and experience.

Rosemary Radford Ruether shaped the concept of free gathering for women in this way, "Precisely because of women's isolation from each other, separated by patriarchal family structures, their deprivation of education, and even of speech, their cultural colonization by an education that incorporates them into a language that they have not defined, but which defines them as inferior and auxiliary to a male dominated world, women need separate spaces and all female gatherings to form the critical culture that can give them an autonomous ground from which to critique patriarchy."[456]

(For those who read these words in a first world country where progress has been made in education for women, awareness of the harm of male-based language, and criminalization of domestic violence, it is important to keep in mind that there are many places on this earth where women still live in virtual slavery, illiterate, subject to violence from men without the possibility of protection. We are sisters to these women.)[457]

First, second, third world, we all need a place to pray where we can pray freely and without fears of retribution, a place to hear ourselves into speech, hear ourselves grow bold in the spirit, a place to exercise prophetic imagination without fear of condemnation.

Diann Neu says, "Women-church feminist liturgies keep alive the memory and imagination of the community of women believers and of those children and men who identify with them." [458]

Before healing memory can be kept alive it must exist for us. WomenEucharist makes possible the creation of alternative memory, the memories-to-be of ourselves as fully equal, fully capable, fully invited to the sacred table. These are memories which begin haltingly as the call of the spirit in the imaginations of first one and then another. These are the prophetic stirrings which call us to know, *in and through* our pain, that there is the possibility of fresh incarnation in our time and in our culture. The imagination which circles what is and then sees beyond it, to what can be, is a frequent way in which God is present to those who are oppressed.

Blessed imagination takes form in the eucharistic acts of these gathered women. We must begin somewhere, in order to take flesh and both become memory (which is past) and stretch out into the future. We step forward to investigate how Jesus enters into feminist community. The prophetic imagination which is embodied in the liturgies of WE is the future being activated, being driven by the Spirit. "Only if some groups work intensely and exclusively on imagining an alternative culture in a way that cannot be controlled or limited by patriarchal culture . . . does the possibility of a genuine transformational dialectic take place."[459]

Free to conspire with the Spirit, and recognized by others as fully the subjects of the salvation event, we can stand free and welcome into our spaces men who wish to be a part of our prayer. Their "lifetime of conditioning in terms of behavior and attitude" is also being inflected by the liberation of women in secular society, and by women in ministry. Gradually we can look to a future in which people are far more likely to comfortably select the time, style and place of worship as well as their companions on the journey.

**I believe that the time will come when I feel sufficiently strong in myself and in my group that I will welcome men freely without worry about their judgments and this will take me feeling like a fully upright woman. I am working toward this future.

**Our feminist worship should never be exclusionary—women must never do to men what they have done to us. That's a big challenge but I think women can meet it and not slip into revenge and resentment mentally.

**Women cannot celebrate life without men. We do not have baby factories yet. Life celebrations and Eucharistic celebrations will always be less than authentic if they are sex-defined. Normalcy is a basic in my evaluation of human process. Soon we may come back to a balance but not until men stop seeing themselves as normative.

**I look to a future where all people can worship together and/or separately as it is appropriate.

OUR LIVES AND OUR LITURGY ✪

**Liturgy will again become connected to the realities of our daily lives. As it is celebrated in the buildings of the institutional Church, liturgy is most often out of touch with the experiences of our lives. Liturgy needs to celebrate and remember the wholeness of our existence. It is too fragmented, perhaps because celibate males make the rules governing our celebrations.

**We will come more and more to honor the diversity of our groups, so that no one will feel herself an outcast. This is something we need to practice every time we meet. Being without judgment allows the spirit of Jesus to show itself in every human form, in every human experience.

**We'll continue appealing to those men and women who have felt disenfranchised by the Institution of Church.

**I hope we can continue to grow by adding members. I hope the church will try to have the parishes divide into small communities and try to meet the daily needs of the people.

God is present in the fabric of our lives. This is where the immanent God dwells. Acceptance of God's reality in our experience can allow women's stories of their lives to come forward as gifted material. As we lift the stories up, like the tales of Exodus, and Jesus' parables of human search, we recognize that the dailyness of our lives has power. Spiritual power is present to provide insights to the group of how God permeates us.

Those of us who are disenfranchised can see ourselves and our stories pregnant with God. Those of us who are outcasts, fragmented, we can hope to be welcomed because in our very lives Jesus lives and moves and has his being. We have thought it was dross but find out it is gold. This is the stuff of which prophecy comes, but only if we hear the call to tell our truths. "It is no small matter in the history of civilization to learn that ordinary people are all called to a prophetic vocation. This could truly be the energy that brings about a New Creation, were it believed in, that is *trusted.. . . .* It is a trust not based on human apprehension or human power but on the grace of the Holy Spirit, which is truly poured out on all humankind."[460]

In the future, in small groups we will continue to expand awareness and trust of the role God's presence in our life stories plays in liturgy and liturgy in our lives.

FUTURE IN PRESENT ✪

**We are recreating a wayward church in the Spirit of Christ.

**We have formed an ecumenical women's group as an offshoot.

**We seem to be becoming more bonded and connected as a group and this is exciting to experience. I see this continuing and deepening. We are already transforming the Church. As the institution continues to crumble we are growing and thriving and I would think somewhere in the future the institution will die and we will continue. (We being the WomenChurch movement)

**I am hopeful and excited based on our first eleven years. Not only will it have a positive impact, it DOES have such an impact in the present. This is the future of the Church. Such communities will "keep the faith" while the institution hangs onto celibacy, sexuality, sexism and status. I see the group continuing much the same as it has, fluctuating in attendance, but with a very strong core group. We are changing the church but we have a long road ahead of us.

**Religious practice, like all aspects of social change, is a constantly evolutionary process.

This is a continuum. By the very imagining into action the future is upon us. One woman says she is "hopeful and excited based on our first eleven years." Living, experimenting, praying and worshipping, she has been defining her future for over a decade. She and a multitude of others see themselves as part of those who keep the faith.

The respondents say this is an "evolutionary process," implying its ongoing nature. WE "recreates" and "transforms" the new church of the people of God. This renewal is at the heart of every major step forward that the people of God have made. The pain of what is calls forth the dream of what might be. The participants see this as a part of the call of the spirit of imagination. "What Catholic feminists, especially those who are active in WomenChurch, are contributing to the spirituality of women who are both Catholic and feminist is a whole new repertoire of songs, new liturgical forms for the imagination, a proleptic image of a new church. These women have bravely moved ahead and begun to live what they believe, not waiting for permission or until the rest of the church is ready to move."[461]

Women called by the spirit of imagination to raise their hands in faith over bread and wine will continue to evolve in their understandings. As we grow in trusting the Spirit we will find more areas for growth, more avenues for action.

WHAT ARE OUR HOPES? ✪

**Hopefully we will endure and grow.

**I hope we will continue for a long time.

**I hope we'll stay dynamic, ever changing, attracting younger women. Always searching.

**Constantly changing, becoming stronger.

** I only hope we can keep ourselves alive and perhaps be responsive to others who find their needs unmet by the institution.

Just keep on being. That is what many women say. Let these good worship groups just keep being here for us. Let us keep on doing what we are doing now. We are recognizing that a powerful new step is being taken in each celebration, each gathering, each liberation moment of WomenEucharist. In these fervent answers vibrates the hope that our gatherings will not dissolve, but develop and find their spot in the ongoing cycle of spiritual maturing.

The responses speak of both being and changing. Already we are looking forward into what can be the healthy tension between maintaining a sacred gift and finding the growth and change which will keep it vital. The Whiteheads have this insight, " In the never ending cycle of religious maturing, two dynamics seem of especial importance. One is the inner dynamic of change itself: energetic but fragile insights survive only in organized structures. . . . Our best hopes, generated in sudden vision or charismatic insight, only endure by being protected in social structures. The second dynamic is that by which communities slip into stagnation."[462]

There are no certain answers now about how we preserve this amazing Spirit of God present. She stirs us and breathes through us and guides us. An attempt to plan every moment of the future betrays a lack of trust that she will continue to dwell in our tent. Some respondents see that the journey is an act of faith. Be a thankful, faithful, patient people. She will be with us.

**It is very important to keep on doing what we are doing. Gather, pray, be thankful. The Spirit will speak to us as she has done in the past. We would not be where we are if she hadn't spoken already, over and over. Now we need to be patient, sit in the tent with Shekinah. She will guide us. We need to trust that it may not be for this generation to see the fruit of our work.

**I'm not sure how quickly the numbers will grow, but I do think that if we listen carefully to the Spirit and be faithful to God's love we will expand.

**We must trust our Wise Mother, she is gathering her daughters because it is time for us to take the place she has set for us. We will prevail if we listen to Her, remain open and patient and faithful. We may be amazed at what comes.

**Who could have imagined ten years ago that we would be doing this? It amazes me, and it is so wonderful. The Spirit has called us, has "imagined" into us the idea. She is trustworthy and we need to keep being open so she can imagine the next step for us.

DOING JUSTICE ✪

**I would like to see some networking among other WomenChurch groups in our geographical region.

**When Jesus said "do this in memory of me," I believe he meant all sorts of "doing." Do justice, wash feet, feed, visit. Our group needs to continue to work on discernment of our ministries.

**I would like to emphasize the action part of this whole movement. I think that the women involved in gathering, discussing, ritualizing are also women engaging in social justice issues, usually because we see this movement as one of social justice as well as personal development.

**If we test all of our deeds against the Gospel, and they mesh, keep making justice with our associates and whoever else will listen, pray a lot, get footholds in where we can so as to share the Spirit, maintain our hope and resolve by keeping all the supports we have and KEEP LOVING GOD AS WE DO THE WORK, we can keep being church.

**Our group is called, at this time, to help women who are abused. In the future we need to continue to listen to the Spirit. New avenues will open.

**If we believe that through our liturgies we can overcome and outgrow our own oppression, then we must also work for the liberation of women, men and children, anyone who is a victim of unjust power structures.

**No way to avoid it, the messages of Jesus are political, they call for us to pray and then to *act* and to pray again.

**I find in my life and in my worship group the stories of liberation being worked out now. We have a never ending need to be of service to others.

**I am so angry sometimes, as are many members of our group. Liturgy helps me not to feed on that anger but to transform it. Good liturgy gets our feet moving, gets us involved against injustice. The energy of our anger gives us energy to act. This is a gift of Jesus. We read the scriptures as liberation and then our anger can be seen not as a curse but as a gift.

**This feels right. I am excited at the possibilities this brings up. I am warmed and encouraged in my dreams and hopes by these times of celebration with women.

**We hope to become inspired to be more active and broader in our response to so many needs.

**One of our members is elderly and somewhat house bound, but she feels that the message of the Gospel she hears when we gather has empowered her to write to the bishops of the US on a regular basis to remind them of the words of the Gospels and the social justice encyclicals. Each of us is called. It is a profound Gift of Faith to believe that we empower one another as Jesus did.

**It's important to do liturgy, and clean toilets. As soon as we sit around theorizing and praying and think that is more important than getting our hands dirty in the work of the Lord we will lose the thread of the journey. We need to pray and laugh and hope and work and then repeat the process. We need to invite others who are suffering into our homes and listen to their struggles and their wisdom and break bread with them.

**When Jesus said that the poor would always be here, he offered us the possibility of always having someone around with whom we could share our riches. We will always have people, projects, needs which will call us. Our group needs to do more listening so that we can hear the voice of Jesus in our Eucharist and carry that into our daily living.

**Our group holds as central that what we deeply know comes out of our own troubles, struggles and joys. What we can place in the hands of God are those very things. It is through the embrace of our own pain that we can know the pain of other people. Knowing that pain we cannot turn away. Our Eucharist gives us both the forum in which to know that God calls us to life and the springboard for launching the works of mercy. I can't at this time envision that this call will ever be completely finished.

Though passivity was imaged as a woman's virtue, it is through women that life actively becomes. And it is most often through and by women that the social and cultural roles of nurturance take place.

With the growth in awareness and articulation of our awesome power to be life-givers, -shapers, -preservers, we see our futures molded in the stories we tell and the meal we share. The sufferings in our communities and in our world, the threat to life from violence and pollution give great urgency to the call to work for life.

Women, feminist people, are embracing a life-with rather than a power-over the world around us. We more and more often identify with the pain of the world. We see ourselves as more like than different from those around us. It is doing away with dualities, reuniting mind and body, humans and earth that we see as key to the future.

The work of justice recognizes that there is no area which is not worthy of love and concern, not the blessed Body of God which we call Mother Earth, not its smallest creatures.

Joan Chittister reminds us that "a commitment to creation, . . . and a sense of human connectedness is the vision that religion must bring to the peacemaking agenda

for the 90s. We must be a voice for the voiceless, we must be a clear call to cosmic conscience; we must turn the world around one heart at a time." [463]

The women of WomenEucharist testify that their vision of the future is one which not
only prays for life, but works for it.

AND SO . . . ✪

These women's voices ring with fresh insights, incarnations of what the message of
Jesus Christ is in our time. Every one of us is hearing the Spirit and sharing the news: smallness, openness and acceptance of all, men included, honoring the connection between
the stories of our lives and the ways that we pray, trusting, growing, endurance. Above
all, continuing to love God. By our very lives, insights, faith in the words of the scripture
and story, we are living a new creation. We as women know that the sacred table, circle,
banquet continues to promise liberation to us all.

COMMENCEMENT THOUGHTS ✪

We are standing in a wide open welcoming circle facing the living Christ at its center. We have listened hard to how many different women describe their view. Each voice
in sacred perspective.

These women of WomenEucharist are brave. It has been a deep honor to know
them, often not by face, but by the personal and spirit-filled discernments which they
have shared here. They demonstrate the traits which, I believe, we require to keep on
being the Body of Christ in our day.

These women have living imagination. They are willing to reimagine what God's life
in us is all about. Part of the reimagining process is the uncovering of what our theological
assumptions are. These unaddressed assumptions form the basis for our understanding of
what life is about, how God relates to us, how we relate to God. Unchallenged assumptions form the basis for daily judgments, perceptions and style. Bringing these to daylight
allows us to muse about their meanings. This is a long process, fueled by prayer, honest
encounters with others, openness to the possibility of change, willingness to hear what
news Spirit might want to share about how she is present and wants us to behave.

All creation is basically the work of imagination. To recreate the church is a work of the imagination. The radical imagination of these women is an ever-deepening dream of how the love of Jesus will be acted out in our time. Dreaming, envisioning, these are the works of imagination. Inspiration, yearning, desire, just anger, impatience. search, flowering, birth, poetry, justice, anticipation, New Creation.

Through openness to the Spirit we conspire with the Sacred Imagination.

These women have tenacity. Around the sacred circle are our foremothers, our mothers in birth and in mentoring. They held on through centuries of opposition, and their daughters, these responders, hold on still. Giving up is not in the game plan. Surely, we grasp tightly because we believe that Jesus wants us, in the past, present and future, equal around the sacred table. We do not give up on Christ because Christ does not give up on us.

We will need to continue this virtue for the work is long from over. Our Eucharist is food for a long long walk. We are not only called to stand straight and equal ourselves, as God intended, we must help others to do the same, while working for a world both physical and spiritual which is a credit to the Creative Imagination.

These women have hope that these things can be accomplished based on faith. The faith is based in certainty of God, present, immanent, holding us. Through what we discern in Eucharist it is possible to rebuild a world riddled with racism, sexism, classism and ecological destruction. It is possible to find a life in which all are equal and equally beloved. Utopian, yes, the best kind of hope. All things are possible with God.

Feast of Mary Magdalene

INDEX

FOOTNOTES

[1] Winter, Miriam Therese, *Woman Prayer Woman Song*, Meyer Stone Books, Oak Park, Illinois, 1987. p. 186.

[2] In a significant study of women's spiritual journey, *Defecting In Place*, Winter, Miriam Therese, Lummis, Adair and Stokes, Allison, eds.,The Crossroad Publishing Company, New York, 1994, this comment is made, " What women are saying is, we are different, our spiritual needs are different, our experiences and our theology are different, our view of the world and our place in it and our understanding of what God expects of us are very different. Work with us. Listen to us. Share an experience of God with us, but allow us to remain true to the Spirit and to the integrity of grace within us." pp. 179-180.

[3] Dickinson, Emily, *Final Harvest*, Little, Brown and Company, Boston, 1961. p. 231.

[4] Kinsella, John, "Bernard Lonergan, SJ," *America*, September 11,1993. p. 13.

[5] Anderson, Sherry Ruth, and Hopkins, Patricia, *The Feminine Face of God*, Bantam Books, New York, 1991. p. 228.

[6] See Chapter 4,"Feminist Spirituality Groups for Support and Alternative Liturgy," *Defecting In Place*, Winter, Lummis, Stokes. This is a wonderful and human discussion of the flow of women's personal authority over their own spirituality. Many of the women surveyed for this study suffered from the same fears and uncertainties as the women of WE.

[7] Acts 2: 46-47.

[8] Ruether, Rosemary Radford *Sexism and God Talk*, Beacon Press, Boston,1983. p. 193.

[9] Ruether, Rosemary Radford. *Women-Church*, Harper & Row, San Francisco, 1985, p. 61.

[10] Prior to the first mailing, it was obvious that anonymity was going to be a significant issue. Women told me that they could not answer the questions if there was a possibility that their names might be attached. Those who most often verbalized the fear were women religious (who believed their participation in such a group might bring censure from within their orders, or, more frequently, from male clerics in their diocese) and women who were employed by the church as teachers, social workers, etc. They almost universally had witnessed retribution to others who had displeased the clergy. One woman said that when her superior discovered that she was a part of a WE group, she and two of her sisters in religion who also participated were ordered to undergo psychiatric examination.

[11] Definition of the institutional church: The religious and cultural institution which designates and controls the exercise and symbols of power through a web of symbols, creeds, canonized scripture, rubrics of sacramental worship and whose public posture consistently denies the ministerial gifts of women. with thanks to Rosemary Radford Ruether.

[12] Aristotle, *De Generation Animalium*, translator, Gweneth Whitteridge, Oxford, Boston, 1981.

[13] Thomas Aquinas, *Summa Theologica,* Q 75, art. 4, pt. 111, Benziger Brothers, New York, 1984.

[14] Kant, Emmanuel, *Observations on Feeling of the Beautiful and Sublime,* translator, John Goldthwait, University of California Press, Berkeley, 1960.

[15] Nietzsche, Friedrich, *Thus Spake Zarathustra,* translator, Thomas Common, Boni and Liveright, Inc., New York, 1917.

[16] Ratzinger, Cardinal Joseph, as quoted in the *National Catholic Reporter.* Dec. 11, 1987.

[17] Robbins, Marty, "Devil Woman."

[18] Kempton, Sally, "Cutting Loose," *Esquire* 7/1970.

[19] Lerner, Gerda, *The Creation of Feminist Consciousness*, Oxford University Press, New York, 1993. p. 23.

[20] Ibid. p. 44.

[21] Ibid. p. 50.

[22] Ibid. p.195.

[23] Grimke, Sarah M., "Letter on the Equality of the Sexes and the Condition of Women," *Feminism: The Essential Historical Writings,* ed. Schneir, Miriam. Random House, NY, 1972. p. 38.

[24] Chittister, Joan,OSB, *Women Strength,* Sheed & Ward, Kansas City, 1990. p.12.

[25] See Thomas, Susan, Women and Anger, Springer Publishing Company, Inc., New York,1993. p.136.

[26] Millett, Kate, *Sexual Politics,* Doubleday, Garden City, NY, 1970.

[27] Rountree, Cathleen, *On Women Turning Fifty,* HarperSanFrancisco, 1993. p. 3.

[28] Ruether, *Women-Church,* p. 127.

[29] Winter, Lummis, Stokes, op. cit. p. 97.

[30] Thomas, op. cit. p. 45.

[31] Osiek, Carolyn, *Beyond Anger,* Paulist Press, New York, 1986. p. 13.

[32] McEwan, Dorothea,ed.,*Women Experiencing Church,* Fowler Wright Books, Leominster, 1991. p. 35.

[33] Schneiders, *Beyond Patching,* Paulist Press, Mahwah, NJ, 1991. p. 99.

[34] Thomas, op. cit. p. 29.

[35] Ibid. p. 47.

[36] Ibid. p. 46.

[37] Ibid. p. 238.

[38] Ibid. p. 47.

[39] Job 40:32

[40] Thomas, op. cit., p. 73.

[41] *If Any One Can NCAN,* Ware, Ann Patrick SL, National Coalition of American Nuns, 1989. p. i.

[42] Ibid. p. 1.

[43] Ibid. p. 6.

[44] Ibid. p. 67.

[45] Osiek, op. cit. p. 26.

[46] Ibid. p. 28.

[47] Ibid. p. 37.

[48] Ibid. p. 41.

[49] Lummis, Stokes, Winter, op. cit. p. 111.

[50] Jefferson, Margo, "Great (Hazel) Scott," MS, 1974.

[51] Day, Dorothy, *Meditations*, Paulist Press, New York, 1970. p. 41.

[52] Flannery, Austin OP, *Vatican Council II The Conciliar and Post Conciliar Documents*, Liturgical Press, Collegeville, Minnesota, 1980. p. 5.

[53] Ibid. p.162.

[54] FitzPatrick, P.J., *In Breaking of Bread*, Cambridge University Press, New York, 1993. p. 375.

[55] Driver, Tom F., *The Magic of Ritual*, HarperSanFrancisco, 1981. p. 136.

[56] Chittister, op. cit. p. 39.

[57] Schneiders, op. cit. p. 33.

[58] Ruether, *Women-Church*, p. 74.

[59] Ibid. p. 184.

[60] Driver, op. cit. p. 207.

[61] Ibid. p. 182.

[62] Heywood, Carter, "Sexuality, Love and Justice," *Weaving the Visions*, Plaskow, Judith and Christ, Carol P., eds., HarperSanFrancisco, 1989. p. 295.

[63] Ibid. p. 300.

[64] Patterson, Eleanora, "Suffering," *Reweaving the Web of Life*, New Society Publishers, Philadelphia, 1982. pp. 166-67.

[65] Schreck, Nancy OSF and Leach, Maureen, *Psalms Anew*, p. 54.

[66] Hebblethwaite, Peter, "Vatican Bank Scandal Reappears in Venezuela," *National Catholic Reporter*, Dec. 24, 1993, p. 12.

[67] Anderson & Hopkins, op. cit. p. 8.

[68] Winter, Miriam Therese, *Woman Wisdom*, The Crossroad Publishing Company, New York, 1991, p. 293.

[69] Lee, Bernard, SM,"Introduction to the Series," *Alternative Futures For Worship*, The Liturgical Press, Collegeville, Minnesota, 1987. p.13.

[70] Kavanagh, John, "This Is My Body," *America*, December 11, 1993. p. 23.

[71] Luke 1: 37.

[72] Schraffran, Janet CDP and Kozak, Pat CSJ, *More Than Words*, Privately published, Cleveland, 1986, p. 99.

[73] Sarton, May, "A Glass of Water," *Selected Poems Of May Sarton*, W.W. Norton and Company, New York, 1978. p. 110.

[74] See Fiorenza, Elisabeth Schüssler, *In Memory of Her*, The Crossroad Publishing Company, New York, 1992, Especially chapter 5.

[75] Kilmartin, Edward J., "Theology of the Sacraments: Toward A New Understanding Of The Chief Rites Of The Church Of Jesus Christ," *Alternative Futures For Worship*, vol.1, pp. 124-125.

[76] Lerner, op. cit. pp. 46-47.

[77] See Dowell, Sue, "One Unholy and Divided Trinity," *Women Experiencing Church*, p. 156.

[78] Rountree, Cathleen, op. cit. p. 8.

[79] Murphy, Margaret, *How Catholic Women Have Changed*, Sheed & Ward, Kansas City, 1987. p. 116.

[80] Schneiders, pp. 87-89. An excellent short volume on faith and feminism. Also see Carr, Anne E., *Transforming Grace*, Harper & Row, New York, 1990, especially Chapter 10 on Christian feminist spirituality. Plaskow, Judith and Christ, Carol P., eds., *Weaving the Visions,* has a wonderful collection on aspects of feminist spirituality from the perspective of women from varied backgrounds. Anderson, Sherry Ruth and Hopkins, Patricia, *The Feminine Face of God*, excellent for stories of women seeking the sacred within.

[81] Wagner, Clare, "Women's Prayer: How It's Changing," *Praying* Magazine, January-February, 1988, p. 4.

[82] Lee, "Introduction to the Series," p. 15.

[83] Wagner, op. cit. p. 6.

[84] Ibid. p. 7.

[85] Lee, Bernard J., op. cit. p. 17.

[86] See *Defecting in Place*, p. 167, for some wonderful comments on changing spirituality. "Women are preaching from their changed perspective in a language they comprehend. Like yeast, they are there in the communities of believers, desiring transformation, and like bread, their voices are rising. . . . While it may seem that the focus is on the externals, such as language and leadership, such issues are the strategies for approaching and effecting change."

[87] Whitehead, James D. and Evelyn Eaton, *The Emerging Laity*, Image Books, New York, 1988. pp. 174-175.

[88] Gilligan, Carol, "In a Different Voice: Visions of Maturity," *Women's Spirituality*, Joan Wolski Conn, ed., Paulist Press, New York. 1986. pp. 63 ff.

[89] Kerouac, Jack, "Two Poems Dedicated to Thomas Merton," *a MERTON concelebration*, Patnaik, Deba, ed., Ave Maria Press, Notre Dame, Indiana. 1981. p. 27.

[90] Isasi-Diaz, Ada Maria and Tarlengo, Yolanda, *Hispanic Women: Prophetic Voice in the Church*, Harper & Row, San Francisco. 1988. p. 6.

[91] "Declaration on Religious Liberty," *Vatican Council II*, Flannery,ed. 2:15 p. 812.

[92] "3 New York City Students Win Westinghouse Science Awards," *The New York Times*, March 15,1994. p. B3.

[93] King, Martin Luther Jr., *Where Do We Go From Here: Chaos or Community?* Beacon Press, Boston, 1968. p. 170.

[94] Evans, Sara M., *Born For Liberty*, The Free Press, New York, 1991. p. 274.

[95] "Dogmatic Constitution on the Church," *Vatican Council II*, Flannery, ed., op. cit. 1:1 p. 350.

[96] Ibid.1:5. p. 353.

[97] Ibid. 1:5. p. 353.

[98] Ibid. 2:10. p. 361.

[99] Ibid.

[100] Ibid. 2:12. p. 363.

[101] "Decree on the Apostolate of Lay People," Introduction, Flannery,ed., op. cit. 1. p. 767.

[102] Ibid. 3:10. p. 777.

[103] "Dogmatic Constitution on Divine Revelation," Ibid. 6:25. p. 764.

[104] "Instruction on the Worship of the Eucharistic Ministry," Introduction, ibid. 1. p.100.

[105] "Constitution on the Sacred Liturgy," ibid. 33. p.13.

[106] "General Instruction on the Roman Missal," Ibid. Forward,12. p. 159.

[107] Ibid. 66. p. 182.

[108] Ibid. 14. p.160.

[109] "Instruction on the Manner of Distributing Holy Communion," ibid. p.152.

[110] "General Instruction on the Roman Missal," ibid. 1:3, p.162.

[111] "Instruction on the Worship of the Eucharistic Mystery," ibid. 4. p. 105.

[112] Whitehead and Whitehead, op. cit. p. 62.

[113] Ibid. pp. 7-8.

[114] "US Catholicism Trends in the '90s," *National Catholic Reporter*, October 8,1993. p. 23.

[115] See the study done by Kennedy, Eugene C. and Heckler, Victor J., *The Catholic Priest in the United Psychological Investigations*, United States Catholic Conference, Washington, DC. 1972.

[116] 1 Cor. 12:4-7.

[117] Fiorenza, Elisabeth Schüssler, *In Memory of Her*, The Crossroad Publishing Company, New York, 1992. p.130.

[118] Ibid. p.123.

[119] Mk. 4: 10-12; Mk 4: 20; Lk 8: 15.

[120] Mk. 10:42-45.

[121] Lk. 8:1-3.

[122] Lk. 12:1.

[123] Mt. 4:25. [124] See Fiorenza, Elisabeth Schüssler, "Women in the Early Christian Movement," Christ, Carol P. and Plaskow, Judith, eds.,*Womanspirit Rising*, Harper & Row, San Francisco, 1979. For a much more detailed study of women in scripture see Fiorenza's *In Memory of Her*.

[125] Osborne, Kenan B. OFM, *Ministry*, Paulist Press, New York, 1993, p. 110.

[126] Ibid. p. 26.

[127] Hebrews 5: 5.

[128] 1 Peter 2:9.

[129] McBrien, Richard, *Catholicism*, pp. 802-803.

[130] Osborne, op. cit. p. 140.

[131] Tertulian, "De exhortatione castitatis," as quoted by Osborne, op. cit. p.140. Also see Schillebeeckx, Edward, *Ministry*, pp. 50-51.

[132] Tertulian, op.cit. p.140.

[133] Kung, Hans, *Why Priests?*, Doubleday & Company, Garden City, NY, 1972. See section III "Development of Traditional Understanding of Office."

[134] Schillebeeckx, op. cit. p. 53.

[135] Whitehead and Whitehead, op. cit. pp. 4-5.

[136] Hegy, Pierre, " 'The End of American Catholicism?' Another Look," *America*, May 1,1993, pp. 8-9.

[137] *National Catholic Reporter*, October 8,1993. p. 23.

[138] This trend continues even in the face of the 1993 pronouncement on marriage status and sacramental reception.

[139] Kaufman, Philip S., *Why You Can Disagree And Remain A Faithful Catholic*, The Crossroad Publishing Company, New York, 1993. See chapters 6 and 7.

[140] As quoted in: D'Antonio, William, "New world laity casts off chains of command," *National Catholic Reporter*. November 20,1992. p.11.

[141] Pottmeyer, Hermann J., "The Traditionalist Temptation of the Contemporary Church," *America*, September 5,1992. p.100.

[142] Boff, Leonardo, *Ecclesiogenesis*, Orbis, Maryknoll, NY, 1986. pp. 8-9.

[143] Wolff, Sr. M. Madeleva, CSC, "The Education of Our Young Religious Teachers," *National Catholic Educational Association Proceedings and Addresses*, 1949.

[144] Meyers, Sr. Bertrande, D.C., *Sisters for the Twenty-First Century*, Sheed & Ward, New York, 1965. p. 36. Good book for development of transition thought on women religious.

[145] "Decree on the Up-To-Date Renewal of Religious Life," Flannery, ed., op. cit. 4. p. 613.

[146] Ibid. p. 616.

[147] Ibid. p. 621.

[148] Ibid. p. 622.

[149] Weaver, Mary Jo, *New Catholic Women*, Harper & Row, San Francisco, 1985, p. 84.

[150] "Apostolic Exhortation on the Renewal of Religious Life," *Vatican II*, Flannery, ed., op. cit, p. 682 no. 5.

[151] Boff, op. cit. p. 2.

[152] Ibid. p. 4.

[153] Ibid.

[154] Ibid. p. 9.

[155] Chittister, op. cit. p. 151.

[156] Windsor, Pat, "LCWR examines life of religious," *National Catholic Reporter*, September 1, 1989. p. 3.

[157] Tillemans, Sr. Rose, "As old communities die, a call to radical sisterhood," *National Catholic Reporter,* November 20,1987. p.16.

[158] Weaver, op. cit. p. 87.

[159] See Kolbenschlag, Madonna, "John Paul II, U.S. Women Religious, and the Saturnian Complex," *The Church In Anguish*, Kung, Hans, and Swidler, Leonard, eds., Harper & Row, San Francisco, 1986. Vidulich, Sr. Dorothy, "After years of failed reform, synod to bring nuns into line," *National Catholic Reporter,* November 5, 1993. p. 18. Maloney, Sr. Susan, "Religious Orders and Sisters in Dissent," *Christian Century,* March 9, 1988. pp. 238-240.

[160] Chittister, op. cit. p. 45.

[161] Schneiders, Sandra M., "Effects of women's experience on Spirituality," Conn, Joan Wolski, ed., *Women's Spirituality*, Paulist Press, New York, 1986. p. 34.

[162] Wallace, Ruth, *They Call Her Pastor*, State University of New York Press, Albany, 1992. p. 134.

[163] Ibid. p. 137.

[164] Daly, Mary, "Be-Friending," Christ, Carol P. and Plaskow, Judith, eds., *Weaving the Visions*, HarperSanFrancisco, 1989. p. 200.

[165] Hunt, Mary, *Fierce Tenderness*, The Crossroad Publishing Company, New York, 1992. p. 166.

[166] John 15: 13.

[167] This response was written prior to the April,1994, Vatican permission.

[168] The works of Rosemary Radford Ruether, Mary Daly, Gerda Lerner, Mary Jo Weaver, Madonna Kolbenschlag, Joan Chittister, Carol Christ, Carter Heywood, Sandra Schneiders, are just a few of the many.

[169] Ruether, *Women-Church*, p. 57ff.

[170] Fox, Matthew, *Creation Spirituality*, HarperCollins, New York, 1981. p.8.

[171] Ruether, *Women-Church*, p. 59.

[172] "Instruction on the Worship of The Eucharistic Mystery," Flannery, ed., op. cit. I:6. p. 106.

[173] Ruether,*Women-Church*, p. 87.

[174] "Theology of the Sacraments," Kilmartin, Duffy, ed., op. cit. p. 149.

[175] "The Constitution on the Sacred Liturgy," Flannery, ed., op. cit. I:14, pp. 7-8.

[176] Kilmartin, Duffy, ed., op. cit. p. 141.

[177] Jn. 6:53-54.

[178] Ruether, *Sexism and God-Talk*, pp. 208-209.

[179] Boff, op. cit. p. 69.

[180] Cooke, Bernard, "Whose Eucharist Is It?" *Churchwatch*, October, 1992. p. 4.

[181] Shannon, William, "No Circuit-Rider Priest, Please!" *America*, April 16,1994. p.11.

[182] Wallis, Jim, "Keeping Faith Doing Justice Building Community," *Sojourners*, February-March, 1992. p.12.

[183] Kent, Corita, *Silkscreen*, 1965.

[184] Winter, Lummis, Stokes, op. cit. p.186.

[185] Lerner, op. cit. p. 227.

[186] Ibid. p. 233.

[187] Weaver, Mary Jo, *Springs of Water in a Dry Land*, Beacon Press, Boston, 1993. p. 45.

[188] Lummis, Stokes, Winter, op .cit. p. 142.

[189] Ibid. pp. 143-144.

[190] Trickett, David, "Small groups cross faith lines to develop modern ecumenism," *National Catholic Reporter*. October 23, 1992. p.19.

[191] Weaver, Mary Jo, *New Catholic Women*, p. 106.

[192] Chittister, op. cit. p. 166.

[193] Boff, op. cit. p. 4.

[194] Mitchell, Rosemary Catalano, and Ricciuti, Gail Anderson, *Birthings and Blessings*, The Crossroad Publishing Company, New York, 1991, p. 13. The book contains a list of "starting points" for planning which are useful in re-viewing the art and craft of liturgical planning.

[195] Ruether, *Sexism and God-Talk*, p. 208.

[196] Guenther, Margaret, *Holy Listening*, Cowley Publications, Boston, 1992. See Chapter 1, "Welcoming the Stranger," for a presentation on the hospitality of listening.

[197] Whitehead and Whitehead, op. cit. p. 46; and Mat. 18: 20.

[198] "Decree on the Apostolate of Lay People," Introduction, Flannery, ed. op. cit. p. 766-767.

[199] Cooke, Bernard, "Non-Patriarchal Salvation," Conn, ed. p. 279.

[200] Driver, op, cit. p. 213.

[201] Schneiders,op. cit. p. 39.

[202] Ruether,Rosemary Radford, *Womanguides*, Beacon Press, Boston. 1985. pp. x-xi.

[203] Fiorenza, op. cit. p. xx.

[204] Ibid. p. xix.

[205] Winter, op. cit. p. 9.

[206] Isasi-Diaz, and Tarango, op. cit. p. 2.

[207] Ywahoo, Dhyani, "Renewing the Sacred Hoop," *Weaving the Visions*, Plaskow, and Christ, eds. p. 274.

[208] Winter, op. cit. p. 10.

[209] *Woman's Song*, collection, National Sisters Vocation Conference. 1307 South Wabash, #350, Chicago,1986.

[210] Schaffran, Janet CDP and Kozak, Pat CSJ, *More Than Words*, self-published, Cleveland, 1987. Authors' note.

[211] See Fiorenza,*In Memory of Her*, Chapter 5, on women's significance in the house churches of early Christian communities.

[212] Heywood, Carter, "Blessing the Bread-A Litany," *Women's Prayer Services*, Gjerding, Iben and Kinnamon, Katherine,eds., Twenty third Publications, Mystic, CT. p. 22.

[213] Finger, Reta Halteman, "Cooks, Waitresses, and Nurses at the Table of the Lord," *Daughters of Sarah*, Fall, 1993. p. 24.

[214] See Hellwig, Monika K., *The Eucharist and the Hunger of the World*, Sheed & Ward,

Kansas City, 1992, for a good study of the connection of Eucharist and famine.

[215] Lummis, Stokes, Winter, op. cit. p. 175.

[216] It is important to note that Eucharistic theologians include the presbyter as a specific place in which God is present. However, *not one single respondent* mentioned the presider as a locus for the presence of Jesus in a specific way, therefore this is an area not covered in this study.

[217] Power, David N., *The Eucharistic Mystery*, The Crossroad Publishing Company, New York, 1994. p.14.

[218] Mairs, Nancy, *Ordinary Time*, Beacon Press, Boston, 1993. p.180.

[219] Power, op. cit. p. 7.

[220] Luke 24: 29-31.

[221] See Ruether, *Women-Church*, "The Ecclesiology of Women-Church," for an in-depth discussion of bars to the development of God-centered community.

[222] David Power notes, " In all the different modes of celebration noted in postconciliar years, communities want to give the sacrament a public role and to find in it a core expression of what it means to be a Christian in today's cultural settings. There is a deep-seated persuasion that it is the faith community's central confession of faith and the key moment of the presence of Christ and of the Spirit in the Church." p. 8.

[223] Lee, Bernard J., S.M., ed., *Alternative Futures for Worship Volume 3 The Eucharist*, "Celebrating and Living the Eucharist: A Cultural Analysis," Westerhoff, John H. III, The Liturgical Press, Collegeville, Minnesota, 1987. p. 26.

[224] Hunt, op. cit. pp.17-19. Also see Mary Daly's work on Be-Friending as a part of inclusion or belonging, and the anti-hostility which that involves: Daly, Mary, "Be-Friending," *Weaving the Visions*, Plaskow and Christ, eds. 1989.

[225] Hunt, op. cit. p. 166.

[226] Gilligan, Carol, *In A Different Voice*, Harvard University Press, Cambridge, MA, 1982. p. 42.

[227] See Whitehead and Whitehead,op. cit. and Hunt, op. cit. especially "The Power of Women's Friendships."

[228] Fiorenza, op. cit. especially the chapter "Toward a Feminist Model of Historical Reconstruction."

[229] There are always multiple understandings of tradition. Power, op. cit. points out, "In interpreting a tradition, wherever a people or an authority is tied inexorably to one meaning, there is a suppression of others that deserve to be heard." p. 11.

[230] Whitehead and Whitehead, op. cit. p. 120.

[231] Perry, John Michael, *Exploring the Evolution of the Lord's Supper in the New Testament*, Sheed & Ward, Kansas City, 1994. p. 124.

[232] "Instruction on the Worship of the Eucharistic Mystery," Flannery, ed. op. cit. I:9. p. 109.

[233] Russell, Letty, "Searching For a Church in the Round," Winter, Stokes, Lummis, op. cit. p. 243.

[234] John 1:14.

[235] Winter, op. cit. p. 224.

[236] Luke 15:1-2.

[237] Fiorenza, Elisabeth Schüssler, *Bread Not Stone*, Beacon Press, Boston, 1984. p. xi.

[238] Schneiders, op. cit. p. 94.

[239] See *Summa Theologica*, III, Q 31. "The male sex is more noble than the female, and for this reason He took flesh in the male sex."

[240] See "One Thousand Years of Feminist Bible Criticism," Lerner, op. cit. pp.138ff.

[241] Fiorenza, *In Memory of Her*. p.xviii.

[242] Ibid. p.xix.

[243] Fox, Ruth, "Strange omission of key women in lectionary," *National Catholic Reporter,* May 13,1994. pp. 13-14. Fox cites tens of examples of scripture texts which have been shortened by leaving out parts in which women appear in a favorable light in both the weekday and the A,B, and C cycles for Sundays. Her conclusion, based on information provided in the lectionary norms, is, "Thus we can conclude that the passages described above featuring women were omitted or made optional for one of the following reasons: 1.They are of lesser importance; 2. they contain serious literary, critical or exegetical problems; 3. the faithful will not understand them; 4. they are not essential to the meaning of the text; 5. they have lesser spiritual value; 6. they have little pastoral worth; 7, they contain truly difficult questions."

[244] Ruether, *Sexism and God-Talk,* pp. 22-23.

[245] Sleevi, Mary Lou, *Sisters and Prophets,* Ave Maria Press, Notre Dame, IN, 1993. p. 32.

[246] Chittister, op .cit. p. 36.

[247] Accurso, Lina, "Women Ministers:Fundamentally and Literally," *Daughters of Sarah,* vol.19, no. 2. p. 41.

[248] Fiorenza, *In Memory of Her,* p. xiv.

[249] Winter, op. cit. p. 9.

[250] Lee, Bernard J., S.M., "Liturgy of the Word, Shared Homily: Conversation That Puts Communities At Risk," *Alternative Futures For Worship,* vol .3, Bernard Lee, ed. p.157.

[251] See Boff, op. cit. especially the section on "Building a Living Church."

[252] Ibid. p. 41.

[253] Russell, Letty, "Searching for a Church in the Round," Winter, Lummis, Stokes, op. cit.

[254] Whitehead and Whitehead, op. cit. p. 54.

[255] Scripture passages frequently named as favorites: The beatitudes, the feeding stories, the judgment verses which call us to feed and clothe in Matt. 25, the stories of healings.

[256] O'Connor, Sr. Francis Bernard CSC, *Like Bread, Their Voices Rise!,* Ave Maria Press, Notre Dame, IN. 1993. pp.162-163.

[257] Ruether, *Sexism and God-Talk,* p. 23.

[258] See Ruether's "The Feminist Radicalizing of the Prophetic Tradition," in *Sexism and God - Talk,* for a more extensive discussion.

[259] Whitehead and Whitehead, op. cit. p. 61.

[260] Mt 28:20

[261] Winter, op .cit. p. 9.

[262] Ruether, *Women-Church,* p. 135.

[263] Ibid. p. 210.

[264] Zimmerman, Irene SSSF,*Womenpsalms,* St. Mary's Press, Winona, MN. 1992. p. 56.

[265] Day, Dorothy, *Meditations,* Paulist Press, New York, 1970. p.66.

[266] Johnson, Ann, *Miryam of Jerusalem,* Ave Maria Press, Notre Dame, IN. 1991. p.126.

[267] Aquinas, Thomas, *Summa Theologica,* Q 75, art 4, pt. III.

[268] John 6:35-37.

[269] Nelson, Gertrud Mueller, *To Dance With God,* Paulist Press, New York, 1986. p.34.

[270] Fitzpatrick, op .cit. p. 309

[271] Ibid. p. 327.

[272] Compare with the results of a *New York Times* poll reported June 1, 1994, which showed that among Catholics aged 18-45 who took part in the eucharist once a week, 34% believed that the elements actually became the body and blood of Christ, while

63% believed they were symbolic reminders.

[273] See Perry on the "interior experience" of the communication of the Spirit as an affirmation of Jesus' real presence, op. cit. p. 115.

[274] Lk. 22:19-20.

[275] Mt. 26:26-28; Mk. 14:22-24.

[276] 1Cor. 10: 15-17.

[277] The women interviewed have a very uncertain view of the role of ordained priesthood. The Women's Ordination Conference calls for a reordered priesthood which would emphasize the responsibility to service to the community rather than power over the community. The statement of one respondent, "We are all celebrants. . . ." would seem to imply that we are all called to celebrate here, no one is a passive recipient of a sacrament.

[278] Whitehead and Whitehead, op. cit. p. 162.

[279] Ruether, *Women-Church*, p. 78.

[280] "Dogmatic Constitution on the Church," Flannery, ed. especially Chapter IV, "The Laity," in which the authors call for active, eager participation.

[281] For a quick view of the development of Eucharistic theology and the return of the contemporary church to emphasis on certain aspects of early church worship see McBrien, op. cit., pp. 760-765, also Perry, op. cit., for an overview of scripture, community and eucharistic theology.

[282] As quoted by Mitchell, Nathan, "Who Is At The Table? Reclaiming Real Presence," *Commonweal*, January 27,1995. p. 14.

[283] Duffy, Regis, *Real Presence*, Harper & Row, San Francisco, 1982. p. 134.

[284] Ibid. p. 150.

[285] For a survey of belief on what Catholics believe happens at Eucharist see, "Future of Faith Worries Catholic Leaders," *New York Times*, June 1,1994. Peter Steinfels finds that over half of those who attend Mass every week believe that there is only symbolic change in the bread and wine.

[286] Fitzpatrick, op. cit. p. 321.

[287] Perry, op. cit. p. 124.

[288] Jn. 20: 19-22.

[289] In an opposite way of viewing this experience, Bernard Cooke tells a story *(Churchwatch, October,1992)* about having a class demonstration of Mass actions with a Lutheran pastor and an Episcopalian priest. The attempt was only to show students that there could be a eucharist which would be acceptable to all three religious groups. He comments, "We all agreed: we're not going to celebrate Mass. We did say: since we are going to be in a prayerful situation, in the prayer part let's pray. . . . *When we finished, all three of us knew we had celebrated the Eucharist.*" An interesting example of the inner confirmation of the Spirit that Jesus is present, even when he's deliberately not invited!

[290] Acts 4:31.

[291] Hays, Edward, *Prayers for the Domestic Church*, Forest of Peace Publishing, Inc., Leavenworth, KS. 1995. p. 153.

[292] Tom Driver, op. cit. names that stultification of ritual which attempts to ward off every kind of change and preserve power in one human arena as "ritualism." And he calls it a violation of the very nature of ritual.

[293] Ibid. p. 207.

[294] Neu, Diann, "Women-Church Transforming Liturgy," *Women At Worship*, Proctor-Smith, Marjorie and Walton, Janet R., eds.,Westminster/John Knox Press, Louisville, Kentucky,

1993. p. 176.

[295] Ruether, *Women-Church*. p. 5.

[296] Mt. 12:1, also Mk. 2:23-28 and Lk. 6:1-5.

[297] Mt. 9: 9-10; Lk. 19: 1-10.

[298] Schillebeeckx, Edward, *The Church With A Human Face*, The Crossroad Publishing Company, New York, 1985. p. 20.

[299] Mitford, Nancy, *Pigeon Pie*, British Book Centre, New York, 1959. p.17.

[300] Julian of Norwich, *Showings*, Paulist Press, New York, 1978. p. 292.

[301] Hays, Edward, *Prayers for a Planetary Pilgrim*, Forest Of Peace Publishing, Inc., Leavenworth, KS. 1995. p. 91.

[302] Heywood, Carter, "The Enigmatic God," in *Spinning a Sacred Yarn*, The Pilgrim Press, New York, 1982. p.107.

[303] Thought Woman is the creator-image of the Laguna Indians. Ruoff, A. Lavonne Brown, *Literatures of the American Indian*, Chelsea House Publishers, New York, 1991.

[304] Revelation 22:13.

[305] "Song of the Sky Loom" is a prayer of the Tewa tribe. Ruoff, op. cit.

[306] Kipling, Rudyard, "Recessional June 22,1897," *The New Oxford Book of English Verse*, ed. Sir Arthur Quiller-Couch, Oxford University Press, New York, 1955. p. 1076.

[307] Dillard, Annie, *Holy The Firm*, Harper & Row, New York, 1977. p. 71.

[308] Hoffman, Charles, *American Indians Sing*, The John Day Company, New York, 1967. p. 47.

[309] "A Mighty Fortress," hymn by Martin Luther, "Ein' feste Burg."

[310] Manasseh 1,7.

[311] Edwards, Jonathan, "Sinners in the Hands of an Angry God," sermon.

[312] Isaiah 66:11-13.

[313] Romans 12:19.

[314] Isaiah 42:13

[315] Genesis 2:19, 22-23; also, wo-man = wif-man or wife man, implying one who is not complete unless married. *Webster's Third New International Dictionary.*

[316] See Mary Ritchie Key, *Male/Female Language*, The Scarecrow Press, Metuchan, NJ. p. 94, on the use of "she" and other feminines as terms of contempt used by men against other men. Every woman has her favorites, some of them turned around so as to compliment women by referring to them as in some way having "masculine" attributes, e.g., you drive like a man, you throw like a man.

[317] Hammond, Dorothy, and Jablow, Alta, *Women in the Cultures of The World*, Cummings Publishing Company, Menlo Park, CA. 1976. p.12.

[318] Ibid.

[319] Johnson, Elizabeth A., *She Who Is: The Mystery of God in Feminist Theological Discourse*, The Crossroad Publishing Company, New York, 1992. pp. 26-27. Also see Lerner, *The Creation of Patriarchy*, Ruether, *Sexism and God -Talk*, especially Chapter 2, "Sexism and God-Language."

[320] Brazelton, T. Barry, and Young, Grace C., "An example of imitative behavior in a nine-week-old infant," *Journal of the American Academy of Child Psychiatry*, 3:1, January, 1964.

[321] Sociolinguistics studies speech communities, which are groups of people who share a group of rules which control what is acceptable concerning speech, including slang, proper speech, and cultural nuancing. Everyone belongs to at least one speech community. For a good overview see Hickerson, Nancy Parrott, *Linguistic Anthropology*, Holt, Rinehart and Winston, New York, 1980.

[322] An interesting word choice, meaning taking power over or coming into control of a subject.

[323] Key, op. cit. p. 89.

[324] Winter, op. cit. p. 7.

[325] Ferguson, Charles A., "Diglossia," *Word*, 15: 325-340.

[326] Fiorenza, *Discipleship of Equals*, p. 265.

[327] It is inevitable that the study of linguistics, as with many other fields, should be patriarchal in orientation. The relationship of women to speech has often been assumed to be the same as men's. A holistic understanding of sociolinguistics demands that women's speech be studied in as great detail as men's and that women at no time again be considered derivative.

[328] Early studies of female - male language usage carried the preconceived patriarchal notions of their time, so that women language was seen as abnormal, less useful and more simple-minded than its male counterpart. See among others, Otto Jesperson "The Woman," *Language, Its Nature, Development and Origin*, W.W. Norton, New York, 1921.

[329] See Ritchie, op. cit., for a very readable study, along with a great variety of cartoons which illuminate the differences in female and male speech.

[330] Fiorenza, op. cit. pp. 65-66.

[331] Johnson, op. cit. p. 14.

[332] Daly, Mary, *Beyond God the Father,* Beacon Press, Boston, original reintroduction 1985. pp. 8-10.

[333] See Rich, Adrienne, *On Lies Secrets and Silence*, W.W. Norton, New York, 1979. p.11.

[334] 1 Cor.14:34, "Women should keep silent in such gatherings. They may not speak. Rather, as the law states, submissiveness is indicated for them," and 1 Tim. 2:12, " I do not permit a woman to act as teacher, or in any way to have authority over a man; she must be quiet."

[335] See Key, "The Silent Woman: Tyranny in Language," op. cit. pp. 127-138, for a discussion of means by which males have historically kept women in silence in areas of importance while encouraging a reputation of women as voluable about matters of little or no importance. "Silence gives the proper grace to women."

[336] Fiorenza, Elisabeth Schüssler, *Discipleship of Equals,* The Crossroad Publishing Company, New York, 1994. p. 251.

[337] See Daly, *Beyond God the Father,* pp. 150-153, on the concept that women were silenced to keep them from speaking the unspeakable. Also see Lerner. Her whole work documents the struggle against silencing century after century.
For another view of silence, not as a negative but as a positive which is not forced upon us, see Fox, *Original Blessing*, Bear & Co., Santa Fe, 1983, especially theme 11, "Emptying: Letting Go of Images and letting Silence Be Silence."

[338] Johnson, op. cit. p. 15.

[339] Johnson, op. cit. pp. 33.

[340] Walker, Alice,*The Color Purple*, Harcourt, Brace, Jovanovich, New York,1982. pp.164-168.

[341] Daly, *Beyond God The Father*, p. 8.

[342] Johnson, op. cit. p. 36.

[343] See McFague, Sally, *The Body of God: an Ecological Theology*, Fortress Press, Minneapolis, 1993. There is a tremendous amount of material on the honoring of the earth, not a domination over it, as being primal to the feminist theological tradition.

[344] See Warnock, Donna, "Patriarchy is a Killer: What People Concerned About Peace and Justice Should Know," *Reweaving The Web of Life*, Pam McAllister, ed., New Society

Publishers, Philadelphia, 1982. p. 25. The destruction of women on a horrendous level was akin to a holocaust of females. Those most threatened were women who did not live under the protection of a male, or who demonstrated theological ideas which were perceived to be heretical by Church authority. Women mystics were particularly at risk because they sought to have direct religious experience of God, rather than experience mediated through the patriarchy. See Lerner, op. cit., pp. 79-80.

[345] Cavanagh, Joan, "I Am a Dangerous Woman," *Reweaving the Web of Life*, McAllister, ed. pp. 3-4. The book stores and libraries are filling shelf after shelf with the burgeoning feminine voices calling for the revolution away from patriarchalism before it is too late. In addition to *Reweaving the Web of Life*, which is not just a critique of patriarchalism but also a series of essays on taking back our world, Mary Daly's *Gyn/Ecology* is excellent, as well as the work of Barbara Deming,

[346] Johnson, op. cit. p. 7.

[347] Ibid. p. 30

[348] Anderson and Hopkins, op. cit. p. 225.

[349] Bloom, Anthony, *Beginning to Pray*, Paulist Press, New York, 1970. p. 67.

[350] Hardesty, Nancy, *Inclusive Language in the Church*, John Knox Press, Atlanta, 1987. p.16.

[351] See Johnson, op. cit. "the frequency with which Jesus calls God Father breaks down . . .: Mark 1, Q i, special Luke 2, special Matthew 1, John 73. As James Dunn concludes, it is scarcely possible to dispute that, ` here we see straightforward evidence of a burgeoning tradition, of a manner of speaking about Jesus and his relation with God which became very popular in the last decades of the first century.' It is a matter of theological development in the early church rather than abundant use by the actual Jesus who lived." p. 81.

[352] Winter, Lummis, Stokes, op. cit. p. 169.

[353] Craighead, Meinrad, *The Mother's Songs,: Images of God the Mother*, Paulist Press, Mahwah, NJ, 1986. introduction.

[354] Dt. 32:18.

[355] Isaiah 42:14.

[356] Hays, *Prayers for the Domestic Church*, p. 153.

[357] Wilshire, Donna, *Virgin Mother Crone*, Inner Traditions, Rochester, Vermont, 1994. p.118.

[358] Julian of Norwich, op. cit. pp. 292, 298.

[359] Winter, op. cit. p. 206.

[360] Isaiah 66:12-13.

[361] Wilshire, pp.1 20-122. See also Ruether, *Sexism and God-Talk*, especially chapters 1-4 on the early separation experiences of people from nature and from each other in which lie the roots of domination. Also Merlin Stone, "When God Was a Woman," *Womanspirit Rising*, Christ and Plaskow, 1979. pp. 120-130. Also, Moltmann-Wendel, Elizabeth, *A Land Flowing With Milk and Honey*, The Crossroad Publishing Company, New York, 1986. pp. 43-63.

[362] FitzGerald, Constance, OCD, "Impasse and Dark Night," *Women's Spirituality*, Joan Wolski Conn, ed. p. 302.

[363] Maitland, Sara, *A Map of the New Country: Women and Christianity*, Routledge & Kegan Paul, London, 1983. p. 179.

[364] Johnson, op. cit. p. 21.

[365] Heywood, Carter, op. cit. pp. 108-110.

[366] Johnson, op. cit., p. 228. Also see the chapter on "Mutuality," Moltmann-Wendel, for a beautiful picture of positive mutuality with God which is characterized by movement

in relationship, and in which the other remains autonomous, never subsumed or subjectified, always free.

[367] Ruether, *Sexism and God-Talk,* pp. 18-19.

[368] Linn, Dennis, Linn, Sheila Fabricant, and Linn, Matthew, *Good Goats : Healing Our Image of God,* Paulist Press, Mahwah, NJ, 1994. p. 7.

[369] Rae, Eleanor and Marie-Daly, Bernice, *Created In Her Image,* The Crossroad Publishing Company, New York, 1990. p. 63.

[370] A partial list with 71 entries is published in Snow, Kimberly, *Keys to the Open Gate,* Conari Press, Berkeley, California, 1994. pp. 105-107. All were published between 1967 and 1994. More titles are published regularly.

[371] Ruether, *Sexism and God -Talk,* p. 71.

[372] Christ, Carol P., "Why Women Need the Goddess," *Womanspirit Rising,* Christ and Plaskow, eds. p.277.

[373] Rae and Marie-Daly, op. cit. p. 67.

[374] There is much evidence that naming the divine as feminine goes deep into prehistory. The archeological finds of the Neolithic-Chalcolithic (7000BC-3500BC) indicate the sacredness seen in the feminine. See Gimbutas, Marija, *The Goddesses and Gods of Old Europe.* for a reinterpretation of androcentric history.

[375] Johnson, op. cit. p. 49.

[376] Fiorenza, *Discipleship of Equals,* p. 93.

[377] Rae and Marie-Daly, op. cit. p. 78.

[378] FitzGerald, in *Women's Spirituality,* Conn, ed. p. 287.

[379] Rae and Marie-Daly, op. cit. pp. 81-82.

[380] Wind has been translated also as spirit of God.

[381] Moltmann-Wendel, op. cit. p. 97. Also see Fiorenza, *In Memory of Her,* where she clearly sites the Goddess/wisdom language in the language used for Israel's God.

[382] See Pagels, Elaine, *The Gnostic Gospels,* Random House, New York, 1979.

[383] Enno, E.B., "Authority and Conflict in the Early Church," *Eglise et Theologie 7,* as quoted in Fiorenza, *In Memory of Her,* p. 68.

[384] Lerner, op. cit. p. 65ff. Her chapters on women mystics are illuminating.

[385] Ibid. p. 69.

[386] Baker, Hatty, *Women in the Ministry,* C.W. Daniel, London, 1911. p. 48.

[387] Johnson, op. cit. p. 83.

[388] *Inter Insigniores,* 1976. n. 4, as published in *The Order of Priesthood,* no author, Our Sunday Visitor, Huntington, IA. 1978. pp. 8-11.

[389] Schneiders, op. cit. p. 35.

[390] Daly, op. cit. p. 63. The book is a classic and wonderful to read for her insights on phallocentric theology, as well as her arresting use of language.

[391] Mary Collins, "Principles of Feminist Liturgy," points out, "A feminist liturgy is as likely to ritualize human connectedness to the Great Mother or the Great Spirit, to Sophia . . . as to the ineffable Holy One of Israel or the Risen Christ. Feminist liturgy aims to explore and celebrate a new order of ultimate relationships, one that is saving . . . for women insofar as it heals the destructive disorder wrought by patriarchal consciousness." Proctor-Smith, and Walton, eds., op. cit. p. 20.

[392] Winter, Lummis, Stokes, op. cit. p. 172.

[393] Ibid. p.174.

[394] Vanier, Jean, *Be Not Afraid,* Paulist Press, New York, 1975. pp. 38-39.

[395] Anderson-Reed, Joyce, "After All, I'm A Woman," *Womenpsalms,* Ahlers, Broughton,

and Koch, compilers. p.15.

[396] Johnson, op. cit. p. 150.

[397] Hays, *Prayers for the Domestic Church*, p. 59.

[398] Sims, Deborah, "A Letter to My Sisters," *Womenpsalms*, Ahlers, Broughton, and Koch, compilers. p. 19.

[399] Driver, op. cit. p. 50.

[400] Cockrell, Andrea Cook, "Husk," *Womenpsalms*, Ahlers, Broughton, and Koch, compilers. p. 38.

[401] Christ, Carol, "Spiritual Quest and Women's Experience," *Womenspirit Rising*, Christ and Plaskow, eds. p. 227.

[402] Nelson, op. cit. p. 16.

[403] Carr, Anne, "On Feminist Spirituality," Conn, ed., op. cit. p. 50.

[404] Weaver, *Springs of Water in a Dry Land*, p. 100. She also includes some questions we might ask as we explore, "What is it? Where is it? How do I find it? What do I do with it? Why am I sometimes afraid of it? How do I feel about it? How can I use my own experience to articulate it and respond to it?"

[405] Schneiders, op. cit. pp. 87-88. Her chapter, "Feminist Spirituality," is excellent for an understanding of the development of feminist spirituality.

[406] Winter, Loomis and Stokes, op. cit. p. 166.

[407] Ibid. p. 185.

[408] Clement of Alexandria, *The Pedagogue*, III,1; PG, vol. 8. #556C.

[409] Walton, Janet R., "Conclusion," Proctor-Smith and Walton, eds., op. cit. p. 237.

[410] Driver, op. cit. p.166.

[411] Ibid. p. 190.

[412] Winter, Lummis, Stokes, op. cit. p. 179.

[413] Neu, Diann, "Women-Church Transforming Liturgy," Proctor-Smith, and Walton, eds. p.171.

[414] Ruether, *Women-Church*, p. 93.

[415] Chittister, op. cit. p. 77.

[416] Carr, Anne, Conn, ed. op. cit. p. 55.

[417] Winter, Lummis, Stokes, op. cit. p. 188.

[418] Ruether, *Women-Church*, p. 62.

[419] Winter, Loomis, Stokes, op. cit. p. 62ff. All of chapter 3 is filled with quotes from individual women on their struggles.

[420] Whitehead and Whitehead, op. cit. p. 197.

[421] Fox, *Original Blessing,*, p. 260.

[422] Isaiah 61:1-3.

[423] Rukeyser, Muriel, "Käthe Kollwitz," *The Speed of Darkness*, Random House, New York, 1968. pp. 99-105.

[424] Sheedy, Fr. Frank, "Ask Me A Question," *Our Sunday Visitor*, June 11,1995. p. 16.

[425] Replansky, Naomi, "Housing Shortage," *The Dangerous World: New and Selected Poems 1934-1994*, Another Chicago Press, Chicago, 1994. p. 14.

[426] 1 John 4:18.

[427] See Gordon, Margaret T., and Riger, Stephanie, *The Female Fear*, The Free Press, New York, 1989. p. 118.

[428] Schneiders, op. cit. p.106.

[429] Acts 2:18.

[430] "Declaration on Religious Liberty," Flannery, ed.,op. cit. l:3. p. 801.

[431] "Introduction," *Womanspirit Rising*, Christ and Plaskow, eds. p. 16.

[432] Truchses, Darlene Deer, *From Fear to Freedom*, Fulcrum, Inc., Golden, CO. 1989. p. 66.

[433] Collins, Mary, OSB, "Women in Relationship to the Institutional Church," LCWR National Assembly, Albuquerque, NM, August 26, 1991.

[434] Ruether, *Women-Church*. p. 59.

[435] Ibid. p. 60.

[436] Besides Ruether see Sandra Schneiders, op. cit. "(Catholic feminists) both hope for and expect that men of good will will eventually join them in reshaping of a church of all believers. Thus their separatism is neither total or ideological but practical and provisional" (p. 106). She goes on to comment that "no one in the movement thinks that the reintegration will happen anytime soon." Numerous co-celebrating groups are now visible which are attempting to find through praxis the new possibilities of integrated worship groups.

[437] Brotherton, Anne, ed., *The Voice of the Turtledove*, Paulist Press, New York/ Mahwah, 1992. p. 211.

[438] Ibid. p. 215.

[439] Weaver,*Springs of Water in a Dry Land*. p. 45.

[440] Boff, op. cit. p. 33.

[441] Galatians 5:1.

[442] Corpi, Lucha, "Emily Dickenson," Catherine Rodriguez-Nieto, translator, *Palabras de Mediodia/Noon Words.*, El Fuego de Aetlan Publications, Berkeley, CA, 1980.

[443] Corpi, Lucha, "Winter Song," Catherine Rodriguez-Nieto, translator, *Variaciones Sobre Una Tempestad/Variations on the Storm*, Third Woman Press, Berkeley, CA, 1990.

[444] Power, op. cit. p. 335.

[445] Schneiders, op. cit. p. 191.

[446] Ibid. p.108.

[447] Winter, Lummis, Stokes, op. cit. pp. 162-163.

[448] Chittister, op. cit. p. 176.

[449] Mt. 9:10-11.

[450] Hunt, op. cit. p. 29.

[451] Baranowski, Arthur R., *Creating Small Faith Communities*, St. Anthony Messenger Press, Cincinnati, OH, 1988. p. 4.

[452] Boff, op. cit. p. 1.

[453] Russell, Letty, Winter, Stokes, Lummis, eds. op. cit. p. 241.

[454] "Introduction," *Womanspirit Rising*, Christ, and Plaskow, eds. p. 9.

[455] Ps. 137:4.

[456] Ruether,*Women-Church*. p. 59.

[457] Without belaboring the United Nations statistics it is important to remember that women "work two thirds of the world's working hours, represent two thirds of the world's illiterate people and are often physically abused or sexually exploited." Rausch, Thomas P., "The Unfinished Agenda of Vatican II," *America*, June 17-24,1995. p.25.

[458] Neu, Diann, Winter, Lummis, Stokes, eds.,op cit. p.233.

[459] Ruether, *Women-Church*. p. 62.

[460] Fox, *Original Blessing*, p. 259.

[461] Schneiders, op. cit. p. 107.

[462] Whitehead and Whitehead, op. cit. p. 186.

[463] Chittister, op. cit. p. 103.

PERMISSIONS

Material in *The Feminine Face of God,* by Sherry Ruth Anderson and Patricia Hopkins, 1991 reprinted with permission from Bantam Books, New York.

Excerpt from "After All, I'm A Woman," by Joyce Anderson-Reed reprinted from *Womenpsalms* by Julia Ahlers, Rosemary Broughton, and Carl Koch, compilers, 1992,with permission from Saint Mary's Press. All rights reserved.

Excerpt from "Husk," by Andrea Cook Cockrell reprinted from *Womenpsalms* by Julia Ahlers, Rosemary Broughton, and Carl Koch, compilers, 1992, with permission from Saint Mary's Press. All rights reserved.

The excerpt from *Creating Small Faith Communities: A Plan for Restructuring the Parish and Renewing Catholic Life,* third revised edition, copyright (c) 1996 by Arthur R. Baranowski, reprinted by permission of St. Anthony Messenger Press. All rights reserved.

Quotes from *Ecclesiogenesis,* by Leonardo Boff, 1986, reprinted by permission of Orbis Books.

Excerpt from "I Am a Dangerous Woman" by Joan Cavanagh, in *Reweaving the Web of Life,* Pam McAllister, ed., 1982 reprinted with permission of the author.

Material from *Women Strength,* by Sr. Joan Chittister, reprinted by permission of Sheed & Ward, 115 E. Armour Blvd., Kansas City, MO 64141. 1-800-333-7373.

Grateful acknowledgment to Bernard Cooke for permission to reprint from "Whose Eucharist is it?," *Church Watch,* October, 1992.

Material from *Beyond God the Father,* by Mary Daly, 1985, reprinted by permission of Beacon Press.

Permission for material reprinted from "New world laity casts off chains of command," by William D'Antonio, *National Catholic Reporter.* November 20,1992 granted by publisher.

Excerpt from poem 394 in *Final Harvest,* (1961) by Emily Dickinson, reprinted by permission of Little, Brown and Company, Boston.

Grateful acknowledgment to Annie Dillard for permission to quote from *Holy The Firm,* 1977, Harper & Row.

Grateful acknowledgment to Tom F. Driver for permission to quote from *The Magic of Ritual,* HarperSanFrancisco, 1981.

Materials in *Alternative Futures For Worship,* 1987, edited by Regis A. Duffy, O.F.M. (vol. 1), Bernard J. Lee, S.M., (vol. 3), and Michael A. Cowan (vol. 6), copyright (c) 1987 by The Order of St. Benedict, Inc. Published by The Liturgical Press, Collegeville, MN. Used with permission.

From *BORN FOR LIBERTY: A History of Women in America* by Sara M. Evans. Copyright (c) 1989 by Sara M. Evans. Reprinted with permission of The Free Press, a Division of Simon & Shuster.

Excerpts from *In Memory of Her,* by Elisabeth Schüssler Fiorenza, 1992, reproduced by permission from The Crossroad Publishing Company, NY.

Excerpts from *Discipleship of Equals,* by Elisabeth Schüssler Fiorenza, 1994, reproduced by permission from The Crossroad Publishing Company, NY.

Material from *In Breaking of Bread,* by P.J. FitzPatrick, Cambridge University Press, 1993, reprinted with permission of publisher.

Excerpts from *Vatican Council II The Conciliar and Post Conciliar Documents,* Austin Flannery, O.P., ed., copyright (c) 1980 by the Order of St. Benedict, Inc. Published by The Liturgical Press, Collegeville, MN. Used with permission.

Excerpts from *Vatican Council II: The Conciliar and Post Conciliar Documents, New Revised Edition,* edited by Austin Flannery, O.P., copyright (c) 1975, Costello Publishing Company, Inc., Northport, NY are used by permission of the publisher, all rights reserved. No part of these excerpts may be reproduced, stored in a retrieval system, or transmitted in any form or by any means—electronic, mechanical, photo-copying, recording or otherwise, without express permission of Costello Publishing Company.

Grateful acknowledgement to Matthew Fox for permission to reprint material from *Creation Spirituality,* HarperCollins, New York, 1981.

Permission to reprint material from "Strange omission of key women in lectionary," by Ruth Fox, *National Catholic Reporter,* May 13,1994 granted by publisher.

From *In a Different Voice* by Carol Gilligan. Copyright (c) 1982 by the President and Fellows of Harvard College. Reprinted by permission of Harvard University Press.

Material from *Inclusive Language in the Church,* by Nancy Hardesty, 1987, reprinted by permission of John Knox Press.

Grateful acknowledgment to Edward Hays for permission to quote from *Prayers for the Domestic Church,* and *Prayers for a Planetary Pilgrim,* Forest of Peace Publishing, Inc., Leavenworth, KS., 1995.

Material from "Vatican Bank Scandal Reappears in Venezuela," by Peter Hebblethwaite, 1993, reprinted with permission from the National Catholic Reporter.

Excerpt from "The Enigmatic God," by Carter Heywood in *Spinning a Sacred Yarn,* 1982, reprinted with permission from The Pilgrim Press, Cleveland, OH.

Material from *Fierce Tenderness,* by Mary Hunt, 1992, reprinted with permission of The Crossroad Publishing Company, New York.

Material from "This is My Body," by John Kavanagh, *America,* December 11, 1993, reprinted with permission of the publisher.

Material from *Where Do We Go From Here: Chaos or Community? by Martin Luther King Jr.,* 1968, reprinted by permission of Beacon Press, Boston

Material from "Bernard Lonergan, SJ," by John Kinsella, *America,* September 11,1993, reprinted with permission of the publisher.

Excerpt from *Miryam of Jerusalem* by Ann Johnson, copyright (c) 1991 by Ave Maria Press, Notre Dame, IN 46556, used with permission of the publisher.

Material from *She Who Is: The Mystery of God in Feminist Theological Discourse,* by Elisabeth A. Johnson, 1992, reprinted by permission of The Crossroad Publishing Company, New York.

Grateful acknowledgment to Philip S. Kaufman for permission to use materials from *Why You Can Disagree And Remain A Faithful Catholic,* The Crossroad Publishing Company, New York.

From *The Creation of Feminist Consciousness From the Middle Ages to 1870* by Gerda Lerner. Copyright (c) 1994 by Gerda Lerner. Used by permission of Oxford University Press, Inc.

Material from *Ordinary Time,* by Nancy Mairs, 1993, reprinted by permission of Beacon Press, Boston.

Material from *Catholicism, Completely Revised and Updated,* by Richard P. McBrien, copyright (c) 1994 by Richard P. McBrien, reprinted by permission from Harper Collins Publishers, New York.

Material from "Who Is At The Table? Reclaiming Real Presence," by Nathan Mitchell, *Commonweal,* January 27,1995, reprinted by permission from the publisher.

Grateful acknowledgment to Rosemary Catalano Mitchell and Gail Anderson Ricciuti for permission to use material from *Birthings and Blessings,* The Crossroad Publishing

Company, New York, 1991.

Material from *How Catholic Women Have Changed,* by Margaret Murphy, 1987, reprinted with permission of Sheed & Ward, 115 E. Armour Blvd, Kansas City, MO 64141. 1-800-333-7373.

Scripture texts (with the exception of that on p. 66) used in this work are taken from the New American Bible with Revised New Testament. Copyright (c) 1986, and the Revised Psalms of the New American Bible, copyright (c) 1991, by the Confraternity of Christian Doctrine, Washington, D.C. and are used by permission of copyright owner. All rights reserved.

Excerpts from *Like Bread, Their Voices Rise!* by Sr. Francis Bernard O'Connor, C.S.C., Copyright (c) 1993 by Ave Maria Press, Notre Dame, IN 46556, reprinted with permission of the publisher.

Material from *Ministry,* by Kenan B. Osborne, OFM, copyright (c) 1993, Paulist Press, New York, reprinted by permission of the publisher.

Material from *Exploring the Evolution of the Lord's Supper in the New Testament,* by John Michael Perry, 1994, reprinted with permission of Sheed & Ward, 115 Armour Blvd., Kansas City, MO 64141. 1-800 333-7373.

Material from "The Traditionalist Temptation of the Contemporary Church," by Hermann J. Pottmeyer, *America,* September 5, 1992, reprinted with permission of the publisher.

Grateful acknowledgment to David N. Power to use material from *The Eucharistic Mystery,* The Crossroad Publishing Company, New York, 1994.

Excerpts from *Created in Her Image,* by Eleanor Rae and Bernice Marie-Daly, 1990, reprinted with permission from The Crossroad Publishing Company, NY.

Material from "Ratzinger Rejects Quick Fix of Women's Role in Church," by Cardinal Joseph Ratzinger, 1987, reprinted with permission from the National Catholic Reporter.

Material from "The Unfinished Agenda of Vatican II," by Thomas P. Rausch, *America,* June 17-24,1995, reprinted with permission of the publisher.

Grateful acknowledgment to Cathleen Rountree for permission to use material from *On Women Turning Fifty,* HarperSanFrancisco, 1993.

Material from *Sexism and God-Talk* by Rosemary Radford Ruether, (c) 1983,1993 by Rosemary Radford Ruether, reprinted by permission of Beacon Press, Boston.

Excerpts as submitted from *Women-Church: Theology and Practice of Feminist Liturgical Communities* by Rosemary Radford Ruether. Copyright (c) 1985 by Rosemary Radford Ruether. Reprinted by permission of HarperCollins Publishers, Inc.

Excerpt from "Käthe Kollwitz," by Muriel Rukeyser, in *The Speed of Darkness,* 1968, reprinted with permission of Random House, New York.

Quote from *Literatures of the American Indian,* by A. Lavonne Brown Ruoff, 1991, reprinted with permission of Chelsea House Publishers, New York.

Material from "No Circuit-Rider Priest, Please!" by William Shannon, *America,* April 16,1994, reprinted with permission from the publisher.

Material from "Ask Me A Question," by Fr. Frank Sheedy, 1995, used with permission of *Our Sunday Visitor.*

Excerpt from "A letter to My Sisters," by Deborah Sims reprinted from *Womenpsalms* by Julia Ahlers, Rosemary Broughton, and Carl Koch, compilers, 1992, with permission from Saint Mary's Press. All rights reserved.

Grateful acknowledgment to Mary Lou Sleevi for permission to use material from *Sisters and Prophets* 1993, Ave Maria Press, Notre Dame, IN.

Permission to reprint material in "As old communities die, a call to radical sisterhood," by Sr. Rose Tillemans, *National Catholic Reporter,* November 20,1987 granted by publisher.

Permission to reprint material from "Small groups cross faith lines to develop modern ecumenism," by David Trickett, *National Catholic Reporter.* Oct. 23, 1992 granted by publisher.

Material in *From Fear to Freedom,* by Darlene Deer Truchses, 1989, reprinted by permission from Fulcrum, Inc., Golden, CO.

Permission to reprint material from "After years of failed reform, synod to bring nuns into line," by St. Dorothy Vidulich, *National Catholic Reporter,* November 5, 1993 granted by publisher.

Material in "Women's Prayer: How It's Changing," by Clare Wagner in *Praying* Magazine, January-February, 1988, reprinted by permission from publisher.

Excerpt from *The Color Purple,* copyright (c) 1982 by Alice Walker, reprinted by permission of Harcourt Brace & Company.

Quote from "Keeping Faith Doing Justice Building Community," by Jim Wallis, reprinted with permission from *Sojourners,* 2401 15th St. N.W., Washington D.C., (202) 328-8842, (800) 714-7474.

Material from *Springs of Water in a Dry Land,* by Mary Jo Weaver, 1993, reprinted by permission of Beacon Press.

Material from *Virgin Mother Crone,* by Donna Wilshire, reprinted by permission of Inner Traditions, Rochester, VT. 1994.

Most grateful acknowledgment to James D. and Evelyn Whitehead for permission to use material from *The Emerging Laity,* Image Books, New York, 1988.

Permission to reprint material from "LCWR examines life of religious," by Pat Windsor, *National Catholic Reporter,* September 1, 1989 granted by publisher.

Excerpt from "Liturgy," by Irene Zimmerman reprinted from *Womenpsalms* by Julia Ahlers, Rosemary Broughton, and Carl Koch, compilers, 1992, with permission from Saint Mary's Press. All rights reserved.

BIBLIOGRAPHY

Accurso, Lina, "Women Ministers: Fundamentally and Literally," *Daughters of Sarah*, vol. 19, no. 2.

Ahlers, Julia, Broughton, Rosemary, and Koch, Carl, compilers, *Womenpsalms*, Saint Mary's Press, Winona, MN, 1992.

Alternative Futures For Worship, edited by Regis A. Duffy, O.F.M. (vol. 1), Bernard J. Lee, S.M., (vol. 3), and Michael A. Cowan (vol. 6), The Liturgical Press, Collegeville, Minnesota, 1987.

Anderson, Sherry Ruth and Hopkins, Patricia, *The Feminine Face of God*, Bantam Books, New York, 1991.

Aquinas, Thomas, *Summa Theologica*, Q 75, art 4, pt. III., Benziger Brothers, New York, 1948.

Aristotle, *De Generation Animalium*, translator Gweneth Whitteridge, Oxford, Boston, 1981.

Baker, Hatty, *Women in the Ministry*, C.W. Daniel, London, 1911.

Baranowski, Arthur R., *Creating Small Faith Communities*, St. Anthony Messenger Press, Cincinnati, OH, 1988.

Berrigan, Daniel, *Ten Commandments for the Long Haul*, Abingdon, Nashville, 1981.

Bloom, Anthony, *Beginning to Pray*, Paulist Press, New York, 1970.

Boff, Leonardo, *Ecclesiogenesis*, Orbis, Maryknoll, NY, 1986.

Brazelton, T. Barry, and Young, Grace C., "An example of imitative behavior in a nine-week-old infant," *Journal of the American Academy of Child Psychiatry*, 3:1, January, 1964.

Brotherton, Anne, ed., *The Voice of the Turtledove*, Paulist Press, New York/ Mahwah, 1992.

Carr, Anne E., *Transforming Grace*, Harper & Row, New York, 1990.

Carr, Anne, "On Feminist Spirituality," in *Women's Spirituality*, Joan Wolski Conn, ed., Paulist Press, New York. 1986.

Chittister, Joan, OSB, *Women Strength*, Sheed & Ward, Kansas City, 1990.

Clement of Alexandria, *The Pedagogue*, III,1; PG, vol. 8. #556C.

Collins, Mary, OSB, "Women in Relationship to the Institutional Church, " LCWR National Assembly, Albuquerque, NM, August 26, 1991.

Conn, Joan Wolski, ed., *Women's Spirituality*, Paulist Press, New York. 1986.

Cooke, Bernard, "Whose Eucharist Is It?" *Churchwatch*, October, 1992.

Corpi, Lucha, "Emily Dickenson," Catherine Rodriguez-Nieto, translator, *Palabras de Mediodia/Noon Words*, El Fuego de Aetlan Publications, Berkeley, CA, 1980.

Corpi, Lucha, "Winter Song," Catherine Rodriguez-Nieto, Translator, *Variaciones Sobre Una Tempestad/Variations on the Storm*, Third Woman Press, Berkeley, CA, 1990.

Craighead, Meinrad, *The Mother's Songs: Images of God the Mother*, Paulist Press, Mahwah, NJ, 1986.

D'Antonio, William, "New world laity casts off chains of command," *National Catholic Reporter*. November 20,1992.

Daly, Mary, *Beyond God the Father*, Beacon Press, Boston, 1985.

Daly, Mary, *Gyn/Ecology,* Beacon Press, Boston, 1978.

Day, Dorothy, *Meditations,* Paulist Press, New York, 1970.

Dickinson, Emily, *Final Harvest,* Little, Brown and Company, Boston, 1961.

Dillard, Annie, *Holy The Firm,* Harper & Row, New York, 1977.

Driver, Tom F.., *The Magic of Ritual,* HarperSanFrancisco, San Francisco, 1981.

Edwards, Jonathan, "Sinners in the Hands of an Angry God," In *A History of the Work of Redemption,* Presbyterian Board of Publication, Philadelphia, n.d.

Evans, Sara M., *Born For Liberty,* The Free Press, New York, 1991.

Ferguson, Charles A., "Diglossia," *Word,* 15: 325-340.

Finger, Reta Halteman, "Cooks, Waitresses, and Nurses at the Table of the Lord," *Daughters of Sarah,* Fall, 1993.

Fiorenza, Elisabeth Schüssler, *In Memory of Her,* The Crossroad Publishing Company, New York, 1992,

Fiorenza, Elisabeth Schüssler, *Bread Not Stone,* Beacon Press, Boston, 1984.

Fiorenza, Elisabeth Schüssler, *Discipleship of Equals,* The Crossroad Publishing Company, New York, 1994.

FitzPatrick, P.J., In *Breaking of Bread,* Cambridge University Press, New York, 1993.

Flannery, Austin O.P., ed., *Vatican Council II The Conciliar and Post Conciliar Documents,* Liturgical Press, Collegeville, Minnesota, 1980.

Fox, Matthew, *Creation Spirituality,* HarperCollins, New York, 1981.

Fox, Matthew, *Original Blessing,* Bear & Co., Santa Fe, 1983.

Fox, Ruth, "Strange omission of key women in lectionary," *National Catholic Reporter,* May 13,1994.

Gilligan, Carol, *In A Different Voice,* Harvard University Press, Cambridge, Massachusetts, 1982.

Gimbutas, Marija, *The Goddesses and Gods of Old Europe.* University of California Press, Berkeley, CA, 1982.

Gjerding, Iben and Katherine Kinnamon, eds., *Women's Prayer Services,* Twenty third Publications, Mystic, Ct., 1992.

Gordon, Margaret T., and Riger, Stephanie, *The Female Fear,* The Free Press, New York, 1989.

Guenther, Margaret, *Holy Listening,* Cowley Publications, Boston, 1992.

Hardesty, Nancy, *Inclusive Language in the Church,* John Knox Press, Atlanta, 1987.

Hays, Edward, *Prayers for the Domestic Church,* Forest of Peace Publishing, Inc., Leavenworth, Kansas,1995.

Hays, Edward, *Prayers for a Planetary Pilgrim,* Forest Of Peace Publishing, Inc., Leavenworth,KS., 1995.

Hebblethwaite, Peter, "Vatican Bank Scandal Reappears in Venezuela," *National Catholic Reporter,* Dec. 24, 1993.

Hegy, Pierre, " 'The End of American Catholicism?' Another Look," *America,* May 1, 1993.

Hellwig, Monika K., *The Eucharist and the Hunger of the World,* Sheed & Ward, Kansas City, 1992.

Heywood, Carter, "Sexuality, Love and Justice," *Weaving the Visions,* Judith Plaskow and Carol P. Christ, eds., HarperSanFrancisco, 1989.

Hickerson, Nancy Parrott, *Linguistic Anthropology,* Holt, Rinehart and Winston, New York, 1980.

Hoffman, Charles, *American Indians Sing,* The John Day Company, New York, 1967.

Hunt, Mary, *Fierce Tenderness,* The Crossroad Publishing Company, New York, 1992.

Isasi-Diaz, Ada Maria and Tarlengo, Yolanda, *Hispanic Women: Prophetic Voice in the Church,* Harper & Row, San Francisco. 1988.

Jefferson, Margo, "Great (Hazel) Scott," *MS,* March, 1974.

Jesperson, Otto, *Language: Its Nature, Development and Origin,* W.W. Norton, NY, 1921.

Johnson, Ann, *Miryam of Jerusalem,* Ave Maria Press, Notre Dame, Indiana, 1991.

Johnson, Elizabeth A., *She Who Is: The Mystery of God in Feminist Theological*

Discourse, The Crossroad Publishing Company, New York, 1992.

Julian of Norwich, *Showings,* Paulist Press, New York, 1978.

Kant, Immanuel, *Observations on Feeling of the Beautiful and Sublime,* translator by John Goldthwait, University of California Press, Berkeley, 1960.

Kaufman, Philip S., *Why You Can Disagree And Remain A Faithful Catholic,* The Crossroad Publishing Company, New York, 1993.

Kavanagh, John, "This Is My Body," *America,* December 11, 1973 p. 23.

Kempton, Sally, "Cutting Loose," *Esquire* 7/1970.

Kennedy, Eugene C. and Heckler, Victor J., *The Catholic Priest in the United Psychological Investigations,* United States Catholic Conference, Washington, DC. 1972.

Kent, Corita, *Silkscreen,* 1965.

Kerouac, Jack, "Two Poems Dedicated to Thomas Merton," *a MERTON concelebration,* Deba Patnaik, ed., Ave Maria Press, Notre Dame, IN.1981.

Key, Mary Ritchie, *Male/Female Language,* The Scarecrow Press, Metuchan, NJ., 1975.

King, Martin Luther Jr., *Where Do We Go From Here: Chaos or Community?* Beacon Press, Boston, 1968.

Kinsella, John, "Bernard Lonergan, SJ," *America,* September 11,1993.

Kipling, Rudyard, "Recessional June 22,1897," *The New Oxford Book of English Verse,* Sir Arthur Quiller-Couch, ed., Oxford University Press, New York, 1955.

Kung, Hans, *Why Priests?,* Doubleday & Company, Garden City, NY, 1972.

Kung, Hans, and Swidler, Leonard, eds., *The Church in Anguish,* Harper & Row, San Francisco, 1986.

Lerner, Gerda, *The Creation of Feminist Consciousness,* Oxford University Press, New York, 1993.

Lerner, Gerda, *The Creation of Patriarchy,* Oxford University Press, New York, 1986.

Linn, Dennis, Linn, Sheila Fabricant, and Linn, Matthew, *Good Goats : Healing Our Image of God,* Paulist Press, Mahwah, NJ, 1994.

Luther, Martin, "A Mighty Fortress," words to Johann Sebastian Bach, "Feste Burg Is Unser Gott," Kassel, NY, 1989.

Mairs, Nancy, *Ordinary Time,* Beacon Press, Boston, 1993.

Maitland, Sara, *A Map of the New Country: Women and Christianity,* Routledge & Kegan Paul, London, 1983.

Maloney, Sr. Susan, "Religious Orders and Sisters in Dissent," *Christian Century,* March 9, 1988.

McAllister, Pam, ed., *Reweaving the Web of Life,* New Society Publishers, Philadelphia, 1982.

McBrien, Richard, *Catholicism, Completely Revised and Updated,* Harper Collins Publishers, New York, 1994.

McEwan, Dorothea, ed., *Women Experiencing Church,* Fowler Wright Books, Leominster, 1991.

McFague, Sally, *The Body of God: an Ecological Theology,* Fortress Press, Minneapolis, 1993.

Millett, Kate, *Sexual Politics,* Doubleday, Garden City, NY, 1970.

Mitchell, Nathan, "Who Is At The Table? Reclaiming Real Presence," *Commonweal,* January 27,1995.

Mitchell, Rosemary Catalano, and Ricciuti, Gail Anderson, *Birthings and Blessings,* The Crossroad Publishing Company, New York, 1991.

Mitford, Nancy, *Pigeon Pie,* British Book Centre, New York, 1959.

Moltmann-Wendel, Elizabeth, *A Land Flowing With Milk and Honey,* The Crossroad Publishing Company, New York, 1986.

Murphy, Margaret, *How Catholic Women Have Changed,* Sheed & Ward, Kansas City, 1987.

Meyers, Sr. Bertrande, D.C., *Sisters for the Twenty-First Century,* Sheed & Ward, New York, 1965.

National Sister's Vocation Conference, *Woman's Song,* collection, 1307 South Wabash, #350, Chicago,1986.

Nelson, Gertrud Mueller, *To Dance With God,* Paulist Press, New York, 1986.

New American Bible with Revised New Testament, by the Confraternity of Christian Doctrine, Washington, D.C.,1986

The New American Bible, St. Joseph, Edition, copyright (c) by the Confraternity of Christian Doctrine, Washington, D.C., 1986.

New York Times, The, "3 New York City Students Win Westinghouse Science Awards," March 15,1994. p. B3.

Nietzsche, Friedrich, *Thus Spake Zarathustra,* translator, Thomas Common, Boni and Liveright, Inc., New York, 1917.

No author, "US Catholicism Trends in the '90s," *National Catholic Reporter,* October 8,1993. p. 23.

O'Connor, Sr. Francis Bernard CSC, *Like Bread, Their Voices Rise!,* Ave Maria Press, Notre Dame, Indiana, 1993.

Osborne, Kenan B. OFM, *Ministry,* Paulist Press, New York, 1993,

Osiek, Carolyn, *Beyond Anger,* Paulist Press, New York., 1986.

Inter Insigniores, 1976. n. 4, as published in *The Order of Priesthood,* no author, Our Sunday Visitor, Huntington, Indiana, 1978.

Pagels, Elaine, *The Gnostic Gospels,* Random House, New York, 1979.

Pennington, M. Basil, *Vatican II We've Only Just Begun,* The Crossroad Publishing Company, New York, 1994.

Perry, John Michael, *Exploring the Evolution of the Lord's Supper in the New Testament,* Sheed & Ward, Kansas City, 1994.

Plaskow, Judith and Christ, Carol P., eds., *Weaving the Visions,* HarperSanFrancisco, San Francisco, 1989.

Plaskow, Judith and Christ, Carol P., eds., *Woman Spirit Rising,* Harper & Row, San Francisco, 1979.

Pottmeyer, Hermann J., "The Traditionalist Temptation of the Contemporary Church," *America,* September 5, 1992.

Power, David N., *The Eucharistic Mystery,* The Crossroad Publishing Company, New York, 1994.

Proctor-Smith, Marjorie and Walton, Janet R., eds., *Women At Worship,* Westminster/John Knox Press, Louisville, Kentucky, 1993.

Quiller-Couch, Sir Arthur, ed., *The New Oxford Book of English Verse,* Oxford University Press, New York, 1955.

Rae, Eleanor and Marie-Daly, Bernice, *Created In Her Image,* The Crossroad Publishing Company, New York, 1990.

Ratzinger, Cardinal Joseph, as quoted in the *National Catholic Reporter,* Dec. 11, 1987.

Rausch, Thomas P., "The Unfinished Agenda of Vatican II," *America,* June 17-24,1995.

Replansky, Naomi, "Housing Shortage," *The Dangerous World: New and Selected Poems 1934-1994,* Another Chicago Press, Chicago, 1994.

Revised Psalms of the New American Bible, the Confraternity of Christian Doctrine, Washington, D.C., 1991.

Rich, Adrienne, *On Lies Secrets and Silence,* Norton, New York, 1979.

Rountree, Cathleen, *On Women Turning Fifty,* HarperSanFrancisco, San Francisco, 1993.

Ruether, Rosemary Radford, *Sexism and God Talk,* Beacon Press, Boston,1983.

Ruether, Rosemary Radford, *Women-Church,* Harper & Row, San Francisco, 1985.

Ruether, Rosemary Radford, *Womanguides,* Beacon Press, Boston. 1985.

Rukeyser, Muriel, "Käthe Kollwitz," *The Speed of Darkness,* Random House, New York, 1968.

Ruoff, A. Lavonne Brown, *Literatures of the American Indian,* Chelsea House Publishers, New York, 1991.

Sanford, Linda Tschirhart and Donovan, Mary Ellen, *Women & Self Esteem*, Penguin

Books, New York, 1987.

Sarton, May, "A Glass of Water," *Selected Poems Of May Sarton*, W.W. Norton and Company, New York, 1978.

Schaef, Anne Wilson, *Women's Reality*, HarperCollins, New York, 1992.

Schillebeeckx, Edward, *The Church With A Human Face*, The Crossroad Publishing Company, New York, 1985.

Schillebeeckx, Edward, *Ministry*, pp. 50-51.

Schneiders, Sandra M., *Beyond Patching*, Paulist Press, Mahwah, NJ, 1991.

Schneir, Miriam, ed.,*Feminism: The Essential Historical Writings*, Random House, NY, 1972.

Schraffran, Janet CDP and Kozak, Pat CSJ, *More Than Words*, Privately published, Cleveland, 1986.

Schreck, Nancy OSF and Leach, Maureen, *Psalms Anew*, Saint Mary's Press, Winona, MN, 1986.

Shannon, William, "No Circuit-Rider Priest, Please!" *America*, April 16,1994.

Sheedy, Fr. Frank, "Ask Me A Question," *Our Sunday Visitor*, June 11,1995.

Sleevi, Mary Lou, *Sisters and Prophets*, Ave Maria Press, Notre Dame, Indiana, 1993.

Sowell, Thomas, *A Conflict of Visions*, William Morrow and Company, NY, 1987.

Spinning a Sacred Yarn: Women Speak From the Pulpit. The Pilgrim Press, New York, 1982.

Steinfels, Peter, "Future of Faith Worries Catholic Leaders," *The New York Times*, June 1,1994.

Thomas, Sandra P., *Women and Anger*, Springer Publishing Company, Inc., New York, 1993.

Tillemans, Sr. Rose, "As old communities die, a call to radical sisterhood," *National Catholic Reporter*, November 20,1987.

Trickett, David, "Small groups cross faith lines to develop modern ecumenism," *National Catholic Reporter*. Oct. 23, 1992.

Truchses, Darlene Deer, *From Fear to Freedom*, Fulcrum, Inc., Golden, CO. 1989.

Vanier, Jean, *Be Not Afraid*, Paulist Press, New York, 1975.

Vidulich, Sr. Dorothy, "After years of failed reform, synod to bring nuns into line," *National Catholic Reporter*, November 5, 1993.

Wagner, Clare, "Women's Prayer: How It's Changing," *Praying Magazine*, January-February, 1988.

Walker, Alice,*The Color Purple*, Harcourt, Brace, Jovanovich, New York,1982.

Wallace, Ruth, *They Call Her Pastor*, State University of New York Press, Albany, 1992.

Wallis, Jim, "Keeping Faith Doing Justice Building Community," *Sojourners*, February-March, 1992.

Ware, Ann Patrick SL, *If Any One Can NCAN*, National Coalition of American Nuns, 1989.

Weaver, Mary Jo, *New Catholic Women*, Harper & Row, San Francisco, 1985.

Weaver, Mary Jo, *Springs of Water in a Dry Land*, Beacon Press, Boston, 1993.

Wepman, Dennis, *Desmond Tutu*, Franklin Watts, New York, 1989.

Whitehead, James D. and Evelyn Eaton, *The Emerging Laity*, Image Books, New York, 1988.

Wilshire, Donna, *Virgin Mother Crone*, Inner Traditions, Rochester, Vermont, 1994.

Windsor, Pat, "LCWR examines life of religious," *National Catholic Reporter*, September 1, 1989.

Winter, Miriam Therese, *Woman Prayer Woman Song*, Meyer Stone Books, Oak Park, IL. 1987.

Winter, Miriam Therese, *Woman Wisdom*, The Crossroad Publishing Company, New York, 1991.

Winter, Miriam Therese, Lummis, Adair and Stokes, Allison, *Defecting in Place*, The Crossroad Publishing Company, New York, 1994.

Wolff, Sr. M. Madeleva, CSC, "The Education of Our Young Religious Teachers," *National Catholic Educational Association Proceedings and Addresses*, 1949.

Do you want to buy a copy of this book?
Tell your friends it's wonderful!!!

Write to :
WovenWord Press
811 Mapleton Avenue
Boulder, Colorado 80304

$16.95 + $3.00 postage and handling. Colorado residents
add 3% sales tax.